Seven Hundred Years of
ORIENTAL CARPETS

KURT ERDMANN

Seven Hundred Years of
ORIENTAL CARPETS

edited by Hanna Erdmann
and translated by
May H. Beattie and Hildegard Herzog

UNIVERSITY OF CALIFORNIA PRESS
Berkeley and Los Angeles

University of California Press
Berkeley and Los Angeles, California
© English Translation by
Faber and Faber 1970
First published in Germany in 1966
under the title 'Siebenhundert Jahre Orientteppich'

Library of Congress Catalog Card
Number = 69–12473
ISBN 0–520–01816–8

Printed in Great Britain

Foreword

For the last five hundred years the Oriental carpet has been a favourite objective of wealthy connoisseurs and collectors and, since the turn of this century, it has assumed an important position in scholarly literature.

F. R. Martin's comprehensive work *A History of Oriental Carpets before 1800* (Vienna, 1908) which had been preceded by few publications, was followed by a veritable flood of articles and books. The bibliography in Kurt Erdmann's *Oriental Carpets – an Account of their History* (London, 1962) contains more than 620 titles. Although in the past fifteen years alone about twenty books on carpets have appeared, most of these are concerned with the carpet production of the last 150 years. Among the German handbooks on the antique carpet, the most important are still *Antique Rugs from the Near East* by Wilhelm von Bode and Ernst Kühnel (Brunswick/Berlin, 1958) and the book by Kurt Erdmann mentioned above.

The history of the present volume by Kurt Erdmann goes back to 1960. At that time, the journal *Heimtex* asked my husband to become its consultant on antique carpets – a position left vacant by the death of Heinrich Jacoby. When he agreed neither he nor the publisher anticipated that this would result in a series of fifty-one monthly articles, the continuation of which was only interrupted by the sudden death of the author. In January 1962 the wish was first expressed to put these articles together in book form but the idea did not take definite shape until 1964. The negotiations with the publishers were far advanced and the division of the book into five sections was already agreed on when my husband died in September 1964. For me, therefore, it was no mere duty to prepare this work for publication, and to see it through the press.

Kurt Erdmann had already written an outline for the introduction of the book and this showed how aware he was of the difficulty of defining its purpose. It was to be more than a popular book but not quite a manual or complete history of the carpet. It is a many-sided work put together as a mosaic and the complicated problems and questions concerning the Oriental rug are fully surveyed. Among the subjects are those often lacking in handbooks, such as the development of the systematic study of carpets and the history of their exhibitions. Indeed large sections are written in handbook style, notably the extensive series on the Turkish carpet, which was never completed. The first comprehensive account of the Berlin carpet collection, which includes the record of its war losses and its present state, is an important contribution to the history of German carpet collections in general.

The value of the studies presented here lies not so much in the ordered unity of the whole, as in the clarification of details, which provide a new basis for an understanding of the entire subject. These collected works are to be considered the mature fruits of many years preoccupation with the whole art of the Orient and with its carpets in particular.

Originally the text was accompanied by numerous footnotes. The essential information contained in them, mainly concerned with provenance, comparative material and literature, has been included in the list of illustrations at the end of the book. In two chapters which would otherwise be difficult to understand, the notes have been retained with the text. Information concerning the measurements and the owners of carpets has been given wherever possible. In certain instances the bibliography has been amplified.

For their kindness in permitting the illustration of their carpets in this book I am indebted to many museums and collectors especially to the Islamic Department of the Berlin State Museums who, for the first time, have allowed colour reproduction of their carpets.

Finally, I wish to thank my publisher for bringing out the book in this form and in illustrating the text so lavishly with over three hundred plates of which twenty are in colour.

Berlin, July 1966   HANNA ERDMANN

7

Translators' Note

The translators, one an Oriental rug specialist (M.B.) the other an art historian whose native language is German (H.H.), worked as a team. The aim was to produce a translation that would present the subject clearly to the reader. The criterion used was that difficult rug problems should be easily understood by the non-technical member of the team. This, at times, necessitated some modification of the text. In addition, after discussion with Dr. Hanna Erdmann, small errors were corrected.

M.H.B.

Sheffield, 1968   H.H.

Contents

CONTENTS

PERIPHERAL PROBLEMS

EUROPEAN PRODUCTION

Colour Plates

For the English edition of this book, the sequence of text chapters has been altered, and this has affected the numbering of many illustrations which, therefore, do not have the same Fig. numbers as in the German edition where colour plates were also given Fig. numbers. In order to help the reader who may wish to refer to the German text the Pl. and Fig. numbers of the German text are included in square brackets in the lists on pp. 219–233. In addition a concordance of Fig. numbers in the German edition and illustration numbers in the English edition appears on p. 234.

THE BEGINNINGS OF
CARPET STUDIES

Early Carpets in Western Paintings

In 1886 Wilhelm von Bode bought in Rome the carpet illustrated in Fig. 1, which is supposed to have come from a church in Central Italy. This small piece is damaged on the right side, but probably only the border is missing. It has a field of two squares in each of which is represented the same pair of animals in combat. The larger, lower one can without difficulty be recognized as a dragon. The upper one is more stylized. It has three tail feathers and is therefore a bird, perhaps even a phoenix, with a triangular body and a board-like head with four eyes and a split tongue. This is a strange metamorphosis of a Chinese motif and the brilliant yellow ground on which the animals stand also points to China, where yellow is the Imperial colour. It is obviously Turkish work, but when was the carpet produced? No second piece is known. There were no clues until it was discovered that a carpet with a similar unique design was represented in a fresco (Fig. 2) in the orphanage in Siena. This fresco was painted by Domenico di Bartolo between 1440 and 1444. At that time, therefore, such carpets must have been known in Italy, and so the Berlin one was probably produced before 1440; this supposition was later confirmed by the discovery of the same design in other paintings.

The representations of carpets in pictures of the fifteenth and even of the fourteenth century are important as an aid to dating and as a source of information about other early Turkish carpets of which little was known in 1886.

Various groups can be distinguished and can be arranged chronologically since the pictures are datable. The strange fact emerges that we know more about early Anatolian carpets, of which virtually nothing has survived, than we know about some later groups of which we have many examples but no dates.

The renderings in the paintings are summary, but, since we have several portrayals of most of the types, one serves as a control for the other and we are therefore fairly certain of what the early rugs looked like. Another question is whether all types of this animal group of carpets – which in my opinion originated in north-west Anatolia – are represented and are from the fourteenth and fifteenth centuries. One has to consider that only part of the production found its way to Europe and of this part only a selection, probably the most popular and widespread types, was portrayed in paintings. Until a short time ago all this was supposition because no such carpets were known to have survived, but the situation changed when by chance R. M. Riefstahl saw an insignificant fragment for sale in Cairo and asked where it came from. The dealer said that such fragments often turned up at excavations in Old Cairo but were thrown away because they had no commercial value. Riefstahl bought this and several other pieces at a low price. At one stroke the

situation changed. Naturally, it was immediately noised abroad in the bazaar that a 'crazy foreigner' had bought carpet fragments and this gave them a 'trade value'. Since then they have appeared more frequently on the market and the price has risen rapidly. Certainly not everything that came to light –

1. Anatolia, about 1400.

2. Anatolian carpet in an Italian fresco, 1440–4.

always small pieces – was of importance, but through these finds we possess today something like a hundred fragments of fourteenth- and fifteenth-century carpets, of which unfortunately only part has been published.

In this way a check on the portrayal of carpets of the period in European paintings becomes possible. The result is interesting. Geometric designs predominate in the fragments from Old Cairo. Such designs, of course, are not lacking in European paintings but they are rare when compared with animal designs. On the other hand the designs of the animal style from the Old Cairo fragments show a complexity which is uncommon in the paintings.

Obviously the principle of selecting rugs for the European market had misrepresented the real state of affairs. Firstly, carpets with animal designs were popular in Europe and were therefore imported in greater numbers. Secondly, painters wishing to enrich their pictures with carpets chose figural designs which accorded more with their own taste, in spite of the fact that the designs of actual Anatolian carpets of the fourteenth and fifteenth centuries were more usually geometric.

Carpets in pictures of the early period always show the same creatures in each square. Especially popular were two birds standing on either side of a highly stylized tree (Fig. 3) and an original rug of this type (Fig. 4) came to light in a small Swedish village church. In other carpets the squares contain birds, which judging by their long tail feathers may well be stylized cocks, and the colour of the birds is alternately light on a dark background and dark on light.

A small fragment (Fig. 5) from Old Cairo, which is now in the Metropolitan Museum in New York, obviously comes from a carpet of this sort. The neck of the bird with the retroverted head and a single tail feather is easily recognized. On the other hand we still have no sure original of another type in which

3. Anatolian carpet in a painting by Sano di Pietro, fifteenth century.

4. Anatolia, beginning of the fifteenth century.

standing quadrupeds (Fig. 6) fill the squares. On two fragments from Old Cairo, now in Berlin and Athens, the strangely stylized feet of such animals seem to have been reproduced, but too little is preserved to be certain.

During the fifteenth century the rug designs in paintings became richer. In the individual fields several quadrupeds are depicted, the earlier ones standing peacefully side by side, the later fighting with each other, as in the Dragon and Phoenix carpet. Some years ago a fragment from Old Cairo, belonging to a carpet with the same basic plan, but with six or eight squares, was added to this group. Such carpets seem to indicate the end of the type since no new ones appear in paintings. Instead, towards the end of the fifteenth century, geometric filling of the field, which had been used in the past as well as animal designs, became more frequent and eventually supplanted the latter. After 1500 no such animal carpets seem to have been represented in a European painting and we may therefore assume that, in the course of the fifteenth century,

6. Carpet in a Sienese painting, fourteenth century.

not by way of the Mediterranean, but by the overland route.

We also know from documentary sources that Pope Benedict XII, who resided in Avignon in the fourteenth century, was extremely fond of carpets and insisted that a rug with parrots and white swans should always lie before his throne. In a fresco in the Palace of the Popes in Avignon, a carpet is portrayed which shows birds in individual fields, and in these, with a little effort, one can recognize white swans (which, however, look more like peacocks). Unfortunately, the fresco is poorly preserved. More important is a panel painting by Giovanni di Paolo (Fig. 7) in the Stoclet Collection in Brussels. It represents the visit of Saint Catherine of Siena to the Pope in Avignon to persuade the Holy Father to return to Rome. The Saint and her companion

5. Anatolia, fourteenth century.

their production came to an end. The reasons for this are not difficult to guess. In this group we are dealing undoubtedly with Anatolian products. In the thirteenth and fourteenth centuries Anatolia was ruled by the Turkish Seljuks who took kindly to the representation of figures in their art. In the fifteenth century the Ottomans, who were also Turks, became the rulers and to a great extent dispensed with figures. This was certainly on religious grounds because according to strict Muslim teaching the representation of men or animals is forbidden, for this would mean trespassing on the rights of Allah who alone is the Creator. In some periods, such as the Seljuk, observation of this prohibition was lax; in others, like the Ottoman, it was strict.

Anatolian Animal carpets occur in Italian paintings only, apart from one instance when a Spaniard, Jaume Huguet, portrayed such a rug. Those which are found in paintings of the Netherlands school show mainly geometric but also some other designs. It is difficult to conclude from this whether these originated in another district of Anatolia or reached the West

7. Carpet in a painting by Giovanni di Paolo, about 1440.

stand before the throne of the Pope, who gives them his blessing. Three cardinals and two monks assist as his scribes. The Papal throne stands on a two-stepped podium, which is covered with one of those Anatolian Animal carpets under discussion here and which is, furthermore, one of the few examples known with only one bird in each field. In the picture three such birds can be recognized, which, because of their curved beaks, could well be parrots. Could this be the carpet belonging to Pope Benedict XII? It would seem to be too good to be true. The scene is an historical fact, but the visit of the Saint occurred in the year 1376, about forty years after the death of Benedict XII, and was

paid to his successor Gregory XI, and it is he, presumably, who is depicted. Furthermore, the picture was not painted till seventy years later, that is, about 1440. The supposition, however, should not be lightly dismissed. Why should not the carpet of Benedict XII have been used by his successor? If it were already so famous that the chroniclers mentioned it, perhaps the painter, although he could scarcely have known the carpet from the original but only from a reproduction which we no longer possess, represented it to give the painting local colour. This is only a supposition, but diverting and perhaps even correct.

Oriental Carpets in Paintings of the Renaissance and the Baroque

The portrayal of Oriental carpets in Western paintings does not cease with the Renaissance, because real enthusiasm for the Oriental carpet began only in the sixteenth century. This is also expressed in painting. The number of carpets depicted is almost beyond belief but the situation has changed. Representations of carpets in paintings are the most important source of information for the fourteenth and fifteenth centuries. With their help we can get a broad view and classify those few originals which have survived only in unimpressive fragments. After 1500 the situation is exactly reversed. From this period we possess original carpets in great number and their representations in pictures do not present us with much that is unknown. Nevertheless, they are still of value for the chronological arrangement of the material since carpets themselves are dated only in rare instances.

A whole series of new carpet types now makes its appearance in originals as well as in paintings. Most carpets so far have come from north-west Anatolia but now the district of Ushak in the centre of western Anatolia becomes important, as well as Egypt, which has emerged as the homeland of the Damascus carpet. In the seventeenth century Persian and Indian carpets are occasionally depicted, but even in later times most of the rugs in paintings are still of Turkish origin.

In the fourteenth century only paintings from Italy and the Netherlands show Oriental rugs, but in the sixteenth century they are widespread. The genre painters of seventeenth-century Holland have also depicted many carpets, among them types not now extant but which, from their frequent appearance in paintings, must have been numerous. Brigitte Scheunemann in her article 'An Unknown Carpet Type', *Kunst des Orients*, Wiesbaden, 1959, III, pp. 78 ff., has reconstructed a carpet of this type.

In the fourteenth and fifteenth centuries carpets are portrayed mainly in religious paintings. They adorn the room in which the Virgin Mary receives the Annunciation of the Archangel Gabriel. They lie on the floor of the church, or rather the synagogue, where she is betrothed to Joseph, and always before her throne where she sits, adored by the saints. During the Renaissance, with the coming of secular subjects, a change occurs. The altar-piece still retains the Oriental carpet, but in addition it is now used in other ways, especially in portraits, either as a table cover or as a decoration for a balustrade.

The painters of the fourteenth and fifteenth centuries took great care to depict their carpets as clearly as possible, and in this they were helped by the simplicity of the early designs. From the sixteenth century onwards, however, the carpet designs became more complex, while the artists' style of reproduction became freer. Paolo Veronese was not concerned with depicting the many details in the design of his Persian silk carpet but aimed at incorporating it as effective decoration in the magnificent surroundings of his *Marriage at Cana* (Fig. 8) now in the Louvre. As a result, many of these paintings of carpets of the later Renaissance and of the Baroque are not so valuable and fruitful as source material as the earlier ones. The Dutch genre painters of the seventeenth century are an exception. They reproduce their examples faithfully, but like to introduce the carpet in an 'artistic' way, either rumpled or draped, which of course makes it difficult if not impossible to recognize its design.

A large group of Anatolian carpets, of which hundreds are still preserved, is named after the German painter Hans Holbein the Younger. These so-called Holbein carpets show how desirable the inclusion of Oriental rugs in paintings was considered to be during the Renaissance. It is not particularly apt to call a carpet type after a European artist just because he has represented such pieces in his paintings. It would be acceptable if he were the first or the only one to paint the type, but these carpets had been depicted long before Holbein and more clearly by Italian masters such as Raffaellino del Garbo and Domenico Ghirlandaio. Indeed one of the three types belonging to this group – the carpets with brilliant yellow design on a red ground

8. Persian carpet in a painting by Paolo Veronese, 1562–3.

21

9. Anatolia (Ushak), seventeenth century.

10. Bird Carpet in a painting of the Clouet school, probably 1560–70.

– was never depicted by Holbein. These are now called Lotto carpets after the Italian painter Lorenzo Lotto, whose famous painting in the Zanipolo church in Venice shows a good example (Fig. 107).

Last, but not least, these Holbein carpets are not a homogeneous group. Those with large, geometrically filled squares, as in his portraits of Burgomaster Meyer (Darmstadt) and the Ambassadors (London) were produced in north-western Anatolia, probably in the Bergama district, where the designs continue in the carpets of Chanakkale and Ezine to the present day. In Turkey these two groups are definitely considered to be

the successors to the large-pattern Holbein carpets. They are known as Bergamas in Europe. The pieces with the small-pattern design, such as the carpet in the portrait of the Merchant Gisze in Berlin, and the Lotto carpets, come from the Ushak district.

In spite of lack of precision, pictorial renderings in later centuries are of value in the study of carpets. It can be shown, simply because their representation stops, that the Damascus carpets, which today are more correctly called Mamluk, continued only to the middle of the sixteenth century. This is confirmed by inventories and can be proved by the many extant originals. Later they were replaced by Turkish Court carpets, now known as Ottoman carpets (e.g. Figs. 165 and 166), which apparently were never depicted in paintings. From the sixteenth century onwards the evolution of Oriental rugs may be studied from:

1. originals which have survived in great number but which are unfortunately 'silent', except in rare cases such as dated carpets (pp. 167 ff.), and therefore tell nothing of their place and time of origin;
2. extensive documentary sources mostly in the form of estate inventories but sometimes travel descriptions and other reports;
3. portrayal of Oriental carpets in Western paintings.

These possibilities should be used in conjunction with each other, which is not always easy. No great problems are presented in associating 1 and 3 but there are difficulties in reconciling 2 with 1 and 3, since the information from documentary sources is far from clear. It should certainly not be assumed that a Turkish carpet lurks behind every 'tapis de Turkie' or 'Turkey carpet' or 'türkisch tebich' because in the sixteenth, seventeenth and eighteenth centuries these terms simply meant 'Oriental carpet'. In inventories of this time one often finds 'tapis de Turquie persan' and even the Indian carpet, proved to have been ordered by Sir Robert Bell in Lahore for the Girdlers' Company in London, was called a 'Turkey carpet' (see the chapter 'Carpets with European Blazons', (Fig. 265).

The value of such investigations seems proved by my study of carpet making in Cairo, though the problem here – the transition from Mamluk (formerly Damascus) carpets to Ottoman (formerly Turkish Court) carpets – is particularly complicated and must be treated carefully. With the help of original carpets,

documentary sources and representations in paintings, it was possible to give a complete and convincing picture of the evolution of this group and a similar procedure ought to succeed with others.

It is of great value that in the picture *The Doge's Ring*, which was painted in 1530 by Paris Bordone and is now in the Accademia in Venice, a classically designed Star Ushak is represented for the first time. It is a red-ground piece with dark-blue medallions, of a type preserved in a number of originals (Fig. 139). There also exist three European copies of Ushak carpets with the Arms of the Montagu family (Fig. 262). Two are dated 1584 and 1585 respectively, which proves that this particularly attractive Ushak group was already exported to Europe and copied there at that time. In actual fact, as the Bordone picture proves, this type stems from the beginning of the century. One is inclined to ascribe the less attractive white-ground Bird carpets (Fig. 9), also from the Ushak district, to the seventeenth century. Written sources mention white-ground carpets earlier, without giving descriptions of the design. The reproduction in pictures by Alessandro Varotari, Peter Candid and Cornelis de Vos give a dating towards the end of the sixteenth century. The picture (Fig. 10) of the Clouet school in the Lazaro collection in Madrid is undated and is probably a late copy of an original which, from the shape of the armour and the helmet, must date from about 1560–70. Unless one assumes that this carpet was depicted a few years after it was made, which is unlikely, this type of Anatolian carpet originates in the first half of the sixteenth century.

New finds and new observations continually change the overall picture. It is fascinating that while we believe we know the Oriental carpet so well, we actually know remarkably little about it.

Carpets in Oriental Miniatures

The portrayal of rugs in European art has been of value in classifying surviving antique pieces. It is questionable whether similar help can be expected from Oriental sources. Because of the iconoclastic nature of the Muslim religion, paintings in the European sense are unknown in the Orient. On the other hand carpets are represented in profusion in Oriental miniatures, and are found in those of Persia in the fourteenth century at about the same time as they first appear in Europe. At first they are infrequent, in the fifteenth century they become more numerous and in the sixteenth and seventeenth centuries they occur in Turkish and Indian miniatures as well as in Persian. Compared with European renderings, the Oriental are more faithful. The Italian painters, in spite of all their endeavours, give only a summary picture of the rug, evidently avoiding complex designs, and even with simple models rarely convey the ornamental character of the motifs, whereas the Oriental miniaturists do not shrink from involved compositions. One has the impression that they usually portray their model correctly, but we cannot be certain of this. Because two intact and some fragmentary carpets still exist it is possible to compare them with rugs

11. Persian miniature, c. 1420.

depicted in European paintings, which at an early period were exclusively Turkish. This is not possible in the case of Oriental miniatures as these at first always show Persian carpets, and no Persian carpets from the fourteenth and fifteenth centuries have survived – not even a fragment. The possibility that one day some may come to light is remote. Our only source of information is from the miniatures and it is very fortunate that the two groups of paintings complement each other so happily, the European showing only Turkish, and the Oriental miniatures only Persian designs.

The differences are striking. While in the early Turkish carpet animal figures play an important role, the early Persian carpet is geometrically designed throughout. Only once in a miniature, the famous Demotte *Shahnameh* which today is in the Freer Gallery in Washington, is an animal, a quadruped facing to the right, depicted, but this carpet differs so greatly from all other representations that it is considered to be a piece imported into Persia and most probably belongs to the group of Anatolian Animal carpets. Such differences must not be exaggerated since the impression given by European paintings is obviously not entirely accurate. As the fragments from Old Cairo prove, geometric patterns were also prevalent in Turkey, but painters represented these less often than designs of living creatures. Taking this into consideration it appears that the differences between the two groups are not great for in some cases one can turn to Persian carpets for an explanation of the Turkish. A small-pattern, geometric field design and a relatively richly interlaced Kufic border are characteristic of most carpets in Persian miniatures of the fourteenth and fifteenth centuries. In the carpet (Fig. 11) on which Prince Humay lies, having fainted upon looking at the picture of the beautiful Princess Humayun, the field design is simple and reminiscent of tiles. Later these became more complex (Fig. 12) and rows of crosses or stars, joined by interlacing, alternate with rows of rosettes which fill the small squares formed by the crosses or stars. This becomes especially obvious whenever these squares are differently coloured, usually red and green. In principle, this is the same design construction as in the small-pattern Holbein carpets. These also show two alternating rows of different motifs in which the crosses or stars assume more the shape of a lozenge and are no longer interlaced but are connected by small additional rosettes, while those which fill the squares have become octagons with interlaced outlines. Just as in the carpets in miniatures, this Anatolian group occasionally shows an alternation of colour in the field, giving the impression of a pattern of small squares. Both groups have in common borders with a heavily interlaced Kufic script, and therefore were probably

24

12. Carpet after a Persian miniature of 1485.

14. Medallion carpets in a miniature of 1525.

13. Anatolia (Ushak), sixteenth century.

related. The small-pattern Holbein carpets (Fig. 13), whose fore-runners have not survived, must have resembled the Persian carpets depicted in the miniatures.

Although one cannot record in detail the many variations which carpets depicted in miniatures have undergone during the course of the fifteenth century, the basic principle of design remains the same. They therefore give an archaic impression, in marked contrast to textiles and ceramics, which have progressed stylistically and which are depicted in the same miniatures. The only explanation can be that carpets obviously adhered to older forms, while in other arts a new style emerged which incorporated Chinese influences.

A change occurs at the end of the fifteenth century. Geometric cross, star and rosette designs are replaced by medallions and scrolls; instead of small patterns in rows and squares there are large patterns which emphasize the middle of the field (Fig. 14), characteristic of the classical Persian carpet of the sixteenth century. This is a complete change of style. In practice, towards the end of the fifteenth century the method of production changed and the designing of the cartoons was entrusted to miniature painters, so that elements typical of book art were transferred to rugs. This led to the creation of new groups of medallion and scroll carpets. About 1500 this process seems to have been completed and the designs depicted in later miniatures are found in actual carpets.

Carpets intermediate between the two styles appear in miniatures of the last decade of the fifteenth century when this change took place. These retain the interlaced Kufic borders of the older types but medallions appear in the field. The designs are more complex than those which were finally adopted and which became models for surviving carpets. No originals of the intermediate group are known and it is questionable whether such transitional pieces were ever made, or whether the designs were the creations of the painters as suggestions for modernizing the old-fashioned geometric styles. Perhaps Bihzad, the most famous of the Persian miniaturists, was concerned with this problem but it cannot be proved.

The Discovery of the Antique Carpet

If one recalls the role played by the Oriental carpet in Europe in the fifteenth, sixteenth and seventeenth centuries, how passionately it was sought after, how indispensable it was for court and church ceremonial occasions, how closely associated it was with the urban way of life, and if one recalls the hundreds of inventories of great collections and the thousands of portrayals in pictures, it is difficult to understand how, in the second half of the nineteenth century, a 'discovery' was possible. It must of course be understood that this was a 'rediscovery', not of the Oriental carpet as such, but of the 'antique' Oriental carpet, that is of pieces which in the sixteenth and seventeenth centuries had aroused admiration in Europe but which in fact had been as good as forgotten during the eighteenth and nineteenth centuries.

Undoubtedly Oriental carpets always remained popular. The possession of a 'genuine Persian' was *de rigeur* for our great-grandparents and the demand was not lessened by the establishment of carpet factories in Europe; but the carpets now imported from the Orient were different. The reason was that most of the great Oriental workshops had closed their doors in the eighteenth century. The weavers had either succumbed to disasters or had emigrated. In remote districts, which had suffered less from political events, carpets which preserved traditional forms were still woven, but in these there is a decline in the precision of drawing, the richness of colouring and the care in production. In the Ushak and Smyrna districts in 1865 this trend reached its lowest point, when, against Muslim resistance, Christians forced their way into the carpet industry not as weavers but as organizers. This did not lead to the setting up of actual workshops – even today in the East each carpet is made by hand and usually in the home. But the industry was now organized by giving orders to families in villages, supplying the weavers with materials and collecting the finished articles for export to Europe. Consequently after some time a certain amount of interference in production took place. The buyer's taste had to be considered: patterns not popular in Europe were suppressed and successful designs were encouraged. More and more frequently the weavers were supplied with cartoons which were either copies of existing carpets by designers of varying ability, or completely new patterns. This led to the uprooting of the age-old local types; weavers steeped in traditional skills were converted into mechanical operatives.

Not only were the old designs discarded, but the ancient lore of the dyers was lost. The organizers of the industry considered it unreasonable to retain the old vegetable dyes when work could be done so much more quickly and cheaply with the newly discovered anilines. A merchant's matter-of-fact account of the 1870s illuminates this: 'At first these dyes were employed as supplements to the old dyes (vegetable colours) to make them more brilliant and fiery; now it has also been discovered how to use the new dyes by themselves but the degree of fading which may result from exposure to air and light has not been taken into consideration, a state of affairs which is by no means advantageous to the ancient and renowned craft of the dyer. It must be noted that dye houses do not just use aniline colours because these simplify the dyeing processes. Another reason for the use of these Western products is modern taste. People are no longer content with the simple, old designs for which traditional methods of dyeing are adequate. Complicated designs, richer colour contrasts and brilliant shades are demanded and these can only be achieved by means of artifically produced colours.'

The difficulties involved in the use of aniline dyes are now long past. The dyes have been altered; they have lost their harshness and unstable colours and can no longer be detected simply by rubbing with a damp cloth. Also, in the Orient there is a return to the old vegetable dyes. This means that the early aniline-dyed carpets have acquired 'scarcity' value. They were produced so carelessly that they did not last more than a couple of decades.

Probably the unsatisfactory state of the carpet industry caused a return to earlier carpets for inspiration. Julius Lessing, Director of the Kunstgewerbe Museum in Berlin, in his book *Altorientalische Teppichmuster nach Bildern und Originalen des XV–XVI Jahrhunderts*, which was published in 1877, wanted to provide better models for carpet designers. He was unsuccessful. The merchants took care not to follow his suggestions because at that time their clients would not have shown the slightest interest in strictly classical designs.

Lessing's book contains forty-seven designs, of which forty-two are taken from carpets shown in paintings and only three from actual antique carpets of which, in Lessing's opinion, very few examples had survived.

What had happened to the wealth of carpets in the West? The survival of a carpet is threatened on two counts. If in use, sooner or later it will be ruined by our barbarous custom of wearing outdoor shoes in the house, which no Oriental would think of doing. If it is not in use, it may be damaged by moth and vermin.

It is to the great credit of Wilhelm von Bode that he recognized as antique those carpets which in his time were removed from churches and palaces as useless old rags. He writes in his memoirs: 'In Italy, at that time, they lay practically in the streets and could be had for a song.' He did not hesitate to act and so

15. Anatolia (Ushak), sixteenth century.

When in his eighties, going through the carpet galleries of his museum, he recalled with satisfaction how he had bought a unique Spanish carpet for 60 crowns from the verger of a village church in the Tirol and an enormous Caucasian carpet for 120 lire on a gondola trip to Burano near Venice. There is a delightful story of the unique Turkish prayer rug illustrated in Fig. 15, which in 1904 Bode acquired from the widowed daughter-in-law of the Viennese collector von Angeli with whom he had been friendly. It cost 1,000 crowns and was destined for the Islamic Department of the Berlin Museum which he had just established. 'I enquired as to the provenance of the carpet, to which he [von Angeli] replied that of all people I should know this best. I had bought the carpet for him in Venice for 35 lire when we stayed there together in the spring of 1871.' The increase in price was justifiable, for when the carpet was sent to an exhibition in the thirties it was insured for 250,000 marks. The entire Berlin collection was acquired originally for not more than the cost today of one of its more ordinary pieces. It is too little known what fantastic assets have accrued to the State in the past, and still do today, through skilful museum purchases.

Bode did not remain the only carpet collector for long. The Florentine antique dealer Bardini bought a sixteenth-century silk Hunting carpet from the Marchese Torrigiani for a mere 150 francs. Baron Maurice de Rothschild had to pay him 30,000 for that piece. Today it could hardly be acquired for a million francs. To avoid spoiling the market these transactions were obviously not advertised; so, almost unnoticed by the public, the great collections were founded not only in Berlin but also in London, Paris and Lyons.

In the nineties two events put an end to such opportunities. To begin with, the first exhibition of Oriental carpets, which was held in 1891, centred round the magnificent collection of the Imperial House of Hapsburg and was augmented by many privately owned carpets. The second event, more important than the first, was the carpet exhibition which took place in London in 1892 and the purchase of the Ardebil carpet for £2,500. With this the opportunity for acquiring carpets at bargain prices was past. Carpets had become collectors' pieces.

originated his famous collection which he later presented to the Berlin Museums and which, to a great extent, was destroyed during the last war.

The 'Holy' Carpet of Ardebil

In 1892 an article appeared in *The Times* under the heading 'An extraordinary carpet: At the Galleries of Messrs. Vincent Robinson and Company of Wigmore Street, there will be on view in the afternoons of the next few days what may probably without any exaggeration be called the finest Persian carpet in the world. This is the Holy Carpet of the Mosque of Ardebil, in Persia; a carpet which for size, beauty, condition and authenticated age is entirely unrivalled by any known example.'

The notice in the *Manchester Guardian* was similar: 'Lovers of beautiful things should on no account miss a unique opportunity which is about to offer itself. Tomorrow and for about a fortnight there will be on view at Messrs. Vincent Robinson's establishment a collection of Persian carpets which should start every true believer in beauty on an instant pilgrimage to Wigmore Street. . . . But the crowning glory is a magnificent carpet from the Mosque of Ardebil, now exhibited for the first time in Europe, and which entirely beggars description. One can only say that it is beyond doubt the finest carpet known to modern times.'

The carpet firm of V. J. Robinson was in those days one of the most reputable in London. In past years they had offered for sale valuable antique pieces. Carpet literature is indebted to them for the first two publications to contain coloured reproductions of antique rugs. They handled important pieces such as the North Persian Cartouche-mosaic carpet, which reached the Metropolitan Museum in New York through the Yerkes Collection (cf. Pl. XIX), and the Indian carpet (Fig. 266) with the arms of the Fremlin family which is now in the Victoria and Albert Museum. This exhibition, however, was outstanding because of the 'Holy' carpet of Ardebil, so christened by journalists even though not quite apt, for no Muslim would ever think of calling a carpet 'holy'. In comparison with it the rest of the exhibition was unimportant; but an Indian silk carpet of the seventeenth century with rows of trees and a Persian Animal carpet of the sixteenth century were also exhibited. The other twenty rugs were more modern pieces.

There is no doubt whatsoever that this carpet from Ardebil (Fig. 16) is one of the most important Persian carpets of the sixteenth century and, as it measures 11·50 m. × 5·34 m., it is also one of the biggest. Its area is 61·5 square metres and its knot count about 32,000,000. A yellow medallion filled with scrolling tendrils which end in arabesque leaves and which are interwoven with richly curved cloud bands occupies the centre of a dark-blue field. At the tips of this medallion sixteen ogees are arranged radially. Those on the main axes have a green ground. Of the three between these the central one has a red ground and the two

flanking it are yellow. At both ends a large, red mosque lamp is suspended by four chains from the ogee on the main axis. A quarter of the same medallion with corresponding ogees appears in the corners of the field but without the mosque lamp. The ground is filled with floral scrolls of great complexity (Fig. 17) which finish at the edge of the field and do not contain the arabesque leaves and cloud bands of the medallion design. A clear distinction is made between the design of the field and the medallion. Strangely enough the border is not symmetrically constructed. The main stripe shows alternating red cartouches and green multifoils. The outer guard stripe has, on a red ground, a broadly designed reciprocally arranged design of palmette blossoms between pairs of arabesques, both in light blue. The inner guard stripe shows, on a yellow ground, a loosely drawn intermittent scrolling tendril and red cloud bands. A second red guard stripe with continuous tendrils is introduced next to the field. A rectangular cartouche with an inscription (Fig. 18) appears at that end of the carpet which was woven last. The design is so precisely executed that it must have been woven from a cartoon of the same size. Its composition shows that the carpet belongs to the large group of North Persian Medallion rugs. The radial arrangement of oval cartouches and the mosque lamp is unique in this example and therefore leads to the assumption that it was a special order. A special order from whom, to whom and by whom?

Here the inscription cartouche, which is also unique in this form, gives us some clues. It reads:

I have no refuge in the world other than thy threshold
There is no place of protection for my head other than this door
The work of the slave of the threshold
Maqsud Kashani in the year 946.

This inscription has been much discussed. The year is definite. 946 of the Hijra corresponds to A.D. 1539/40. As the inscription appears at the end of the carpet which was woven last it represents the date when the work was finished. The first two lines come from a poem by Hafiz. The 'threshold' and the 'door' could refer to the mosque of Ardebil, the shrine of Sheikh Safi, ancestor of the Safavid dynasty which ruled in Persia at that time. It was therefore highly venerated at court. But who was Maqsud Kashani? The weaver? No, for naturally several weavers were engaged on a carpet of this size. The designer? This would have been the first instance of a designer being named, and in any case 'maker' is not applicable to a designer. The donor? It is most unlikely that a piece of this importance would be donated by a private individual. There is agreement that only Shah Tahmasp, who reigned at that time, could have

16. Persia (Tabriz), dated 1539–40.

commissioned and given the carpet. Only one role is left for Maqsud: he was the entrepreneur, the head of the workshop where the piece was woven. Kashani means 'the man from Kashan'. Some scholars have assumed that the carpet was made in Kashan in central Persia, especially since, in the sixteenth century, it was an important centre of carpet production. In general the rule seems to have been that artists only stated their native place while working elsewhere. Maqsud came from Kashan and was possibly brought from there by the Shah for this particular task. As the style of the carpet indicates, he must have worked in a North Persian workshop, hardly in Ardebil itself, but perhaps in Tabriz or Qazvin.

The Ardebil carpet, therefore, was most likely made to the order of Shah Tahmasp in the years before 1539/40 for the ancestral shrine in Ardebil. It was probably woven in a North Persian workshop under the direction of a master weaver who came from Kashan perhaps specially for this purpose. In Europe quite fantastic speculations have been indulged in concerning the time taken to weave the carpet. In fact the work need not have taken more than three years.

Everything suggests that when completed, it was immediately taken to the mosque where in 1843 it was seen by the English traveller Holmes. 'On the floor of the long lofty ante-chamber to the principle tombs' he writes, 'were faded remains of what was once a very splendid carpet. At one extremity was woven the date of its make, some three hundred years ago.'

The events that led to the 'faded remains' of the carpet which lay in Ardebil in 1843 being shown to an enthusiastic public in London in 1892 are known in broad outline. In the eighties of last century the Ardebil mosque was in need of repair. The vault of the prayer hall had collapsed. According to the inscription 'Ibrahim, the master builder from Tabriz, did the renovation of this venerated place on the order of His Highness Mohammed Takichan Muizz al Mulk and it was completed in the year of the Hijra 1307 [A.D. 1889/90] by the industry and care of the chief master builder Sadik Beg.' (F. Sarre, *Persische Baudenkmäler*, Berlin, 1910). In order to raise the money the mosque authorities decided to sell some carpets. The negotiations were undertaken by the Manchester firm of Zieglers, active as importers in Sultanabad since 1883. From dealing only occasionally in carpets, they went into production on their own account and by about 1900 had some 2,500 looms at work in Persia. The Ardebil carpet was bought in 1888 by the London firm of V. J. Robinson. It seems to have taken four years to have reached its state of 'perfect preservation'. At about the same time as the Mullahs of Ardebil could use their mosque again, thanks to the carpet which they had sacrificed, it was put on show in London, or more precisely, offered for sale. The price was £2,500. In 1892 that was an unheard-of sum for a carpet. No museum in the world could think of raising so much, but Sir A. W. Franks and William Morris launched a purchase fund which was amazingly successful. In 1893 the Victoria and Albert Museum in London was able to record the acquisition

17. Persia (Tabriz), dated 1539–40.

of the Ardebil carpet as Inv. Nr. 272 of that year – a proud achievement and one rich in consequences.

The sensation caused by the 'Holy Carpet of Ardebil', for the journalists of 1892 had rightly recognized this as such, had far-reaching results. At one stroke the carpet collections of the Victoria and Albert Museum surpassed all others. Only once again did it achieve an acquisition of similar importance: the so-called Chelsea carpet (Fig. 231). As a result of the Vienna Exhibition of 1891 which had caught the imagination of a wide public, interest in the Oriental carpet was intensified but now the time for bargains was past. Prices soared and shortly afterwards £2,500 caused no sensation at the sale of a carpet worth barely a tenth of the Ardebil, in so far as one can use the price of that unique piece as a measuring rod.

The tale of the Ardebil carpet is not yet ended. Its public presentation in 1892 was skilful, but this was not difficult with an object of such importance. It is still a source of satisfaction that in the end the Victoria and Albert Museum was the winner;

18. Persia (Tabriz), dated 1539–40.

19. Persia (Tabriz), dated 1539–40.

but things were not quite what they seemed. Mr. Stebbing, a Director of Vincent Robinson's who promoted the carpet in such convincing terms, did not tell the truth about its excellent state of preservation. This, of course, was known to the Director of the Museum.

The report about the visit of W. R. Holmes in 1843, cited above, was correct, but the description 'faded remains' was somewhat pessimistic. In reality in the eighties V. J. Robinson acquired from Ardebil through the agency of Zieglers not one, but two carpets of the same design. It is well known that in Persia carpets were woven in pairs. In London care was taken to conceal this: apparently a single, well-preserved unique carpet was worth more than a damaged pair. During several years of tedious work one was made from two – and that is the carpet that came to the Victoria and Albert Museum.

At first the remains of the other (Fig. 19) which consisted of the intact middle section (720 × 405 cm.) was hidden and later, at an unknown date, sold to Yerkes who at that time was one of the most enterprising private collectors of Oriental carpets in America, apparently on condition that this fragment was never to be shown in England. Yerkes kept to this undertaking and the carpet did not become known until 1910 when his collection was published. At the auction it passed to Captain de Lamar from whom it was acquired by Sir Joseph Duveen in 1919 and thereby became known. It was exhibited in Cleveland and St. Louis in 1920, in Chicago in 1926 and in Detroit in 1930. In 1931 the ban on exhibiting in England was lifted and it was given a prominent place in the great exhibition of Persian art at Burlington House. It is true it is a ruin, but, when washed, brilliant in its depth of colouring and therefore almost superior to its big brother in the Victoria and Albert Museum which is too big to be washed. Later it reached the collection of J. P. Getty and today is in the County Museum, Los Angeles.

It should be added that oddments remained from the work done in London between 1888 and 1892 when the one complete carpet was made from the two damaged ones. These are mostly small pieces, several of which I have come across: in the Rietberg Museum in Zürich (R. Akerat Loan), in the Museum in Glasgow (Burrell Collection) and in Teppichhaus Carl Hopf in Stuttgart, but it has never been possible to acquire one for Berlin.

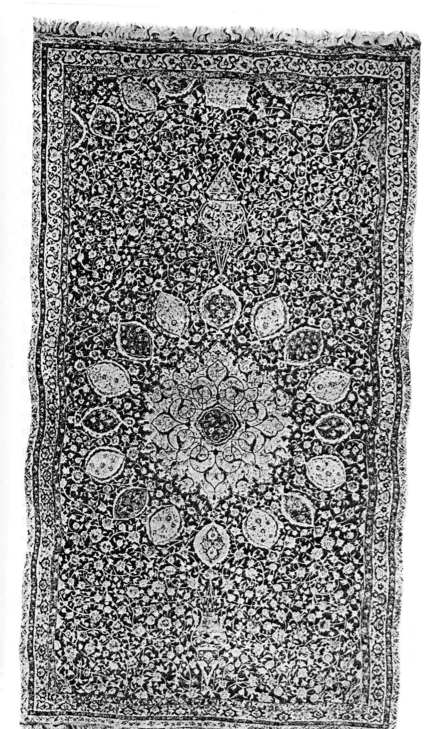

19. Persia (Tabriz), dated 1539–40.

illustrated book already mentioned (*Altorientalische Teppiche nach Bildern und Originalen des XV–XVI Jahrhunderts* published in 1877) wanted to make designs available to the carpet industry of his day. In 1881 J. von Karabacek's *Die persische Nadelmalerei Susandschird* was published in Leipzig. Though full of information, this study was unreliable and, furthermore, was entirely theoretical, so that reading it today, even though it is still stimulating, it is questionable how many carpets the author had ever seen in the original.

In 1890 this changed abruptly. A. Riegl's *Altorientalische Teppiche* is still purely theoretical, but his publication 'Ältere Teppiche aus dem Besitz des Allerhöchsten Kaiserhauses'[2] presents a vast amount of carefully worked out material. In the same year W. von Bode's article 'Ein altpersischer Teppich im Besitz der Kgl. Museen zu Berlin' appeared.[3] It represents one of the great achievements of this expert who towered above his contemporaries and the article endures today as the 4th edition of Bode-Kühnel's *Antique Rugs from the Near East*. One must include with these the publications of Robinson (1882 and 1893)[4] and of E. Stebbing[5] mentioned in the preceding chapter, and also that of M. W. Conway, 'The Lesson of a Persian Carpet',[6] which, undeservedly, has been forgotten.

In the midst of these events in the book world, the 1891 exhibition 'Ausstellung orientalischer Teppiche' was arranged in the Imperial Austrian Trade Museum and, as the first of its kind, has acquired an almost legendary reputation. Wilhelm von Bode, however, writes in his memoirs: 'The exhibition was very

20. The famous Vienna exhibition of 1891 probably looked something like this.

in museums is eventually solved, the importance of carpet exhibitions will not diminish, but they will become more specialized.

Looking back, the year 1890 may be considered a turning point in our knowledge of the Oriental carpet. Though twenty years before that it had been discovered that carpets from earlier times existed, this fact had not yet been publicised and before 1890 the only two publications concerning antique carpets were written by workers in other fields. Julius Lessing in his

mixed and tastelessly arranged. Unimportant modern pieces hung next to magnificent old carpets in as much confusion as in an ordinary Turkish bazaar.' A glance at the catalogue confirms this. Of the 515 pieces listed, numbers 1–300 were trade pieces mostly loaned by Vienna dealers. Numbers 300–429 were 'antique' carpets of which fourteen were Hapsburg possessions, twenty-four from Vienna museums and many others predominantly from Austrian private collections. The descriptions do not always allow of an opinion, because there are hardly any reproductions. One therefore suspects that even in this category not everything was old. There were also oddities like number 399 'Silk portière, gift of the Shah to Prince Metternich, probably European work with orientalizing ornaments on a red ground and gold brocaded field'.

In the catalogue entries 431–515 later pieces predominate, but there are treasures among them such as the silk carpet, now in the Gulbenkian Collection, which Bode had just acquired in Milan at that time. This exhibition is still clearly remembered because of the three-volume folio publication edited by A. Riegl in which a hundred of the most important pieces are illustrated, some of them in colour.[7] In 1908 a supplement was added, and this illustrated, frequently in colour, the most important of those carpets which had come to light since 1891.[8]

The first exhibition of Islamic art was arranged in Paris in 1903. In G. Migeon's publication in connection with this, Plates 71–85 show carpets, all of which are good Persian pieces of the classical period.[9]

The small exhibition of carpets in the Landesgewerbe Museum in Stuttgart in 1909,[10] was followed in 1910 in Munich by the huge exhibition of masterpieces of Muhammadan art. There were more than 3,500 exhibits of which 229 were carpets catalogued by F. Sarre. A comparison with the Vienna catalogue of 1891 shows the progress made in carpet studies in these twenty years. The provenance is clear, the classification sure and the nomenclature precise. This was also followed by a three-volume commemorative folio, the first volume of which deals with carpets.[11]

Contemporaneously with the Munich exhibition, W. R. Valentiner arranged a carpet exhibition in the Metropolitan Museum in New York.[12] The fifty carpets, all illustrated in the catalogue except No. 1 which was not in the exhibition, came from North American owners who, even at that time, possessed remarkable treasures. The catalogue, carefully edited and provided with a long historical introduction, represents one of the best publications of early carpet literature.

An exhibition arranged by the Kunstgewerbe Museum in Budapest in 1914[13] did not get full recognition because of the outbreak of the first world war. The 'Special Loan Exhibition of Carpets and other Textiles from Asia Minor', shown in the Pennsylvania Museum in Philadelphia in 1919, is important as the first attempt to deal with a single area. The 126 carpets all came from American owners, predominantly from the Collection of James F. Ballard. The 1919–20 'Oriental Rug Ex-

hibition' in the Cleveland Museum of Arts, contained important pieces among the eighty-nine items but unfortunately the catalogue is inadequate. There were only a few carpets in the exhibition in Alexandria in 1925.[14]

An important event was the exhibition arranged in 1926 by the Art Club of Chicago. Most of the fifty-five pieces were illustrated in the catalogue, Loan Exhibition of Early Oriental Carpets, which was written by A. U. Pope and is a standard work of carpet literature.

The 'Tentoonstelling Islamischer Kunst' in the Gemeente Museum in the Hague in 1927 contained only a few carpets. Another important exhibition was arranged in the Metropolitan Museum in 1930 by M. S. Dimand. It was carefully catalogued by him as a Loan Exhibition of Persian Rugs of the so-called Polish Type.

The international Exhibition of Persian Art arranged in 1931 at Burlington House in London was sensational. Among the numerous exhibits were 153 carpets including remarkable pieces like the Hunting Carpet from the Poldi Pezzoli Museum in Milan, the silk carpet from the castle in Warsaw and the carpet of the Dukes of Anhalt which had just come to light. The loans from the shrines of Qum, Meshed and Ardebil[15] caused special interest. During the exhibition only a small illustrated souvenir was sold.[16] The six volume Survey of Persian Art,[17] which did not appear until 1938 and in which A. U. Pope dealt with the carpets in 200 pages with 168 plates,[18] was a final and fitting tribute.[19]

The 1932 exhibition 'Türkische Kunst aus sieben Jahrhunderten' organized by the Vienna Sezession was much more modest in scope. Among the thirteen carpets, however, was a fragment of a Konya carpet of the thirteenth century.

The exhibition of Spanish carpets in Madrid in 1933[20] was a pioneer in dealing with one group of carpets. The catalogue, edited by José Ferrandis Torres, is a handbook of the first order. Smaller events of interest on account of local loans, were held in the Gewerbe Museum in Basle, 1934,[21] in the Iparmüvészeti Museum in Budapest, 1935,[22] in the Kunstgewerbe Museum in Graz, 1936[23] and in the Iparmüvészeti Museum in Budapest, 1937.[24] The 'Exhibition of Islamic Art' of the same year, arranged in the De Young Memorial Museum in San Francisco, contained a number of less well-known carpets in American possession. On the other hand there were no carpets in the 1938 exhibition 'Les Arts de l'Iran, l'ancienne Perse et Bagdad' in the Bibliothèque Nationale in Paris.

The great 'Exhibition of Persian Art'[25] organized in New York in 1940 by the Iranian Institute, did not get the recognition it deserved on account of political events.

The war, of course, interrupted the holding of exhibitions. The first post-war exhibitions took place in 1946 in Stockholm[26] and in Amsterdam.[27] In 1947 the Art Institute of Chicago held an exhibition[28] which was particularly well supported by American Museums and collectors. A special theme was treated in the 'Dragon Rug' exhibition in the Textile Museum in

Washington in 1948.[29] In the same year an exhibition took place in the Museo Civico in Turin. It comprised sixty carpets from Italian sources and was therefore not very extensive, but was commemorated by the organizer, V. Viale, in an excellent catalogue which appeared in 1952.[30]

The year 1949 saw exhibitions in Delft[31] and Groningen,[32] and that organized in the Kunst und Gewerbe Museum in Hamburg in 1950 was designed to put on record what had survived the war from German collections which had once been so extensive.[33] This was shown in The Hague in 1951 and supplemented in the same year by another in Stuttgart,[34] which was somewhat different in character.

In 'Splendeur de l'Art Turc', the great Paris exhibition of 1953,[35] about eighty carpets were shown, some of them important examples from the Türk ve Islam Eserleri Museum in Istanbul, whereas the exhibition '7000 Ans Art Persan' contained hardly any.[36]

Later exhibitions and their catalogues are only listed for the sake of completeness:

1961 Hamburg, Kunst und Gewerbe Museum *Kaukasische Teppiche*.[37]

1961 New York, Asia House Gallery, *Peasant and Nomad Rugs* by M. S. Dimand.

1962 Frankfurt, Kunstgewerbe Museum, *Kaukische Teppiche*.

1963 Harlem, Frans Hals Museum, *Tentoonstelling van Antieke Oosterse tapijten uit een particuliere Nederlanse Collectie* with an introduction by P. Otten, fifty-one entries with sixteen illustrations.

1963 Beirut, Lebanon, Musée Nicolas Sursock, *Exposition de Tapis d'Orient*, with an introduction by Henri Seyrig and ninety illustrations.

NOTES

1. Trade exhibitions are not included in the following survey. There may be omissions but it is hoped that everything of importance has been included. There are no catalogues for temporary exhibitions in the Textile Museum in Washington or at meetings of the Haji Baba Club.

2. *Jahrbuch der Kunsthistorischen Sammlungen*, Vienna, 1892, XIII, pp. 267 ff.

3. *Jahrbuch der preussischen Kunstsammlungen*, Berlin, 1892, XIII, pp. 43 ff., 108 ff.

4. V. J. Robinson, *Eastern Carpets*, London, 1882 and 1893.

5. E. Stebbing, *The Holy Carpet of the Mosque of Ardebil*, London, 1892-3.

6. *The Art Journal*, London, 1891, pp. 371 ff.

7. A. Riegl, *Orientalische Teppiche*, Vienna, 1892-5.

8. F. Sarre, *Altorientalische Teppiche*, Leipzig, 1908.

9. G. Migeon, *Exposition des arts musulmans au Musée des Arts Décoratifs*, Paris, 1903.

10. C. Hopf, *Die Teppiche des Orients*. Relative to the exhibition of old oriental carpets held in the Landesgewerbe Museum, Stuttgart, 1909.

11. F. Sarre, F. R. Martin, *Die Ausstellung von Meisterwerken mohammedanischer Kuns München 1910*, Munich, 1912.

12. W. R. Valentiner, *Catalogue of a loan exhibition of early oriental rugs*, New York, 1910. See also W. R. Valentiner in *The Bulletin of the Metropolitan Museum*, 1910, V, p. 221 and K. Ruge in *Kunst und Kunsthandwerk*, Vienna, 1911, XIV, p. 205 ff.

13. K. Csány, S. Csermelyi, K. Layer, *Erdelyi török szönyegek kiállitásának*, Budapest, 1914.

14. G. Migeon, *Exposition de l'art musulman*, Alexandria, 1925.

15. For the textiles of this exhibition see A. F. Kendrick in *The Burlington Magazine*, London, 1931, LVII, pp. 15 ff.; C. E. C. Tattersall in *Apollo*, London, 1931, XIII, pp. 1 ff., 82 ff.; K. Erdmann in *Dedalo*, Milan, 1932, XII, p. 707.

16. *Persian Art. An Illustrated Souvenir* (Anon.).

17. ed. A. U. Pope, Ph. Ackermann, Oxford, New York, 1938.

18. Plates 1107-1275.

19. See extensive discussion by K. Erdmann in *Ars Islamica*, Ann Arbor, 1941, VIII, p. 121 ff.

20. J. Ferrandis Torres, *Exposición de alfombras antiguas espãnolas*, Madrid, 1933.

21. Basle, Gewerbemuseum, *Der orientalische Teppich*, exhibition 1934.

22. K. Layer, *Régi Kisazsiai Szönyegek Kiállitása*, Budapest, 1935.

23. See little-known publication by G. Wolfbauer, 1937, *Die Ausstellung Alt-Orientalischer Teppiche in Graz*, Summer 1936, with original photographs of the fifty pieces exhibited.

24. K. Layer, *Régi Perzsa Szönyegek Kiállitása*, Budapest, 1936.

25. Ph. Ackermann, *Guide to the Exhibition of Persian Art*, The Iranian Institute, New York, 1940.

26. Nationalmusei Utställningakatolog Nr. 124, *Orientaliska Mattor*, 4-27 Oct., Stockholm, 1946.

27. *Catalogus van de Tentoonstelling van Oostersche Tapijten in het Rijksmuseum van 13 July tot 3 September*, Amsterdam, 1946.

28. The Art Institute of Chicago, *An Exhibition of Antique Oriental Rugs*, February-March 1947.

29. With thirty-seven items.

30. M. and V. Viale, *Arazzi e Tappeti Antichi*, Turin, 1952. See K. Erdmann in *Ars Orientalis*, Ann Arbor, 1957, II pp. 571 ff.

31. *Tentoonstelling Oosterse Tapitjten in het Museum 'Het Prinzenhof' te Delft*, 18 December, 1948-30 January 1949.

32. *Catalogus Tentoonstelling van Oosterse Tapitjten in Gebouw 'Pictura' te Groningen*, 9 April-1 May 1949.

33. K. Erdmann, *Orientteppiche aus vier Jahrhunderten*, Hamburg Exhibition, 1950.

34. *Katalog zur Austellung alter und antiker Teppiche des Orients in Stuttgart*, arranged by Teppichhaus Carl Hopf, 26 November-1 December 1951.

35. Arranged by the Musée des Arts Décoratifs.

36. This exhibition which in 1962-3 went from Paris to Essen, Zurich, The Hague, Vienna and Milan was in some cases enriched with additional material.

37. See also the book published at the same time under the same title by U. Schürmann.

The Development of Carpet Studies

Anyone who looks through carpet literature today is surprised to find that the favourite and most reliable books are the early ones. 'Bode-Kühnel', the fourth edition of which appeared in 1955 (English translation, 1958) is a good example.[1] The starting point for this book was an article which Wilhelm von Bode wrote[2] in 1892 and expanded to book form in 1901.[3] The book was revised by Ernst Kühnel in 1914, 1922 and 1955. It has certainly changed in the course of sixty-three years, but it is amazing how much in the original version of 1892 is still valid today.

When Bode gave such a comprehensive picture of Oriental carpets in his first article he had already done a vast amount of work on the subject. According to his memoirs his preliminary studies must have covered more than two decades. We know virtually nothing about this period. From 1870 to 1890 knowledge of the existence of antique carpets was kept secret[4] in order not to spoil the chance of cheap purchases. Not a line was written at that time.[5] After the Vienna exhibition (1891) and the sale of the Ardebil carpet (1892) the silence was broken. A year before Bode's article, Riegl's book *Altorientalische Teppiche*[6] appeared, though it is now more or less forgotten, since it dealt with the subject quite theoretically, whereas Bode wrote his article from practical experience based on his many carpet

21. Arrangement in the Islamic Department of the Kaiser Friedrich Museum, Berlin, c. 1910.

purchases and certainly on numerous conversations with dealers and collectors.

It is a pity that it will probably never be known what passed during these inaugural discussions. A sufficient differentiation between Persian and Turkish carpets had already been achieved and Spanish carpets could also be identified. Indian carpets were still classified as Persian and the Caucasus was not discovered as a producing centre until later. As evidence for dating, the representation of carpets in paintings was of special help to Bode, who was an outstanding expert on European pictures, and the chronology which he established by this means is on the whole still valid today.

Carpet literature begins with the publications by Riegl, Bode and Lessing.[7] Since then an extensive literature has accumulated. In 1960 a bibliography containing 550 titles[8] was compiled and this lists only outstanding works. *Old Oriental Carpets*, by Sarre and Trenkwald,[9] was one of the most sumptuous of all the publications. The first volume contains sixty plates of the best pieces in the Vienna collection, and the second has sixty plates showing important carpets in other museums.

Carpet exhibitions, of which the more important were listed in the previous chapter together with their catalogues and the resultant publications, form the great reservoir of carpet study-material. Apart from short lists, catalogues of museum carpet collections[10] hardly exist. The Textile Museum in Washington is exceptional in that two volumes of its catalogue have already been published.[11] The largest carpet collection in the world, in the Türk ve Islam Eserleri Museum in Istanbul, contains more than a thousand pieces and is virtually unknown,[12] and even the world's most important carpet collection, that of the Metropolitan Museum in New York, still awaits a catalogue.[13] The same applies with a few exceptions to private collections like the Yerkes,[14] Ballard[15] and Petag.[16] Auction catalogues occasionally fill a gap but of course cannot claim to be of value to the serious student.

Really scholarly work such as the discussion of definite problems appears, as is customary, in articles. In the early period, the question of the so-called Armenian or Dragon carpets and that of the so-called Polish carpets were important themes, in recent times the Damascus or Mamluk carpets, the representation of carpets in paintings and miniatures, the finds of fragments in Old Cairo and the Seljuk carpets in Asia Minor.[17]

All the material from exhibitions and articles was incorporated in comprehensive accounts at the outset. The Riegl book of 1891 may have been forgotten, but the Bode of 1892 has, as 'Bode-Kühnel', accompanied carpet studies like a faithful friend for seventy years. In 1922 the Kendrick-Tattersall[18] was added and recently several more companions have joined them.[19] There are also others like the Martin of 1908[20] which contains the greatest wealth of material of any rug book ever written. Unfortunately it appeared several decades too soon and it is of such lavish and monumental make-up that it was only within the reach of a few purchasers and because of its size could hardly be handled. Another is Pope with his chapter 'The Art of Carpet Making' in *A Survey of Persian Art*,[21] which of course deals only with Persian carpets.[22] The latest contributor still awaiting judgement is myself with the present volume and *Oriental Carpets – An Account of their History*, the second edition of which, with little change, appeared in 1960 (an English translation was published in 1962).

If one wants to know how carpet studies developed in the last sixty years one finds that Bode-Kühnel is still the most reliable gauge because, in Kühnel's careful hands, the original text has been preserved as far as possible. It is striking to note the strange hardening or simplification of concepts that occurred at first. The ever-widening discussion had led to the introduction of carpet names or designations. Those terms first tentatively used for easier understanding by Bode in 1901 – 'Holbein', 'Dragon', 'Polish', 'Bird', 'Portuguese', 'Damascus', 'Garden', 'Medallion', 'Vase', 'Animal' and the rest – gradually developed into type designations. Originally these names had only been thought of as labels to simplify discussion. Most of them are meaningless. Holbein has nothing to do with carpets named after him except that two of the three groups are occasionally represented in his pictures. Dragons certainly occur as a dominant motif in a certain group of Caucasian rugs but numerous pieces belonging to this group do not show them.

'Polish' carpets are not so called because they were made in Poland, but because, for a brief period about eighty years ago, it was assumed that they were. The error was rectified in 1894.[23] 'Bird' carpets owe their name to misinterpretation of their principal motif, a misconception which was finally cleared up in 1925.[24] The 'Portuguese' carpets have not yet been properly classified, but nobody today still believes that they come from Portuguese Goa. The 'Damascus' carpets have been recognized as Cairo work,[25] but, as regards the 'Garden', 'Medallion', 'Vase' and 'Animal' carpets Pope has said very aptly that one might just as well write a history of western paintings based on Madonnas, Portraits, Landscapes and Still-Life. It should be understood that there is no real foundation for these names and it is annoying that they are still used. Perhaps this will be remedied in time.

As studies progress, a new and more correct attribution warrants a new name which should be so meaningful and striking that it supersedes the old one. The 'Damascus' carpets have been successfully renamed 'Mamluk' but it has been more difficult to replace the term 'Polish' by 'Shah Abbas'. The new name, though better than the old one, is almost correct but rather long. These carpets were not all made during the reign of

Shah Abbas (1587–1629), but they are in a style characteristic of the times, and one which persisted well into the seventeenth century. For some time 'Isfahan' carpets were called 'Herat', a name which was intended to indicate East Persia rather than the city, but this term is no longer fashionable.

None of this is of fundamental importance if one realizes that only too often the name given to an Oriental carpet is nothing but a matter of convenience.

What is important, however, is that in the last few decades emphasis has shifted from the Persian to the Turkish carpet and the latest edition of Bode-Kühnel takes this into account. As a result, a thesis which I have propounded for fifteen years has been accepted.

I cannot, nor would I, conclude this short survey of the development of carpet studies without mentioning a class of book which, though certainly not without importance since it concerns everybody connected with Oriental carpets, is not directly concerned with our theme. These – the manuals for carpet buyers – are often more attractive and even more important than the whole literature which has been discussed. There are many of them, good and bad, in every language in the world, but they are too numerous to mention. I must assume that every reader of these pages has one or more available and

22. Arrangement in the Islamic Department in the Pergamon Museum, Berlin, 1932.

I would not wish to give offence to owners or authors of such books by mentioning or omitting titles. Much valuable information concerning the important subject of connoisseurship is contained in them.

NOTES

1. *Antique Rugs from the Near East*, Fourth revised edition, translated by Charles Grant Ellis, Brunswick, 1958.

2. 'Ein altpersischer Teppich im Besitz der Kgl. Museen zu Berlin.' *Jahrbuch der preussischen Kunstsammlungen*, Berlin, 1892, XIII, pp. 26 ff., pp. 108 ff.

3. *Vorderasiatische Knüpfteppiche aus älterer Zeit*, Leipzig, 1901.

4. See chapter: Carpet Exhibitions since 1890.

5. An exception is V. J. Robinson, *Eastern Carpets*, London, 1882.

6. Leipzig, 1891.

7. J. Lessing, *Orientalische Teppiche*, Berlin, 1891.

8. K. Erdmann, *Oriental Carpets – An Account of their History*, translated by Charles Grant Ellis, London, 1962.

9. F. Sarre and H. Trenkwald, *Old Oriental Carpets*, Vienna and Leipzig, 1926 and 1929.

10. A. F. Kendrick, *Guide to the Collection of Carpets*, London, Victoria and Albert Museum. – C. E. C. Tattersall, *Fine Carpets in the Victoria and Albert Museum*, London, 1924. – K. Erdmann, *Orientteppiche*, Bilderhefte der Islamischen Abteilung, Berlin, 1935. – S. Troll, *Altorientalische Teppiche*, Vienna, Angewandte Kunst Museum, 1951.

11. E. Kühnel and L. Bellinger, *Catalogue of Spanish rugs*, Washington, 1952; idem, *Catalogue of Cairene rugs*, Washington, 1955.

12. See K. Erdmann, *Der türkische Teppich des 15. Jahrhunderts*, Istanbul, 1957.

13. A catalogue of the Metropolitan Museum Collection is being prepared by M. S. Dimand and one for the Berlin Collection is also in preparation.

14. J. K. Mumford, *The Yerkes Collection of Oriental Carpets*, New York, 1910.

15. J. Breck, F. Morris, *The James F. Ballard Collection of Oriental Rugs*, New York, 1923; M. S. Dimand, *The Ballard Collection of Oriental Rugs in the City Art Museum of St. Louis*, 1935.

16. H. Jacoby, *Eine Sammlung orientalischer Teppiche*, Berlin, 1923.

17. Relevant literature in my book (Note 8).

18. A. F. Kendrick and C. E. C. Tattersall, *Handwoven Carpets Oriental and European*, London, 1922.

19. P. M. Campana, *Il Tapetto Orientale*, Milan, 1945; F. Mazzini, *Tappeti Orientali*, Leghorn, 1947.

20. F. R. Martin, *A History of Oriental Carpets before 1800*, Vienna, 1908.

21. A. U. Pope, 'The Art of Carpet Making', in *A Survey of Persian Art*, London, 1939, Vols III and VI.

22. See my exhaustive discussion in the journal *Ars Islamica*, Ann Arbor, 1941, VIII.

23. A. Riegl, 'Zur Frage der Polenteppiche', *Mitteilungen des K. K. Österreichischen Museums für Kunst und Industrie*, Vienna, 1894, pp. 225 ff.

24. R. M. Riefstahl 'Turkish "Bird" Rugs and their Design', *The Art Bulletin*, Providence, U.S.A., 1925, pp. 91 ff.

25. K. Erdmann, 'Kairener Teppiche', *Ars Islamica*, Ann Arbor, 1938, V, pp. 179 ff. and 1940, VII, pp. 55 ff.

INDIVIDUAL GROUPS OF CARPETS

26. Central Anatolia, thirteenth century.

25. Central Antolia, thirteenth century.

'The photographs I reproduce I owe to the courtesy of H.R.H. Prince William of Sweden who, when visiting Konya, asked the Governor-General to have such made for this work, and by order of H.H. the Grand-Vizier Ferid Pasha, they were executed.'

In Note 247 Martin explains this: Herr Loytved, the German Consul who was of Danish origin, had been charged by Prince William with the supervision of the photographs and water-colours but he had also had copies made for himself which he sent to Berlin. The carpets which had been lying in a dark corner of the mosque had not been noticed by anybody until he, Martin, had drawn Loytved's attention to their great historical value. Only since then had they become famous and 'objects of the greatest veneration'.

These carpets had, in fact, been unkown until 1905 and no traveller who described Alaeddin's mosque, not even Sarre, mentioned them. When he published them in 1907 he had not yet seen them, as is evident from his text. This was a tricky situation, annoying for Martin, who, as discoverer, had the right of publication, and embarrassing for Sarre, who was suspected of having illicitly acquired someone else's material. The culprit obviously was Loytved who, without divulging for whom or for what purpose the photographs had been prepared, had handed them on to Sarre without Martin's permission.

In publicizing these oldest Turkish carpets there is no doubt that Sarre's article was more effective than Martin's book which, with its limited edition of 300 copies, only reached a small circle of experts. It is a pity that this publication of 1908, containing an astonishing amount of material previously unknown, had so little influence. Even today, though out of date, it still contains a wealth of information. Who, however, can read a book of 67 × 56 cm., with the text volume alone weighing ten kilos, quite apart from the fact that the two volumes are among the greatest rarities of carpet literature and cost more than £85 on publication.

Sarre reproduced these carpets once more, in 1909 in his book *Seldschukische Kleinkunst*, and in 1914 they were incorporated in the second edition of Bode-Kühnel. They have formed part

28. Central Anatolia, thirteenth century.

27. Central Anatolia, thirteenth century.

of the basic material of carpet studies ever since. In the same year they were taken to the newly arranged Evkaf Museum (today the Türk ve Islam Eserleri Museum) in Istanbul, where they still are.

There are, however, neither three carpets, as Sarre says, nor, as Martin says, four carpets and two fragments; but there are three intact though damaged carpets and five fragments. Of the latter two small pieces are parts of large carpets (Fig. 26) and three large pieces are parts of small carpets, two perhaps from the same one (Fig. 106).

Even though these Konya carpets are so important, they are hardly known, yet they have always been on show in the Museum, apart from the war years. Until a short time ago photographs of only a few were available and a reliable technical analysis is still awaited. As far as I know they have only been shown twice outside Istanbul, one of the fragments (Fig. 27) at the Vienna Exhibition of 1932; two of the intact carpets (Figs. 24 and 25) and four fragments at the exhibition in Paris in 1953. Therefore, apart from one intact piece and two fragments, all

have been seen abroad. The three intact pieces have often been illustrated but the fragments hardly at all; recently Aslanapa has reproduced in colour the three intact carpets and the fragments Inv. Nrs. 688, 684, 692 and 678.

A fragment from the Eshrefoğlu Mosque in Beyshehir, which is similar to the Konya carpet Inv. Nr. 685 (Fig. 24) can be added to the eight examples (seven if 692 and 693 are from one carpet) from the Alaeddin mosque in Konya. The design of the Beyshehir piece is dark red on a light-red ground, but in the Konya piece light blue on a dark-blue ground. Further examples have been found in Fostat (Old Cairo). Of the twenty-nine pieces in Swedish possession published by Lamm, five belong to this group. Another fragment from Fostat of the type shown in Fig. 27 is in American private possession. Undoubtedly other examples must exist among the numerous pieces of this sort which have still not been published.

The famous Venetian traveller Marco Polo, who was in Asia Minor in 1271, wrote 'There are three classes of people in Turkomania. The first are the Turkomans. They live in the

29. Central Anatolia, thirteenth century.

30. Central Anatolia, thirteenth century.

mountains and the valleys where there is good grazing for their herds. The two other classes are the Armenians and the Greeks who, with the Turkomans, live in the towns and villages and are occupied with trade and handicrafts. The best and most beautiful carpets in the world are made there.'

Marco Polo had just returned from Persia when he made this statement. In his opinion the Turkish carpet of the thirteenth century was superior to the Persian of the same period, and this had been supported by others. Ibn Said (✝1274) wrote 'In Aksaray are made the Turkoman carpets which are exported to all the countries of the world', and Ibn Batuta, who travelled in Anatolia at the beginning of the fourteenth century, also praised them and maintained that they were being exported to Egypt, Syria, Iraq, Persia, India and China. Even if it was an exaggeration to speak of India and China, Anatolian products of the thirteenth century, obviously exported in great numbers, have been found in Egypt as the fragments from Old Cairo prove.

When the carpets from the Alaeddin Mosque became known they were immediately associated with the literary references just mentioned. This was not surprising since Konya was the capital of the Turkoman Seljuks and the Alaeddin was their principal mosque. Whether the pieces really date from the years 1218–20 during which the extensions to the mosque were completed, and were given by the Sultans as products of a Court manufactory is another question. The term 'Court manufactory' is sometimes used too casually. It is certain, however, that these carpets were made in the thirteenth century though perhaps not during the first decade. Since carpets with an area of more than fifteen square metres cannot be produced in nomadic, semi-nomadic or even village conditions, they must have been made in urban workshops on looms of more than two and a half metres in width. The location of these workshops

must remain an open question; Arab sources speak of Aksaray, and Marco Polo travelled by way of Kayseri and Sivas. Probably carpets of this kind were produced in many of the cities of the Seljuks of Rum and it is not by chance that most of the examples which have been preserved come from Konya and from the Royal mosque of that city.

The designs of these rugs are geometric, proportionately small in relation to the size of the field, and are arranged in offset rows. There are hexagons with simple or hooked outlines, in one case even a stem pattern which gives a floral character to the design. Other designs show gabled squares with a star-filling and opposed designs between them, which are distantly reminiscent of Kufic script. There are also hexagons in lozenges formed of rhomboids and finally lozenges with strongly stylized flowers or leaves as filling. In effective contrast to the small-pattern designs the main border stripes show Kufic script of monumental size. On the whole the importance of the design in the main border stripe is greater than that of the field and a neat continuation of the border design at the corners is never attempted. The colouring is of a sombre beauty which underlines the severity of the design. There is a striking preference for the use of two shades of the same colour next to each other: a deep blue along with a soft, pale blue, a rich wine red with a muted light red. Green also occurs in two shades and to a lesser degree white, brown and yellow, always in muted tones. The knotting is fairly coarse (100,000 knots per square metre or less).

The variety of patterns is astonishing. Among the fifteen known examples the same design occurs three times only. The fragments shown in Figs. 25 and 106 have the same field design but the colour used in the field of one piece occurs in the border of the other. The carpet (Fig. 24) and a fragment from Beyshehir have the same pattern but similarly alternating colour schemes. Only the third example (Fig. 27) and a fragment from Fostat in an American private collection may have the same design.

About twenty-five years after the discovery of the Konya carpets, the American scholar Riefstahl found a second group of carpets of this type in the Eshrefoğlu Mosque in Beyshehir, a town some fifty miles south-west of Konya. He discussed these in detail in *The Art Bulletin*, Providence, U.S.A., 1931, XIII, pp. 1 ff. A small fragment shows exactly the same design as the Konya carpet (Fig. 24) but with different colours on field and border. This might serve as a clue for the dating of the carpets found in the Alaeddin Mosque. The Eshrefoğlu Mosque was built in 1298 and it is unlikely that an old carpet would be used in its furnishings. That points to a dating for the whole group at the end or the second half of the thirteenth century, but this, of course, is not conclusive. A second fragment (Fig. 28) has a lozenge design which does not occur in this form in the Konya carpets, but because of its harmony of light and dark blue is closely related to them. What remains of its border shows the monumental Kufic script characteristic of the group. The third (Fig. 29), which is over five metres long, has a field design in soft, pale blue on dark blue, which is also characteristic of the Konya group but it differs in that its design, although strongly stylized, must represent a plant form. Geometric forms which can be associated with Kufic script are used on a soft violet ground in the broad border (Fig. 30). This fragment undoubtedly belongs to the group, but is probably a little later, that is about 1300 or the first quarter of the fourteenth century. The fourth carpet, which was also fairly large (Riefstahl estimated its original length at over six metres), has been preserved in three fragments. It shows a small-pattern arrangement of squares with an octagon filling and is probably more than a hundred years later in date.

In the introduction to his penetrating study of these four carpets Riefstahl writes: 'I should not like to offer my study, however, without expressing in the very beginning the hope that these interesting and exceedingly rare specimens of Turkish carpet weaving may be transferred by the Turkish authorities to some place more secure and more accessible than the mosque of Beyshehir. It would be of the greatest benefit if they might be made accessible for study in the Museum of Angora or if they might be incorporated into the treasure of ancient fabrics now preserved in the well-ordered and protected museum in the former Tekke of the Mewlewi in Konya.'

When with my students in Konya in 1953, I recalled these words, and we asked in the Mevlana Museum for the carpet fragments from Beyshehir, they were not among the exhibited pieces, but neither were they in the mosque of Beyshehir, nor in the Ethnographic Museum in Ankara. After some time an official remembered that one of the rooms in the large museum contained framed carpet fragments, possibly those from Beyshehir. They proved to be seventeenth- and eighteenth-century pieces of little value, beautifully framed in oak and under glass. One of Riefstahl's published fragments appeared in the fifth or sixth frame. The authorities had taken this

THE SELJUK CARPETS FROM KONYA

Publications and Exhibitions

	Year	Istanbul, Türk ve Islam Eserleri Museum Inventory Numbers						
		678	681	684	685	688	689	692/3
F. Sarre, 'Mittelalterliche Knüpfteppiche' in *Kunst und Kunsthandwerk*	1907		×		×		×	
F. R. Martin, *A History of Oriental Carpets before 1800*	1908		×		×		×	
F. Sarre, *Erzeugnisse islamischer Kunst* II. 'Seldjukische Kleinkunst'	1909		×		×		×	
W. von Bode and E. Kühnel, *Vorderasiatische Knüpfteppiche aus älterer Zeit*	1914		×		×		×	
Vienna Exhibition	1932			×				
Paris Exhibition	1953		×	×	×		×	×
K. Erdmann, *Oriental Carpets*	1962		×	×	×	×		×
O. Aslanapa, *Turkish Arts*	1960	×	×	×	×	×	×	×
K. Erdmann, Articles in *Heimtex*	1960–1964		×	×	×	×	×	×
Darmstadt Exhibition	1965		×	×	×		×	×
Illustrated here	Fig.	25	27	24	26	23		106

warning to heart but since they did not know anything about carpets and did not have his article available they had brought all the old-looking fragments from Beyshehir to Konya and exhibited them there. Three of the Seljuk fragments were saved in this way. Only the fourth, according to Riefstahl five metres long, with plant motifs was not there. We assumed that because of its size it could not be framed and was still in the depot, but nothing was known about it. When at a later date a younger Director took over the museum I was allowed to search the carpet depot myself, but could not find this fragment. I came across it eventually but neither in Konya nor in Beyshehir.

In 1957 a friend in Washington showed me a carpet fragment which he had bought in Cairo; it was from Fostat, about 30 cm. square, and he asked me whether it could possibly be Seljuk.

It actually was, and came from the field of a carpet similar to the fragments (Fig. 27) from the Alaeddin Mosque in Konya. When he proudly told the Director that he owned a piece of Konya carpet, the latter replied that they also had one, or rather, were just in the process of acquiring it. He showed us a photograph. It was the lost piece from the mosque in Beyshehir (Figs. 29 and 30). Naturally when the museum learned the facts the purchase fell through. My pleasure in having spotted the piece proved to be premature. It was offered by an agent who, naturally, would not divulge the owner's name. I only know that it still exists and hope to come across it again under more favourable circumstances.

The Anatolian Animal Carpets

There lived in Constantinople a pious man who wished to offer a gift to St. Nicholas, his patron Saint. Since he had no money he decided to sell his one and only possession, a carpet. On the way to the bazaar he encountered the Saint in disguise. St. Nicholas looked at the carpet, bought it, and gave it back to the poor man's wife, so that her husband found it at home when he returned.

This story is illustrated in a fresco (Fig. 31) in the church of Boiana, eight kilometres to the south of Sofia. The poor man has spread out the carpet for sale and bargains with the Saint whom he does not recognize. The fresco was painted in 1259 and, therefore, a carpet is mentioned in a mid-thirteenth-century tale.

The rug is in the form of a runner some 75 cm. in width and 200 cm. in length. Its field is enclosed in a narrow border, the design of which is not indicated. It contains circular medallions in simple rows, two in the breadth of the field and five in its length. Two further medallions are halved by the end border and there was probably another incomplete pair at the far end. Two medallions in the picture contain stylized eagles with heads directed laterally and the two above them contain quadrupeds striding outwards (Fig. 32). The enclosing bands are unornamented and the field design between the medallions is indicated only summarily.

Such medallions with animals are well known in Byzantine textiles. In a miniature in the Chrysostom Codex of Nicephorus Botaniates a man wears Byzantine court dress of the eleventh century (Fig. 33). The robe is ornamented with quadrupeds facing to the right in interlaced medallions whose enclosing bands contain a continuous tendril design. The analogy can be extended to the embroidered cope (Fig. 34) in Anagni which according to Otto von Falke was made in Cyprus in 1295. The medallions, which are not connected with each other, are filled with eagles (in this case double-headed), striding quadrupeds (obviously griffins) and birds (perhaps parrots) with retroverted heads standing back to back on either side of a flower motif.

In paintings of the Italian school of the fourteenth and fifteenth centuries carpets are often depicted which show the following motifs: double-headed or simple, stylized eagles, striding quadrupeds, similar to those in the fresco of Boiana and the miniature just discussed, and addorsed birds with retroverted heads flanking a tree or shrub. Such motifs are used as fillings for the squares or octagons of these rugs. A double-headed eagle appears in a mid-fourteenth-century Florentine picture in Berlin showing the Madonna enthroned with Saints, stylized eagles in a Sienese picture of the fourteenth century in the Vatican, striding and standing quadrupeds with retroverted heads in a picture of the Madonna (Fig. 35) by Ambrogio

31. Fresco in the church of Boiana near Sofia, 1259.

32. Drawing of the fresco Fig. 31.

33. Byzantine court dress of the eleventh century.

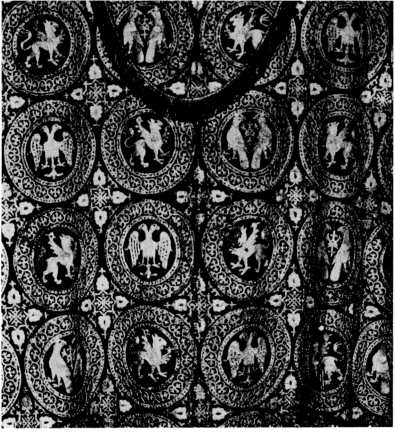

34. Byzantine textile, before 1295.

Lorenzetti and addorsed birds flanking a tree in the Betrothal of the Virgin by Sano di Pietro in the Vatican.

The rugs in these paintings are certainly knotted rugs and, apart from the picture of the enthroned Madonna which might depict a textile, not Byzantine but Turkish work, which is also proved from some extant originals and fragments. It must be assumed that these rugs were made not later than the end of the thirteenth century since they were depicted in paintings at the beginning of the fourteenth century. When in 1929 I listed paintings showing such rugs I called them Anatolian Animal rugs. In time the early examples overlap the later examples of the Konya carpets (Figs. 23–28). Indeed, it appears that the Konya carpets, which disappeared at the beginning of the fourteenth century, were supplanted by the Anatolian Animal carpets which can still be found in pictures of the second half of the fifteenth century.

The existence side by side of these two groups is surprising. The composition of simple rows of identical motifs is certainly the same in both. In the Konya carpets all forms are geometric, even those which hark back to vegetal elements, and figural forms are completely lacking. On the other hand in the Anatolian animal carpets the pattern is based on figures, and geometric elements are found only in borders and guard stripes.

The figural motifs, which from the beginning occur in at least three different designs, have obviously been borrowed from textiles. Even though little is known of the Anatolian-Seljuk silk weaving of the thirteenth century, animal figures occurred frequently in it so that Seljuk influence is possible, but the principal motifs of the Animal carpets, the heraldic eagle, the striding quadruped and addorsed birds standing on either side of a plant, are also found in Byzantine textiles of the eleventh, twelfth and thirteenth centuries in a form so similar that one cannot doubt a connection. If, however, the Anatolian Animal carpets derive their motifs principally from Byzantine textiles, it must be assumed that they originated in a district which had close connections with Byzantium and this was certainly more the case in Western Anatolia than in the Central or Eastern part of the country. There is further evidence for this in the portrayal of these rugs in Italian paintings, which points to an extensive export of rugs to Italy from the interior of Western Anatolia, where the Venetian and Genoese merchants had established their trading stations.

One is thus inclined to assign the older Konya carpets to Central Anatolia, though it must not be assumed that Konya was the only centre of production, while the later Anatolian Animal carpets were made in Western Anatolia. This is feasible because at the beginning of the thirteenth century these districts were still in Byzantine hands, but in the decades after 1220 Turkish pressure on Byzantium increased steadily as a result of the advancing Mongols threatening the Turks in the East. When the Latin Empire in Constantinople came to an end and the Byzantines reconquered the city in 1261 they transferred the centre of their political interest to the Balkans, denuded Asia

Minor of their best troops and thus jeopardized the defence of their Eastern frontier to such an extent that the Turks reached the coast in a few years. It is, therefore, quite possible that at the end of the thirteenth century carpet workshops were established in the region of Ushak, Kula and Ghiordes which later became a centre of carpet production, and possibly also in the vicinity of Bergama. The new type of Anatolian Animal carpet produced here incorporated motifs from Byzantine textiles and can, therefore, be differentiated from the older and in part contemporary Central Anatolian Konya carpets. The representation of Animal carpets in European pictures only provides approximate dates for the originals. The dating is difficult because it cannot be established for how long carpets had to be in circulation in Italy before, for instance, Simone Martini depicted one showing addorsed birds in a painting dated 1317, nor how long a rug had to be in production in Turkey before it was exported to the West. The time-lag may not have been great, but one must assume a period of several decades and a carpet depicted in 1317 may have been made some time between 1270 and 1280. Roughly speaking the portrayal of these rugs in pictures, at first only in the Italian school, and later in the Netherlandish and Spanish schools, occurs between 1300 and 1500. The prototypes must, therefore, have been made between 1270 and 1450. Carpets showing eagles, either double-headed or single and heraldically stylized or in profile, occur only in paintings of the fourteenth century. There are two examples from this period with a pair of birds flanking a tree and five from the first half of the fifteenth century. Striding quadrupeds occur mainly in the fourteenth (six examples) but only once in the fifteenth century. Groups of animals or animals in combat appear only in pictures of the fifteenth century.

The fragments from Old Cairo sometimes show animals in free arrangement as in paintings: rows of confronted, horned quadrupeds alternating with rows of hexagons (Fig. 36), confronted birds on either side of a tree (Fig. 37) or an abstract design that could have been yaken from a Konya carpet (Fig. 24). With few exceptions, Western painters who introduced such carpets into their pictures took the easy way out, by portraying rugs with simple patterns. Either these were preferred by the importers, or perhaps the artists themselves simplified a complex pattern.

It is interesting to note that in one painting only (Fig. 38) a standing cock used as the filling of the octagon occurs in almost exactly the same design in a fragment (Fig. 5) from Old Cairo. The connection between the birds depicted in the Spanish picture (Fig. 39) and those in an actual carpet (Fig. 40) in Konya is less marked, but still close enough to show that they are of the same type, which proves that the carpet now in the Mevlana Museum in Konya dates from the beginning of the fifteenth century.

A similar date can be assumed for the well-known carpet with the dragon and phoenix combat (Fig. 1) in Berlin which came from a church in Central Italy. This type must have been widespread

35. Carpet in a painting by Ambrogia Lorenzetti.

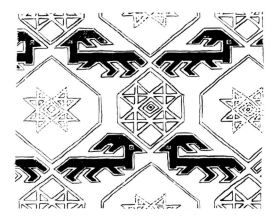

36. Drawing of a design of an Anatolian carpet, about 1400.

37. Drawing of a design of an Anatolian carpet, fifteenth century.

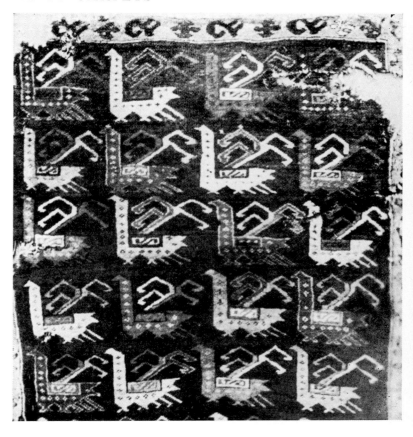

40. Anatolian, fifteenth century.

38. Carpet in a painting by Niccolo da Buonaccorso (1348–88).

9. Carpet in a painting by Jaume Huguet (died 1437–8).

41. Norway, fifteenth to sixteenth century.

in the first half of the fifteenth century because Domenico di Bartolo, between 1440–1444 portrayed such carpets in a fresco (Fig. 2) in Siena and the design also appears in pictures by Baldovenetti, Morone, Hans Memling and, less clearly shown, by Pisanello and Jacopo Bellini. In addition two fragments from Old Cairo exist. One was in the art trade in 1940 and the other is in the Ethnographical Museum in Basle. It is amusing to see how such a carpet has been imitated in a Norwegian cushion cover (Fig. 41). The phoenix has shrunk but the dragon can still be seen clearly. Carpets with these designs must therefore have been known in the Baltic in the fifteenth century.

The So-called Holbein Carpets

In addition to the Anatolian Animal carpets, rugs with fields filled with geometric designs are occasionally found in European paintings of the fourteenth and fifteenth centuries. In general these motifs are drawn in such a primitive way that little can be deduced from them and it is sometimes doubtful whether knotted carpets are represented. This changes in the middle of the fifteenth century. The earliest certain example of geometric field design in a carpet occurs in 1451 in a picture by Piero della Francesca in the church of San Francesco in Rimini, where Sigismondo Malatesta is represented kneeling before his patron Saint. The same type of so-called Holbein rug, appears in Mantegna's altarpiece in the church of San Zeno in Verona painted between 1457 and 1459. A Fra Carnevale miniature in the Vatican library is of the same period. In all three rugs a frieze of Kufic script occurs in the main stripe of the border. It is freely and richly drawn and is known only in one rug fragment (Fig. 184) in Berlin. In a late fifteenth-century picture (Fig. 42), lost in Berlin during the war, a distinctly later version of the border occurs, in which the Kufic script has become an interlace in a form known from many rugs (Figs. 13, 47, 48). The origin of the group, therefore, can be dated to the first half of the fifteenth century and the Berlin fragment (Fig. 184) is the oldest known example. Similar geometric forms also occur both in the border and the field in the fragments from Old Cairo which have already been considered with the Anatolian Animal carpets.

A fragment in the National Museum in Stockholm has a field design of offset rows of octagons, a motif which is known from the Konya carpets (Fig. 23). Another (Fig. 43) in Gothenburg has offset rows in which large octagons and small hexagons alternate within the rows. The geometric border of the carpet which, ultimately, depends on ornaments derived from Kufic script is identical with the fragment (Fig. 44) from the mosque in Beyshehir. The field of the latter piece consists of rows of large lozenges alternating with rows of smaller, more simply drawn rosettes. The large motifs are constructed of a cruciform centre with diagonally radiating, forked arabesque leaves which form the outline of the lozenge. This form is clearly a forerunner of the lozenge motif in the usual Holbein carpets, where an inner arabesque structure is surrounded by a second, outer one. The indication of vertical and horizontal lines, which divide the field into small squares, is strange, but, as a result, each large motif forms the filling of a square while the smaller ones are quartered and become the corner pieces in four adjoining squares. In classical times such a division of the field into squares indicated by means of lines occurs in only one other group of carpets: those formerly regarded as a late phase of the Egyptian Mamluk carpets, although according to recent investigations they may have had their origin in some locality of Anatolia which is not yet known. This unusual arrangement can also be found in several groups of the later Turkoman carpets (Fig. 45).

42. Anatolian carpet in a painting by Raffaellino del Garbo, end of fifteenth century.

43. Drawing of an Anatolian carpet fragment, second half of the fifteenth century.

Holbein carpets, of which about fifty intact and fragmentary examples are preserved, are often to be seen in paintings. The field pattern consists of rows of octagons with interlaced outline alternating with offset rows of lozenges whose outlines are formed of arabesques which proceed from a central cross. Small rosettes are used for the filling of the remainder of the field. Apart from insignificant details in drawing this pattern does not change during its period of production. On the other hand Holbein carpets have been made in many sizes and the number of the motifs appearing in the field varies from 6×13 to 2×3 octagons. As in almost all Anatolian carpets the rule is that the size of the motifs remain constant but the area of pattern used varies with the size of the carpet. The octagons of the Berlin fragment (Fig. 184) are of one colour as are those in the oldest portrayals in pictures. This could be

taken as a sign of an early piece but for the fact that uniformity of colour in the octagons also occurs in later pieces, such as those in the Bavarian National Museum in Munich and in the City Art Museum in St. Louis. Usually the colours of the octagons change within the row and, in the case of offset rows, from row to row (Fig. 46). As far as I know only two colours are used and the colour of the field is usually but not always uniform. Of thirty-seven pieces on which I have colour notes, twenty-five have fields of one colour and of these twelve are dark blue, nine red and four green. In twelve pieces two colours, red and green or red and blue (Fig. 47) are used in the field.

Whenever such a colour change occurs the impression is created of a pattern divided into small squares (Figs. 47, 48, 50) and the octagons act as filling for the individual squares; lozenge

44. Anatolia, beginning of the fifteenth century.

45. Turkestan, nineteenth century.

46. West Anatolia, beginning of the sixteenth century.

47. West Anatolia, beginning of the sixteenth century.

forms are shared among the four adjoining squares as corner-pieces. This influences the colour effect of the carpet. On the other hand in the carpet from the Beyshehir mosque (Fig. 44) although the squares are indicated, the field is only of one colour and the colour of the lozenges is also uniform.

The question now arises how to interpret the pattern of these Holbein carpets. Does it consist, as seems probable, of carpets with a field of one colour, and of horizontal rows of octagons alternating with horizontal but offset rows of lozenges, or, does it consist of small squares rhythmically alternating in colour each with an octagon filling and oblique corners? In the second example (Fig. 47) the interpretation is clear. In the first (Fig. 46) it is possible that if the separation into squares be omitted the

oblique corners in the four adjoining squares fuse into an apparently independent lozenge motif. This interpretation would only be valid, however, if it could be proved that the colour change of the second form (Fig. 47) be the older, and if so that design would be the earlier one. It is, of course, conceivable, though difficult to imagine, that the offset rows in Fig. 46 were subsequently taken to be a small pattern of squares. This is an important but somewhat complex problem which cannot be elaborated beyond what is said in the appendix under Fig. 46.

The field design of these carpets is constant, apart from the area of pattern determined by the size of the carpet and the changes in colour of the lozenges, which occur when that of the field is not of one colour. Two exceptions are known to me. One,

48. West Anatolia, sixteenth century.

49. West Anatolia, sixteenth century.

a carpet formerly in the Dirksen Collection (Fig. 48), contains differently shaped octagons. A multi-rayed star surrounded by double volutes replaces the usual cruciform centre and the whole is framed in an octagon. This motif occurs in the Bergama carpets and may have been borrowed from that district. A similar variant appears in the remains of a carpet (Fig. 49) now used as a chair cover.

Although the designs of the Holbein rug borders seem varied on closer inspection they are remarkably similar. Thirty-eight of the forty-three examples available to me go back to the same basic pattern. This a is stylized frieze of script, also found in other Anatolian groups, but only in five early examples have the shafts of the letters free ends (Figs. 46, 184). Usually the script

has become an interlace which occurs in complex form (Figs. 42, 47) (24 examples) and a simpler form (Figs. 48 and 49) (9 examples). Occasionally there is a row of cartouches in the second border stripe (Fig. 46). Other border designs (Fig. 50) are rare and probably late, although it is difficult to say how late. Carpets of this type first appear in pictures in the middle of the fifteenth century and towards the end of the century the usual interlace border appears. Portrayals of such carpets continue during the whole of the sixteenth century. The latest occurs in the group portrait *The Somerset House Conference* of 1604 in the National Portrait Gallery in London, and in the *Portrait of a Lady* of 1655 by Justus Suttermans, but in both cases the carpets portrayed may have been older possessions.

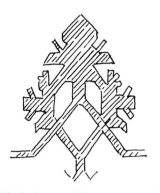

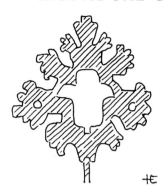

54. Palmette blossom: (a) in a Lotto carpet, (b) in a Medallion Ushak.

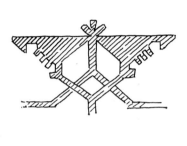

55. Paired arabesque: (a) from a Lotto carpet, (b) from a Medallion Ushak.

tions and wrote: '... the arabesques form quatrefoiled and irregular compartments symmetrically arranged'. This, though still vague, speaks for the first time of pattern construction. I was able to describe it more clearly in 1950, when I spoke of 'A small pattern design of squares, the corners of which have been cut off, results in the coalescing of four squares in the form of a yellow cross. The octagon that fills the space between the crosses consists of simple yellow blossoms arranged around a small central lozenge with a blue star and angular branches with yellow half palmettes.' In 1951 Troll referred to this, speaking of 'stiff, yellow arabesques, forming a tile pattern of crosses and octagons'. The description in the fourth edition of Bode-Kühnel (1955) is less clear, speaking only of 'octagons completely dissolved into geometric tendrils and arabesques, which are so compressed that they can hardly be recognized as such'. In 1955 I amended my description of 1950 to: 'offset rows of lozenge and octagon figures in endless repeat (Fig. 53) and this is the same composition as in the small-pattern Holbein carpets'. The lozenge motifs, in spite of their more cruciform outline, are constructed as in the Holbein carpets: a centre with gabled arabesque leaves 'vertically and much enlarged blossoms

in the Haji Baba Club, a society of carpet lovers, in New York.

Both the small-pattern Holbein carpets (Figs. 46, 47, 48) and the Lotto carpets (Fig. 178, Pl. IX) have in common a design in which layout and size are constant. A law which is valid for almost all Anatolian carpets in repetitive designs is that, with a change in the size of the field there is no change in the size of the design repeat (cf. Figs. 56 and 57). It is strange that the fundamental relationship of the two groups was not recognized sooner even though their similarity was appreciated early. Probably the design of the Lotto carpets was not understood.

The Vienna catalogue of 1891 describes it as 'Clearly arranged angular tendrils with highly stylized blossoms with serrated edges . . .'. Riegl observes 'along with the characteristic stepped figures also certain interlaced tendrils', while Valentiner in 1910 speaks of 'geometrically conventionalized leaf forms'. In the second (1914) edition of Bode-Kühnel's book it is stated on page 131 that the pattern is based on 'tendrils stiffened into angular forms though the flowers of the pomegranate or palmette were the origin of it'. The same uninformative description is repeated in the third edition (1921). Kendrick and Tattersall's handbook (1922) is content with the remark 'showing arabesques' and even such a discerning connoisseur as Jacoby speaks (1923) of 'the red and yellow flame-like arabesques and palmettes'. In 1935 I had not got further than 'strongly geometrical arabesque tendrils'. In 1935 Dimand improved on these descrip-

56. West Anatolia, seventeeenth century.

horizontally. The octagons, however, are of a different shape. They are arranged in a looser, symmetrical structure of full and half palmettes with connecting arabesque leaves which resemble rather a filling of the space between the lozenges than a figure in its own right.' I believe that this description must be retained because the fragmentation of the field into small squares of different colours (Fig. 47) never occurs in Lotto carpets.

In considering where, when and how certain types of Turkish carpet originated, the position of the Lotto carpet is not very satisfactory. They are only depicted in Western paintings from the beginning of the sixteenth century, and do not occur among the fragments from Old Cairo. The oldest, extant originals go back to the early sixteenth century and although Spanish copies exist, they appeared later (Fig. 272). Forerunners of the Lotto design among the older Anatolian types indicate only the composition but not the details.

The Lotto carpets, which were probably made in the same district of Western Anatolia as the small-pattern Holbein carpets, are about a hundred years later and borrow from the Holbein carpets their basic plan of two different shapes arranged

58. West Anatolia, seventeenth century.

57. West Anatolia, late seventeenth century.

in alternating rows, but the actual motifs are different. The yellow palmette blossoms and arabesque leaves without either contrasting outline or ornamentation, are silhouetted on a red ground and recall the field pattern of earlier Medallion Ushaks, especially those with a yellow design on a dark-blue field, but the colouring is enlivened somewhat through the use of darker, usually dark blue, fillings at the base of the palmettes and arabesques. Sometimes the lozenge centres of the crosses are also emphasized by a contrasting colour. Besides the same brilliant yellow, the third similarity consists in the lack of outline and inner ornamentation. The edging of the flowers in the field of the Ushaks are less stiff and have a feeling of movement. In the secondary medallion of these Ushaks palmette blossoms occur which are similarly stylized (Fig. 54) and the arabesques filling the central medallion are often terminated on right and left by a pair which have straight lateral contours and point inwards. In arrangement this corresponds to the strongly stylized pair of arabesque leaves in the Lotto carpets which form the upper and lower limitations of the octagon filling (Fig. 55). Such an unusual construction could hardly have been invented twice. There are obvious connections here and the question as to which form is the earlier may be left open. What is important, however, is that the pattern of the Lotto carpets did not evolve but, like that of the Holbein carpet, was deliberately designed. The traditional scheme of composition, of offset rows of

59. West Anatolia, end of the seventeenth century.

This new design was obviously successful. Not only does it occur again and again in pictures of all the European schools from the beginning of the sixteenth to the end of the seventeenth centuries, but also it is still extant in hundreds of examples amongst which are even some with European coats-of-arms, which proves that they were made to European order (Fig. 144). Grote-Hasenbalg has quite rightly pointed out that such carpets were made in several workshops. Quite marked differences can be noted although the design is constant and this is not always occasioned by differences in date. Versions of compact (Fig.56) and sparse (Figs. 58, 59) designs occur simultaneously and the sizes also vary considerably in contemporary pieces. It is true, for this group as for others, that later carpets are smaller in size. The number of border designs is astonishing. They begin with the Kufic script (Fig. 52) of the Holbein carpets, continue through variation and degeneration of the scheme until there are box borders, cartouches, cloud-bands (Fig. 57), tendril and scroll borders of all kinds, most of which point to Ushak.

There are, however, hardly any different field designs. In a large carpet in Berlin (Pl. IX) single blue or green leaves are used, so that a diagonal effect is produced although the design is otherwise unchanged. In a small piece formerly in the collection of Wilhelm von Bode (Fig. 58), the centre of the octagonal motif is dark blue. Changes in the colour of the field are equally rare. I have only come across two blue-ground examples among at least five hundred carpets of this group, one in the McMullan Collection in New York and the second in private possession in Holland. All the other examples have red fields.

Degeneration of design, so frequent in late examples of other groups, hardly ever occurs (Fig. 59). Apparently the Lotto carpets disappeared as suddenly at the end of the seventeenth century as they had appeared at the beginning of the sixteenth. There is no evidence that even some of their designs survived into the eighteenth and nineteenth centuries. It is as if the workshops which produced them had suddenly closed their doors or had started to make carpets of a different kind.

lozenges, cross forms and octagon motifs respectively, was changed according to the taste of the time. The Lotto carpets, therefore, unlike the Holbeins are not folk art but are the products of manufactories which undoubtedly were situated in Ushak or in the surrounding district.

The Small Silk Carpets of Kashan

The Small Silk carpets of Kashan, which are among the most important of the sixteenth-century rugs of Persia, form a clearly defined group. They were probably woven in the same workshop as the famous Vienna Hunting carpet (Fig. 99) from the Hapsburg Collection, the carpet formerly in the possession of Baron Maurice de Rothschild which is equally well designed but less satisfactory in its colouring, and the Animal carpet (Fig. 102) of the Polish family Branicki which, before the war, was in Warsaw Castle and whose whereabouts are now unfortunately unknown. Riefstahl was the first to group the Small Silk carpets of Kashan when, in 1916, he showed that the three silk carpets of the Altman Collection in the Metropolitan Museum in New

60. Persia (Kashan), sixteenth century.

61. Persia (Kashan), sixteenth century.

63. Persia (Kashan), sixteenth century.

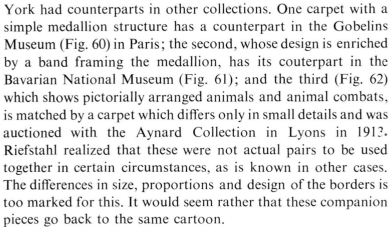

62. Persia (Kashan), middle of the sixteenth century.

York had counterparts in other collections. One carpet with a simple medallion structure has a counterpart in the Gobelins Museum (Fig. 60) in Paris; the second, whose design is enriched by a band framing the medallion, has its couterpart in the Bavarian National Museum (Fig. 61); and the third (Fig. 62) which shows pictorially arranged animals and animal combats, is matched by a carpet which differs only in small details and was auctioned with the Aynard Collection in Lyons in 1913. Riefstahl realized that these were not actual pairs to be used together in certain circumstances, as is known in other cases. The differences in size, proportions and design of the borders is too marked for this. It would seem rather that these companion pieces go back to the same cartoon.

He cites as further examples of this group, though without counterparts, a carpet (Fig. 68) now in the Gulbenkian Collection, formerly in the Schloss Museum in Berlin, and another (Fig. 67) formerly in the possession of Pierpont Morgan, and today as a gift of P. A. B. Widener in the National Gallery in Washington.

Shortly afterwards two further examples came to light: a small piece (Fig. 233) which in 1919 was given to the Louvre by

Peytel and a carpet (Fig. 63) in the usual size of the group which in 1925 was presented to the Art Institute in Detroit by Edsel B. Ford. Both show the pictorially arranged animals and animal combats of the third group and are obviously based on the same cartoon as those. Three, possibly four, hitherto unknown examples have been added lately to these ten pieces and are discussed below.

The carpet exhibition in the Rijksmuseum in Amsterdam in 1946 included a rug (Fig. 64) of normal size (168 × 245 cm.) in the possession of the Portuguese-Israelite community of the city. On the red field is a green central medallion in the form of an octafoil with white outlines, and blue quartered medallions of the same design fill the corners. Palmette blossoms pointing outwards ornament the main green border stripe between an inner yellow and an outer red guard. These are of large size and every second one is framed in a shield. The border design is similar to that of the Widener carpet (Fig. 67) and distantly related to one of the Altman carpets.

The counterpart (Fig. 65) of this carpet which was previously in the John Taylor Johnston Collection, reached the Metropolitan Museum in 1958 as a gift of Mrs. Douglas M. Moffat,

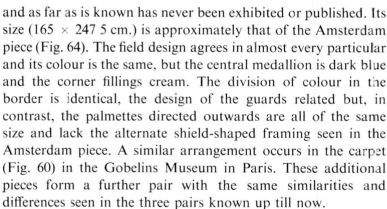

64. Persia (Kashan), sixteenth century.

65. Persia (Kashan), sixteenth century.

and as far as is known has never been exhibited or published. Its size (165 × 247 5 cm.) is approximately that of the Amsterdam piece (Fig. 64). The field design agrees in almost every particular and its colour is the same, but the central medallion is dark blue and the corner fillings cream. The division of colour in the border is identical, the design of the guards related but, in contrast, the palmettes directed outwards are all of the same size and lack the alternate shield-shaped framing seen in the Amsterdam piece. A similar arrangement occurs in the carpet (Fig. 60) in the Gobelins Museum in Paris. These additional pieces form a further pair with the same similarities and differences seen in the three pairs known up till now.

It is more difficult to classify the third piece (175 × 232 cm.) (Fig. 66), given to the Museum of Applied Art in Vienna by the Baroness Clarice de Rothschild. Surrounding a cream-cloured, ogival medallion with pendants on a dark red ground are arranged ten dark-blue cartouches with cloud-band filling, four of which are halved by the side borders and quarters of quatre-foil medallions with blossoms and arabesque leaves fill the cream-coloured corners. An inner red and outer green guard enclose the main cream-coloured border stripe which is orna-

mented with palmettes in shields connected by broad band-like arabesques. The arrangement of the cartouches around the central medallion corresponds closely to that of the Widener carpet (Fig. 67) but in the latter they are joined by a fine tendril. Cartouches in the field do not occur elsewhere in the group. The drawings of the corner fillings is similar to that of the two related carpets, one of which (not illustrated) is in the Altman Collection in New York and the other in the Gobelins Museum in Paris, but in these two the contours are not thickened. In Small Silk Kashans the medallions are always correctly drawn and quarters of the central medallion design fill the corners. This does not apply to the Vienna piece (Fig. 66) which has a central ogival medallion unknown in any other example of this group. Other differences are the thickened chi or cloud-ball edging, the stiff drawing of the arabesque leaves in the field corners and the less elegant, band-like forms in the main stripe of the border. Strictly this piece, a late-comer, does not belong to the group but it is related to it.

In the silk tapestry carpets which are supposed to have been made in Kashan at the end of the sixteenth and beginning of the seventeenth centuries, ogival central medallions often have the

Garden Carpets

Many Persian carpets of the sixteenth and seventeenth centuries are adorned with verses which liken them to a garden where the borders are filled with scented flowers and the trees with twittering birds.

Garden - a magic word in a country which consists largely of steppe and bare mountains.

The garden was beautified again with the sparkle of youth
When the rose laughs the nightingale does not remain silent.

So sings Hafiz of the gardens of Shiraz, and Sadi writes in the 'Rose Garden': 'It happened that I spent the night with my friend in the garden, in that lovely airy abode with beautiful densely entwined trees. It looked almost as if splinters of molten glass had been spread under our feet and as if the tree tops were surrounded with the necklace of the Pleiades.'

Lovely songs in the garden
Clear water in the meadow,
This filled with colourful tulips
And that full of fruits without number.
Rustling through the shady hall of trees
The winds make a shimmering carpet

69. North Persia, eighteenth century.

A continuous thread leads from the 'hanging gardens' of Semiramis by way of the Castle of the Sassanians in Sarvistan, to the cypress garden of the Taq-i-Bustan or garden hall which is one of the most famous monuments of old Persian art, and continues to the garden plans of Shah Abbas the Great in Isfahan, of which at the beginning of the seventeenth century Sir Thomas Herbert left so vivid a description.

It is not by chance that the word 'Paradise', which both Christians and Muslims associate with the idea of a beautiful garden, comes from the Persian.

The Poet Sadi compares the garden to a carpet spread by the night winds in the shadow of the trees. The miniature painters who designed the cartoons for the carpet weavers made the carpet like a garden which could not be harmed by the heat of summer or the cold of winter but where, as in the garden of Paradise, there was eternal spring. A contemporary source states 'During the cold season of the year the carpets are brought from the store and banquets are held on them as if in a garden'.

The painters and weavers of the sixteenth century were not the first to visualize carpets as gardens. Their garden carpets had a famous predecessor, the legendary 'Spring of Chosroes', which the Sassanian King Chosroes Nushirvan had ordered for his audience hall in Ctesiphon and which was described by Arab writers. It is supposed to have been 150 metres long and 30 metres wide. Its field represented a garden with streams and paths, flower beds, blossoms and trees. Gold threads indicated the colour of the earth and crystals the water of the streams. The stems, branches and twigs of the trees were made of silver and the flowers, leaves and roots of silk and coloured jewels. In A.D. 637 when the Arabs conquered Ctesiphon, the carpet was cut up and distributed as booty. Ali, the son-in-law of the Prophet, is said to have sold his share for 20,000 drachma. None of the pieces has survived but the descriptions indicate that it cannot have been a knotted carpet, but a woven one or perhaps even a felt adorned with jewels, embroidered in gold and appliquéd with silk.

This technique lived on in Islamic times. In the ninth century a contemporary writer reports that the mother of the Caliph al Musta'in ordered a precious carpet and tried in vain to interest her son in it. As she insisted, he finally sent two of his servants who contemplated it with astonishment because 'all that was beautiful in the world was depicted in it'. Ahmed ibn Hamdun reports: 'I myself took a golden gazelle whose eyes were of rubies into my hand and hid it up my sleeve. Then we returned to the Caliph and described the beauty of what we had seen and my companion said "Oh Ruler of the Faithful, he has stolen something from it" and he pointed to my sleeve. When I showed

70. North Persia, eighteenth century.

71. North Persia, second half of the eighteenth century.

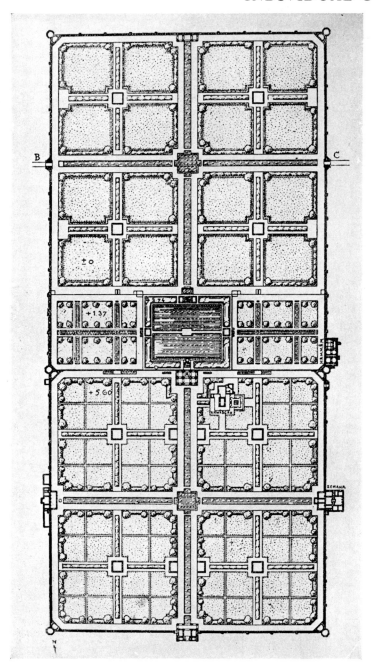

73. North Persia, eighteenth century.

72. Plan of an Oriental garden.

him the gazelle the Caliph said "Upon my soul, go back and take what you wish." And we did so.'

One cannot easily steal a figure from a knotted carpet, and therefore the carpet of the Caliph's mother must have been appliquéd like the 'Spring of Chosroes'. In fact the knotting technique hardly reached Persia before the eleventh century and obviously at first did not supplant the valuable floor coverings made in a different way.

Not until the sixteenth century did Persian weavers attain the mastery which enabled them, in collaboration with miniaturists to create carpets comparable with the 'Spring of Chosroes'. In many of the carpets of Tabriz, Qazvin and Kashan the field becomes a garden (Fig. 103). Flowering trees alternate with

dark cypresses at whose base a spring arises. Birds live in the branches and all kinds of animals gambol among the trees. Such perfect representations only occur in the classical period, that is in the sixteenth and early seventeenth centuries. They disappear with the decline of the great workshops, but the 'garden' theme is not lost. It is found in later North Persian carpets in a simplified form. In the field flowering trees and cypresses stand in rows and a new motif appears, a tree with drooping branches, possibly a willow (Figs. 69, 180). Few animals are depicted, apart from small birds whose squat forms recall their lively forerunners in earlier carpets. The small rosette-like blossoms which without rhyme or reason appear in the cypresses hark back to the branches of flowering trees, which in carpets of the

I. Persia, seventeenth century.

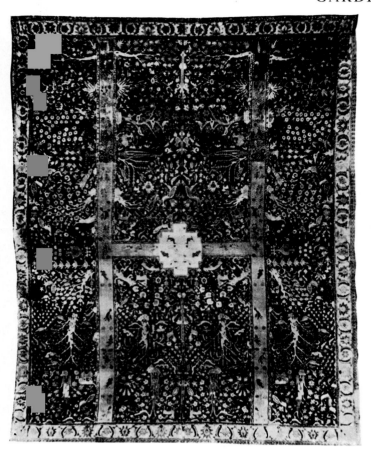

74. North Persia, beginning of the eighteenth century.

75. North Persia, before 1632.

classical period (Fig. 103) overlie and enliven the dark green of the cypresses. In spite of the stiffening of the motifs the 'garden' theme lives on.

It seems possible that the 'Spring of Chosroes' survives in these carpets of the sixteenth (Fig. 103) and eighteenth (Fig. 69) centuries. The descriptions of the fabulous carpet in the palace of Ctesiphon definitely speak of trees and flowers, paths, streams and flower beds. This recalls another North Persian type of carpet of the eighteenth century of which a number are still extant. The fields of these carpets (Fig. 70) can be said to represent the plan of an Oriental garden seen from above (Fig. 72). Ducks swim in the central pool, and stylized fish in the broad channel where zigzag lines represent cascading water.

Subsidiary channels branch off at right angles. Flowering shrubs grow in square beds and trees drawn in profile shade the paths. Finally, where the channels intersect, there are bridges (?) which in actual gardens often support a pavilion.

Carpets of this group, which are more justifiably called Garden carpets, are often large and sometimes more than nine metres in length. I well recall the one (Fig. 71) in a New York private collection the catalogue of which I compiled some years ago. In order to spread out the carpet in the room where I was working the chairs had to be removed so that no seat was available for the venerable owner when he came to discuss the work. Without hesitation he seated himself cross-legged on the carpet, which was natural to him as he had grown up in Kayseri

69

in Turkey. Seated next to him and talking, it was amazing how the illusion of being in a garden became stronger and stronger. This illusion is lost in later pieces because they are not large enough to show more than a small section of the design (Figs. 73, 180) which may no longer be understood. In the latest pieces of the type (Fig. 193) only rows of flower beds remain.

Stylized Garden carpets do not occur before the eighteenth century, but there must have been forerunners in earlier periods. A large piece (187 × 151 cm.) of the seventeenth century which was acquired by the Angewandte Kunst Museum in Vienna from the Figdor Collection (Pl. I) bears little relationship to the main group apart from the design of the water channels with fish. There are closer connections in the case of a large piece (Fig. 74) first recorded in the art trade in Constantinople about 1900. It disappeared soon after, but recently came to light in the Burrell Collection now in the Glasgow Museum. This carpet lacks paths and flower beds but has a freer arrangement of water channels and trees with animals and birds. The design lies somewhere between carpets illustrated in Fig 103 and Fig. 69. Undoubtedly there is a relationship with the real Garden carpets but the Glasgow piece cannot be considered a pre-

76. South Persia, before 1632.

decessor of the later group but rather a variant which itself presupposes the existence of the Garden carpet design a good century before the known pieces of this type were made.

The discovery of a large carpet (840 × 370 cm.) (Fig. 75) in a locked store room in the castle of Amber in India and now in the Jaipur Museum clarifies this somewhat complicated situation. Like a number of carpets belonging to the Maharajah of Jaipur it has on the underside a cloth label with the inventory description. The oldest of the labelled carpets at Jaipur goes back to 29th August 1632 and describes the piece as 'Foreign carpet with garden divided into four squares'. Because of its structure, colouring and design, especially that of its border, this must be assigned to the group of Persian Vase carpets probably from Kerman in South Persia. A further proof is that Abu Fadl, the chronicler of the Moghul Emperor Akbar who reigned from 1556 to 1605, mentioned that at that time carpets from Kerman, Joshegan and other Persian places were imported into India. The Jaipur carpet, where the central pool has a pavilion with a throne (Fig. 75), shows the same water channel system as the later North Persian Garden carpets. On the other hand the drawing of the trees by the paths and in the beds is richer and more lively and animals are also introduced (Fig. 76).

Thus although there are still gaps, the origin of the Garden carpet design is made clearer. It originated in South Persia and the Jaipur piece acquired in 1632 is the earliest known example though undoubtedly the design is older. The Figdor carpet (Pl. I, *facing p.* 68) is probably fifty years later than the Jaipur piece. The design migrated to North Persia and the Glasgow carpet (Fig. 74) is intermediate between the Vienna piece and the stylized Garden carpets (Figs. 70 and 72).

These, therefore, represent the terminal stage of a development whose beginning is represented by the Jaipur carpet of 1632. Perhaps some new discovery may enable us to trace the evolution of the design still farther back. But it can hardly be expected to bridge the gap between the Jaipur carpet and the 'Spring of Chosroes' although there is some evidence that this legendary carpet of the sixth century A.D. was similar in design to that of its descendant of some thousand years later.

Figure Carpets

Among Oriental carpets there is a small group in which human figures are represented. This seems to contradict the widely held belief in the West that in the art of Islam the representation of animate forms is forbidden. There is no such edict in the Koran, not even a prohibition to represent God because Allah was considered to be so sublime that no Muslim would ever think of portraying him.

During the first centuries of Islam there were, even in the house of the Prophet, hangings and cushions adorned with figures and the first Caliphs had their castles richly painted throughout and had statues made of themselves. Not until the ninth century did Islam move closer to the spirit expressed in the Mosaic Law: (Deuteronomy v. 8) 'Thou shalt not make thee any graven image, or any likeness of anything that is in heaven above, or that is in the earth beneath, or that is in the waters beneath the earth:' which is found as the second Commandment of the Christian catechism. It is further stated in both religions 'Thou shalt not bow down thyself unto them, nor serve them:' This edict is clearly directed against the worship of idols. The Arab theologians of the ninth century considered that God was the sole Creator and that man would be acting against His wishes by creating images of mortal creatures and thereby perhaps bestowing some degree of immortality upon them. But their edicts had only a limited effect because they could not be found in the Koran and, therefore, were not 'the Word of God'. There was never any representation of God and pictures of Saints, Angels, Prophets, Muhammed and even his earthly successors the Caliphs were forbidden. Equally observed has been that custom, which goes back to the beginnings of Islam, not to introduce figures into places of worship. In all other respects figures have been used, though since neither God nor the ruler could be represented they did not play such an important role as in Classical and Christian art.

The Islamic art of Persia has always included the portrayal of figures and a rich school of miniature painting developed which naturally could not do without them (cf. Figs. 11 and 14). When in the fifteenth and sixteenth centuries the miniature painters were given the task of designing carpets (Figs. 77–84 and Pl. I) figures were woven into carpets. This could have led to aesthetic difficulties since carpets are not book pages, but articles of furniture intended to cover the floor of a room. European standards cannot be applied here: in the West the use of tables, chairs, benches and cupboards almost rob the floor of its proper significance as a firmly enclosed or defined space. In the East, where furniture as used in the West is lacking, the floor dominates the room and everybody sits on it, whereas in our houses the sitter on his chair is high above the floor. In the West the most important part of the room is the wall, which is decorated with pictures and in front of which are placed artistically carved cupboards and chests. In the Orient, however, the floor is the significant area and the whole impression of

77. Persia (Kashan), first half of the sixteenth century.

78. Persia (Kashan), first half of the sixteenth century.

82. Persia (Tabriz), sixteenth century.

83. India, seventeenth century.

offered a bowl of fruit by a servant and lute and tambourine players stand in the shadow of a tree near a stream playing for a dancer, while a fourth beats time with his hands.

Similar scenes occur in a whole series of sixteenth-century Persian carpets from the workshops of Tabriz and Kashan. Usually the figures are either winged and represent houris, or wingless and are, therefore, boon-companions of this earth. These figures are introduced into the central medallion, the corners and the border, while the field is enlivened only with animals. Occasionally there are rows of oval plaques in the field (Fig. 81) in which earthly and heavenly themes alternate.

A unique carpet fragment (Fig. 82) which has disappeared since the war was formerly in the collection of Baron Hatvany of Budapest. Here the ogival field medallion shows a garden

scene, stylistically close to a miniature. Unfortunately the fragment represents only a quarter of the carpet and it is almost impossible to determine what the complete medallion looked like since no other example of such a pictorial scene in a carpet has survived. A pleasure pavilion occupies the centre and in it sits a figure facing right, his left hand extended to receive something offered by another figure whose right hand only is preserved. Behind the railing which encloses the garden stand two people and in the doorway leading into it squats a bearded man with a staff, who is probably the guardian of the gate. Five musicians and two servants appear in the foreground, the one in front carrying a bowl and the one behind a long-necked bottle. The white field of the carpet shows the customary garden landscape with animals. The corners, one of which (Fig.

220) is preserved in fragmentary form in the museum in Brooklyn, show four winged figures, so that even here, in spite of the naturalism of the central scene, the idea of Paradise is re-echoed.

Somewhat similar scenes were favoured in Indian carpets of the sixteenth and seventeenth centuries. A famous carpet of this type (Fig. 83), in the Museum of Fine Arts in Boston, has a field resembling the illuminated page of a manuscript and it can hardly be imagined that it was used as floor covering. A fragment with two elephants in combat (Pl. II), formerly in the Sarre Collection, may be from a carpet of the same type. Other examples are in the Widener Collection in the National Gallery of Art, and in the Textile Museum in Washington. In a Persian type of the seventeenth century, extant in a few examples, figures occur only in the corners of the field (Fig. 84). The scene is always the same: one or two ships complete with crew, obviously European, a man swimming and fish. The iconography of this scene that also occurs in similar form in Persian textiles of the seventeenth century has not yet been explained. Perhaps it is the story of Jonah. The occurrence of Europeans in such works has given them the name 'Portuguese Carpets' and they have been ascribed to Goa in Western India. The style of representation is reminiscent of Indian miniatures of the Mogul period, but these carpets are neither Indian, nor even, as was assumed at one time, South Persian but North Persian. The same design, though without ships in the corners, continued in carpets of the eighteenth and nineteenth centuries which must be ascribed to the Caucasus. The primitively drawn human figures which are sometimes found in later Caucasian carpets are not derived from these examples of the seventeenth century which are based on miniature paintings, but are borrowed from the realm of folk art, where they are popular in textiles and kilims.

84. North Persia (?), c. 1600.

Persian Carpets of Turkish Provenance

One of the best known and most valuable carpets in the Victoria and Albert Museum in London is a blue-ground carpet (Fig. 85) with a red central medallion and an exceptionally finely designed scrolling pattern filling the field. There are no corner pieces. A group consisting of a lion in combat with two dragons is used instead. On the light-green ground of the border are red cartouches containing verses by Hafiz. This large piece (1·65 × 2·32 m.) is knotted in wool on a silk foundation and has more than 11,000 knots per square decimetre. Some details are brocaded in silver. The carpet, which was published for the first time in 1883, later came into the possession of the Museum with the Salting Collection and is, therefore, known in literature as the 'Salting Carpet'. From the very beginning it aroused feelings of admiration and mistrust. As early as 1908 Martin wrote that it was too well preserved and the colours too brilliant.

When I saw this carpet for the first time in 1931 I made the following notes: 'Very dark-blue field with lustrous and, therefore, rather light green border. The central medallion dark red with light-red (!) floral scrolls. This relationship is reversed in

85. Anatolia, nineteenth century.

86. Anatolia, middle of the nineteenth century.

II. India, seventeenth century.

87. Anatolia, nineteenth century.

the outer guard-stripe because here dark-red scrolls appear on a light-red ground. The border cartouches are of the same colour as the central medallion. Inner guard-stripe white with a light-brown scroll (!) (a colour which does not appear elsewhere in the field). Much is unusual in the design which shows a profusion of closely packed and brightly coloured leaves and flowers, yellow scrolls and green parrots. Hardly a mistake; much too good; wonderful work. An indication of how to explain these incongruities is the brown lion in combat with two dragons, a motif which appears in the four corners and shows East Asian influence. Perhaps a workshop existed where immigrant Chinese artists produced this carpet and related pieces (!?).'

My attempt to explain the peculiar features of this carpet was not successful. A new edition of the *Guide to the Collection of Carpets* in the Victoria and Albert Museum appeared in the

88. Anatolia, nineteenth century.

In spite of some differences all these carpets were obviously made in the same workshop, with the possible exception of the carpet from the Baker Collection in the Metropolitan Museum. The Salting, Labanow-Rostowski and the Marquand carpets came from Istanbul and are reputed to have been gifts of the Turkish Sultan. The fact that one piece of the group is still in the Saray in Istanbul may not be purely fortuitous but it is insufficient proof to consider the group Turkish.

A. U. Pope had realized that some of the Persian prayer rugs of the sixteenth and seventeenth centuries which were known in 1938 – there were hardly a dozen – had some similarities with the Medallion and Animal carpets of the Salting group. He also knew that pairs to some of them, such as the carpet (Fig. 87) which the Metropolitan Museum in New York acquired from the Fletcher Collection, were in the Top Kapi Saray Museum. What he did not know, however, was that the Top Kapi Saray Museum, which contains the possessions of the Ottoman

same year and this piece is illustrated on Plate VIII. Although in earlier editions it was described as 'Persian, sixteenth century' the following description is given in the edition of 1931: 'Though strongly Persian in character, and hitherto attributed to Persia, it has become very doubtful whether carpets of this kind were actually woven there. A mass of evidence makes it likely that they were made in the neighbourhood of Constantinople not earlier than the eighteenth century.'

Several other famous carpets belong to the same group – the carpet of Prince Labanow-Rostowski in Leningrad, a carpet in the Czartoryski Museum in Cracow, the carpet from the Marquand Collection (Fig. 86), today in the Philadelphia Museum of Art, a carpet presented to the Metropolitan Museum in New York by Mr. G. F. Baker, one similar to the Salting Carpet in the American trade, a carpet from the Goupil Collection in the Musée Historique des Tissus in Lyons, and finally, a carpet in the Ali Bey Ibrahim Collection in Cairo and one in the Top Kapi Saray in Istanbul.

89. Anatolia (Hereke ?), nineteenth century.

Sultans, possesses no fewer than thirty-seven of such prayer rugs. Thanks to the kindness of Tahsin Öz, the Director at that time, I was able during my stay in Istanbul in 1937 to study these intensively and the result was published in 1941.

'Most of the carpets' I wrote at that time 'are of medium size, finely knotted in a fairly hard wool, usually on a silk foundation and sometimes have small parts brocaded in silver. Their state of preservation is unusually good in every case. The careful drawing shows Persian designs of the sixteenth and seventeenth centuries. The colour scheme is striking but strange even considering that its freshness is due partly to the good state of preservation. In a few pieces only an impression of a Persian palette emerges. The colours of the majority are disturbingly bright. A discordant note is often struck by a combination of brilliant white and a harsh, light green associated with a light carmine and blue. Just as unusual although not quite so jarring is the use of light blue on a black field. In a numerically smaller

91. Anatolia (Hereke ?), nineteenth century.

group the colouring is restricted to a few shades lacking in contrast. There are even carpets in which, apart from a few details, only two colours have been used. Monochrome scrolling stems whose leaves and blossoms appear as silhouettes are particularly popular and the pattern is in a lighter shade of the field colour (Fig. 88). Especially common is a combination of white and drab brown which produces a dull effect. All these pieces are Persian in design but other patterns occur which can only be explained as variations of Anatolian motifs. The carpets which show the latter are usually somewhat smaller, sometimes even strikingly so, and are somewhat coarser in knotting. This is evident in the piece illustrated in Fig. 89 whose brown niche is filled with black scrolls with light-blue blossoms which in their loose arrangement and marked isolation from the field recall the Anatolian patterns in the manner of the Transylvanian carpets. The carpet in Fig. 90 shows, in the upper part of the niche, a paraphrase of a Damascus carpet and in the border a customary Anatolian design. That in Fig. 91, the

90. Anatolia (Hereke ?), nineteenth century.

A Carpet 'Unmasked'

In June 1964 the journal *Heimtex* published the following notice based on reports in the English press:

'An Oriental Carpet Fake:

An unusual event in the history of the Oriental carpet occurred recently when an antique piece was removed from exhibition in the Victoria and Albert Museum. This was a Turkish carpet [Fig. 92], hitherto considered to be about three or four hundred years old, and it had been exhibited in the Islamic Gallery since the thirties. The first doubts about this carpet were expressed in 1962 by the American specialist, Mr. Nessim Cohen. When experts of the Museum examined it closely it was found that the carpet had been produced at the end of the nineteenth or the beginning of the twentieth century and not, as previously assumed, in the sixteenth or seventeenth centuries. It had come from the Schwarzenberg Collection in Vienna and bore the Tamerlane arms which had contributed to the erroneous attribution.'

It is not unusual that a carpet on display be removed and disappear into store. What was unusual in this case was the publicity attached to it and the fact that the Director of the Museum on the representations of an outsider submitted a carpet, hitherto considered genuine, for chemical tests, a happening which is all too rare. In the case of the carpet in the Victoria and Albert Museum the chemical investigation showed that parts of the warp which could not possibly come from a later restoration were dyed with a colour not produced until the end of the nineteenth century.

There are few museum directors who have never in their lives bought a fake, and probably there are a dozen more White-ground Anatolian carpets in European and American museums and in private possession which could be 'unmasked'; but few owners would be as courteous and helpful as Mr. Wingfield Digby of the Victoria and Albert Museum in London. It can only be to the advantage of carpet studies if some of the 'black sheep' which during the last few decades have infiltrated the ranks of the White-ground carpets could be eliminated in this way.

The story is that in the year 1933 the Victoria and Albert Museum acquired from a little-known dealer a large White-ground carpet (178 × 290 cm.) with a pattern of black spots and stripes. It was, therefore, a piece belonging to that small group formerly called Chintamani carpets (Fig. 93) because it was believed that the design was derived from the Chinese Chintamani. Later they were called Tamerlane or Timurlenk carpets because it was assumed that the design represented the arms of Tamerlane. Neither derivation can be proved and today

they may be called 'spot and stripe' carpets. It is unlikely that the press notice connecting the design with Tamerlane misled the museum experts. When the possessions of Wilhelm von Bode were auctioned in Berlin in 1929, they included the carpet (Fig. 94) that subsequently appeared on the London art market as 'Bode's Tamerlane rug'. This was his well-known Chintamani carpet. It cannot have been cheap, and the Victoria and Albert Museum failed to acquire it. What probably happened, therefore, was that when an almost identical carpet, likewise well documented, was offered to the Museum, doubtless at a lower price, the opportunity was seized. It could hardly have been suspected that this was a fake since it is a well-known fact that the first examples of really good fakes are nearly always accepted as genuine. Suspicion is not aroused until the third or fourth piece appears by which time sufficient material exists to prove the deception. One could, however, reproach the Victoria and Albert Museum for accepting the documentation 'Prince Schwarzenberg' in good faith. The Schwarzenberg Chintamani carpet (Fig. 95), first mentioned in 1724 in the inventory of the collection, was exhibited in Vienna in 1891 and in Munich in 1910 and was, therefore, not unknown. If a careful comparison had been made of photographs of the Schwarzenberg carpet and of the London piece, differences could have been detected. There would still have been the possibility that two carpets in the same design existed in the Palais Schwarzenberg, and indeed in 1891 that collection had a second White-ground carpet although in the Bird design. It is embarrassing in such cases to enquire of the previous owner, since it is not known what prompted the sale. There remained the dealer's attribution which certainly contributed to the fact that no doubts arose as to the authenticity of this piece.

In *Europa und der Orientteppich* (Mainz, 1962, pp. 136–140) I described from my own experience a similar occurrence which it should be noted may well be related to the London sale.

'Generally experts and forgers fight a constant battle without ever meeting each other. The forger operates through a middle-man and remains in the background. Usually the experts are one step ahead, but often not even that. Therefore, they may temporarily lose ground when the forgers branch out in a new direction. This happened in the carpet market a number of years ago. Up to then the most common forgeries were of carpets of the great workshops of the sixteenth century and were confined to the designs of the best-known pieces of that period. Naturally these were not restricted to simple copies but combined motifs from different carpets in a new design. This, however, easily produced inaccuracies and mistakes which were not likely to

asked for a written authentication. Thereupon the carpet was carefully examined, even more carefully than was customary because it differed a little in colour from the usual type of which there are about fifty examples in collections and museums. This, however, could have been the result of unskilful chemical treatment. Otherwise everything was in order and no doubt existed as to its genuineness. So the certificate was given and the Assize judge departed well satisfied. Some three months later a carpet dealer appeared with three Asia Minor prayer rugs of the eighteenth century, ordinary pieces, which occur commonly and which at that time cost £200 to £300 each. He also wanted a certificate of authenticity; but the three rugs, which judging from their designs originated in different districts, had a fatal

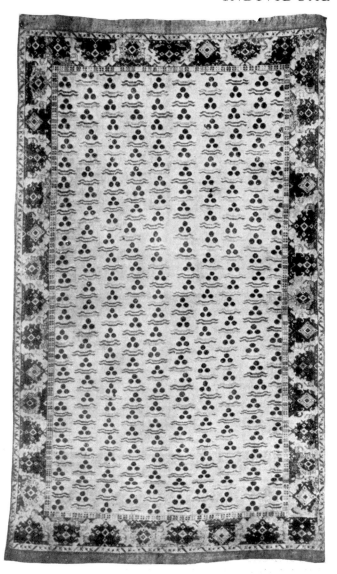

92. Forgery, end of nineteenth or beginning of the twentieth century.

deceive anybody who had a comprehensive knowledge of genuine, old carpets.

'Suddenly, however, the forgers' tactics changed and carpets were produced in the manner of seventeenth and eighteenth century commercial rugs, so that detection based on the design was no longer possible. The margin of profit was much smaller, for such carpets did not cost more than £4,000 to £5,000. At this figure a profit of £500 to £1,000 would be made if they could be sold as genuine. In addition, it was hoped to put on the market more pieces of this kind than the former types, which could be sold only in single examples, but it was necessary to have written authentication from well-known specialists.

'One day such an expert received a visit from a serious, elderly gentleman – according to his card a retired Assize judge – who showed a beautiful seventeenth-century Bird carpet. The piece was supposed to be an old family possession and he did not want to sell it, but would be interested to know what it was. This information was given, but he was still not satisfied and

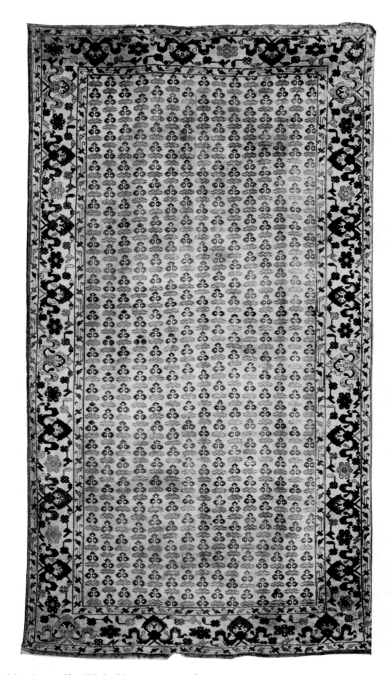

93. Anatolia (Ushak), seventeenth century.

resemblance to each other. It was suspicious. On closer examination it transpired that a good coloured reproduction in well-known handbooks existed for each of these carpets. This could have been mere chance because carpets of the kind were produced in great numbers, but misgivings were strengthened. This and other factors resulted in a refusal of the certificate. The dealer was taken aback and became excited; the carpets came from a church in Transylvania, and must, therefore, be genuine and, in any case, a short time ago was not a certificate provided for a Bird carpet coming from the same source? The man realized too late that he had given the show away. The "retired judge" was as much of a fake as his "old family carpet". The refusal to give these certificates caused a commotion among experts.

95. Anatolia (Ushak), seventeenth century.

Nobody was inclined to regard these three carpets as forgeries. It was argued that fakes of carpets of this type had never occurred before and could hardly be profitable considering the low prices. The forgers too, and in particular the middlemen, did not give up, but tried to gain their ends by different means. A few months after the first failure a gentleman from Vienna appeared with ten old carpets and a certificate with many official stamps in which it was stated that ten of the carpets of the church in X had been sold to Mr. Y. Unfortunately the expert had heard of the intention of that church to sell carpets, and had acquired photographs of those pieces. He read through the proffered document, asked to see the carpets and then proved to the speechless man, with the help of his photographs that only one of his pieces really came from that church. Nine had been substituted and of these six or seven were forgeries.

'The contest continued. Again and again fakes of this type appeared in the trade and again and again collectors were deceived. One more attempt was made to get certificates. The elderly gentleman who had his carpet spread out by a servant created a dignified impression but it seemed doubtful whether his visiting card, which bore the name of a famous and noble Hungarian family, well known on account of its carpet collection, was more genuine than that of the Assize judge who had produced carpets from "old family possessions". This happened a number of years ago. Today this new group of fakes is generally well recognized.'

These events happened between 1929 and 1933. The important feature of all four attempts was to gain certificates of authenticity, not to sell carpets to the museum. The first attempt with the Bird carpet succeeded, but not the others. The carpets submitted were mostly smaller pieces of the Transylvanian group among which were many White-ground rugs of the Bird type. A Caucasian Dragon carpet did not appear until the last group. In the end such carpets were no longer submitted in Berlin for certificates because it was realized that there was no possibility of these being granted. This, of course, did not mean that buyers could not be found elsewhere.

Forgeries were easy enough as long as they reproduced the usual simple Transylvanian designs. According to rumour a workshop existed somewhere in the Balkans with the misguided

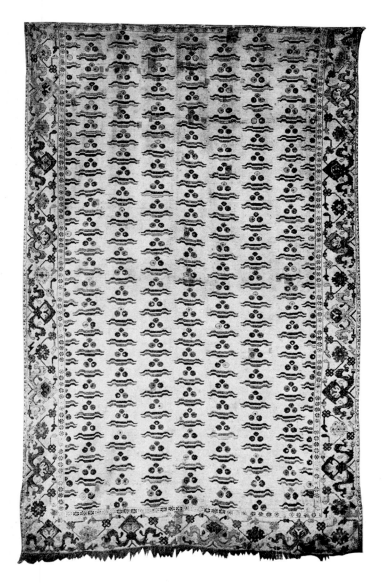

94. Anatolia (Ushak), seventeenth century.

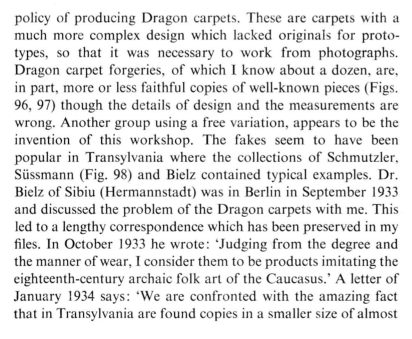

97. Forgery, end of nineteenth or beginning of the twentieth century.

96. Forgery, end of nineteenth or beginning of the twentieth century.

policy of producing Dragon carpets. These are carpets with a much more complex design which lacked originals for prototypes, so that it was necessary to work from photographs. Dragon carpet forgeries, of which I know about a dozen, are, in part, more or less faithful copies of well-known pieces (Figs. 96, 97) though the details of design and the measurements are wrong. Another group using a free variation, appears to be the invention of this workshop. The fakes seem to have been popular in Transylvania where the collections of Schmutzler, Süssmann (Fig. 98) and Bielz contained typical examples. Dr. Bielz of Sibiu (Hermannstadt) was in Berlin in September 1933 and discussed the problem of the Dragon carpets with me. This led to a lengthy correspondence which has been preserved in my files. In October 1933 he wrote: 'Judging from the degree and the manner of wear, I consider them to be products imitating the eighteenth-century archaic folk art of the Caucasus.' A letter of January 1934 says: 'We are confronted with the amazing fact that in Transylvania are found copies in a smaller size of almost

all the large Dragon carpets well known abroad, which, in spite of their different periods of design, seem to have been made at one time which, with some reservations, I must suppose to be the eighteenth century.' In March 1935 he writes: 'Like you I am now convinced that we are dealing here with skilful forgeries which were foisted onto us in the beginning. I also believe that the workshop is to be sought in Bucharest. Clues which I hoped to follow up suddenly disappeared so I am only left with a supposition.'

I was in Budapest in the summer of 1935 where my host Dr. Delmar made it possible for me to see most of the carpet collections in the city, among which were some remarkably beautiful pieces. We only once came across a Dragon carpet fake and I asked Dr. Delmar what sort of a carpet this was. He said 'Oh, that is a Duduk carpet. These are forgeries which are made in Rumania. Some years ago the market was flooded with them but as you can see not many of them remain in our collections.' This was undoubtedly so, but the Duduk car-

IV. Egypt (Cairo), *c.* 1500.

pets, although they may have moved elsewhere, are still in existence.

In one of my books, when discussing degeneration in Caucasian production at the beginning of the nineteenth century and the strange persistence of older motifs, I illustrated such a rug, which was once in the possession of Count Lichnowsky. There had been doubts about this piece thirty years ago when it was submitted for opinion and recently it has been shown to be a fake. In the next edition of my book it was replaced by the carpet dated 1689 (Fig. 211) from the Textile Museum in Washington. Who was this Mr. Duduk or Toduk or Tudoc? It is certain that he sold his forgeries only through middlemen who probably often did not realize the origin of their wares. Mr. Tuduc, which is the correct spelling, was, so I am assured by those who knew him, a small but well-respected carpet dealer in Bucharest, who had excellent pieces in his shop and also in his private collection. His agents bought old carpets, irrespective of their state of preservation, in the provinces, especially in Transylvania. At that time these were still in good supply and cheap. They were restored in his workshop where he employed a small number of skilful weavers. Perhaps these restorations were the beginnings of the whole business and later led to the weaving of his own designs into much damaged carpets. Good prototypes for all Transylvanian groups were plentiful and it was not difficult to copy the Chintamani carpets and Bird carpets with their simple designs and colouring. The production of this workshop must have been extensive. The copying of unfamiliar designs such as those of the Dragon carpets was less successful. It is not known when the workshop ceased to operate but apparently it did not survive the second world war.

This does not mean that new forgeries do not come to light. Strangely enough their provenance still points to the Balkans where, since the last war, they have of course been labelled 'refugee possessions'. Emil Schmutzler, well known through his beautiful book on Transylvanian carpets, is supposed to have rescued them by the wagon load even though, according to my information, he was no longer alive at the end of the war. It is immaterial that he even becomes a Baron in the imagination of dealers, for the names of the Hungarian nobility are still attractive. Half the fun would go out of carpet collecting if there were no fakes or forgeries or at least no wrongly attributed

98. Copy, twentieth century.

pieces. The public reacted quite properly during the Weinmüller auction in Munich (15 March 1961) when it did not bid for pieces offered by an obscure dealer; but neither dealer nor rejected carpets have disappeared.

It is much more difficult to unmask forgeries once they have been accepted. Not every museum director or private collector is as reasonable as Mr. Wingfield Digby of the Victoria and Albert Museum whose name is mentioned once again in gratitude.

SOME COLLECTIONS AND MUSEUMS

99. Persia (Kashan), first half of the sixteenth century.

100. East Asia, eighth century or earlier.

101. India, seventeenth century.

and public ownership: the Textile Museum in Washington D.C. owed its foundation to the passion for collecting of the late G. H. Myers, who died in 1957. From the very beginning this collection was planned as a gift and although it contains the most important study material in the U.S.A. it cannot of course rival the possessions of the Metropolitan Museum, since even the resources of a millionaire are limited.

America, Austria, Germany, England, France, Italy, Denmark — what is left? Spanish museums offer hardly anything, although Count Welczek had assembled an important collection of Spanish carpets. Portugal is supposed to have good Isfahans in public and private collections, which are unknown to me. The Swiss museums have only a few carpets. In the Balkans the Iparmüvészeti Museum in Budapest has a con-

90

siderable collection of Turkish carpets and before the last war there were a number of discerning collectors who assembled interesting material. The carpets of the Transylvanian churches are known through the publication of E. Schmutzler, *Altorientalische Teppiche in Siebenbürgen*. These are all Turkish and date mostly from the seventeenth century. The Benaki Museum in Athens also possesses some interesting pieces.

It is disappointing that the further east one goes, the fewer antique Oriental carpets one finds. The museums in Poland possess some important pieces but the wonderful silk carpet of the Branicki family, formerly in Warsaw Castle, is believed to have disappeared during the war. There is not much in Russia. The Hermitage in Leningrad, a museum on a par with those of Paris, London and the combined Berlin Museums, possesses only a few pieces and carpets played no part in the Persian exhibition of 1935–36 which occupied more than seventy rooms in the Hermitage. The carpets in the Museum of Oriental Culture in Moscow are more of ethnological interest and there are collections, unknown to me, in provincial museums in south-eastern Russia. The National Museum in Tehran possesses

a few carpets, a collection which has come into being by rescuing pieces in danger of being lost. This is by no means representative when compared with the other excellent departments of the Museum. Bearing in mind the Ardebil carpet, those from the shrines of the mosques in Qum and Meshed were disappointing when shown in London in 1931.

Not until the gift of Ibrahim Pasha did the Arab Museum in Cairo acquire its own collection of predominantly Turkish carpets. There is nothing in Baghdad, Beirut or Damascus. There are, however, three outstanding collections in the East: in Japan, in the eighth-century temple treasure of the Shosoin in Nara, the carpets, of great interest on account of their early date, are not knotted but are made of felt (Fig. 100) and are from the T'ang period; in India there is the seventeenth-century carpet collection of the Maharaja of Jaipur, whose pieces often have labels on the reverse giving information such as the place of purchase and acquisition date (Fig. 101); in Istanbul the Türk ve Islam Eserleri Museum, with more than a thousand carpets, has by far the richest collection in the world.

Carpets as Turkish Booty

The evening after the battle of Vienna, in which the Turks were forced to raise the siege, the Polish King Jan Sobieski sat in the tent conquered from the Turkish Wazir Kara Mustapha and wrote to his wife: '. . . it is impossible to describe the refined luxury which prevails in the tents of the Wazir. Baths, little gardens, fountains, rabbit warrens and even a parrot. . . . The Wazir had taken a beautiful ostrich from a royal castle, and had had its head cut off so that it would not again fall into the possession of the Christians. . . . It is impossible to describe everything that belongs to my booty.' Undoubtedly many carpets were included in it.

It is not surprising, therefore, that a number of carpets in Polish possession have been associated with the name of this king. The Shah Abbas ('Polish') carpet of the church of St. John in Studziana is supposed to have been given by him, as well as the three similar carpets in Frauenburg Cathedral (which were still there in 1900 but have since been destroyed by vermin). This may be true. Less probable is the traditional story that the large white-ground Animal carpet, one half of which is today in

102. Persia (Kashan), mid-sixteenth century.

the sacristy of the cathedral in Cracow, while the other is in the Musée des Arts Décoratifs in Paris (Fig. 103), was a present from the Polish king, because it was made a good hundred years before the relief of Vienna.

Strictly speaking we know of only one carpet that was taken at the seige of Vienna, a Shah Abbas carpet now in the W. H. Moore Collection, which has on the back written in ink the following information: 'A. D. WILKONSKI XII Septembris 1683 z pod Wiednia.' We do not know who Wilkonski was, but that he acquired the carpet on 12th September at the battle of Vienna (Wiednia) is certain. The silk tapestry carpet (Fig. 142) in the Landesmuseum in Karlsruhe may have belonged to the booty of the Margrave Ludwig Wilhelm von Baden (1655–1707), known as Turkish Louis. A similar piece formerly in possession of the Royal House of Saxony, acquired by the Metropolitan Museum in 1931, probably also comes from this source.

Such an origin is doubtful in the case of other important pieces. European arms five times repeated appear in a large Shah Abbas carpet (Fig. 260) formerly belonging to the Czartoryski family in Cracow and now in the Metropolitan Museum in New York. It was therefore made to Western specification, and is unlikely to have been taken from the Turks at the battle of Vienna. Another, in the Czartoryski Museum, can be ruled out because it is a nineteenth-century Turkish copy (cf. Fig. 85) of a sixteenth-century Persian Animal carpet. The magnificent silk carpet (Fig. 102) of the Branicki family, which appeared about forty years ago and was bought by the Polish government for Warsaw Castle, where apparently it perished during the last war, dates from about 1540–1550 and was therefore nearly 150 years old when, in 1683, it was taken as booty at Vienna.

In the West carpets might last for centuries if their worth was recognized and they were used only occasionally. The most beautiful example is the Coronation carpet (Fig. 104) at Rosenborg Castle in Copenhagen, a Shah Abbas carpet, which is in a state of such perfect preservation that it might have been made yesterday. This carpet, first mentioned in 1685 in the estate of Queen Sophie Amalie, has only been used on the occasions of the Coronation of the Kings of Denmark.

In the Orient, carpets have never been regarded as rarities and we can hardly assume that an Ottoman Wazir at the siege of Vienna would take about with him a carpet 150 years old. Contemporary pieces would have been used and this may have happened in the case of two early seventeenth-century carpets. One, an Animal carpet probably from Kashan, in the possession of Prince Sanguszko, is at present on loan to the Metropolitan Museum. The other, an imposing yellow-ground Medallion carpet (Fig. 105) which was found a good many years ago in the

V. Persia (Kashan), seventeenth century.

103. Persia (Tabriz), sixteenth century.

104. Persia (Isfahan), seventeenth century.

loft of the castle at Dessau, was probably acquired as Turkish booty by the Duke of Anhalt, and recently was bought by the Metropolitan Museum reputedly for more than a million dollars.

It is worth noting that all pieces associated with the victory of 1683 are of Persian origin. This is probably no mere accident for, although Turkey had its own extensive carpet production, Sultans and high dignitaries seem to have had a taste for Persian rugs and preferred them to the local products.

105. Persia (Tabriz), c. 1600.

94

Venice and the Oriental Carpet

Venice's relations with the Orient, and therefore also with the Oriental carpet, go back to the early Middle Ages. In long-drawn-out competition with south Italian ports such as Bari, Amalfi and Salerno, which had a more favourable geographical position, and later with the great rivals of the west coast, Genoa and Pisa, the City of the Lagoons established her claim to leadership. The decisive date was the year 1204, when Doge Dandolo succeeded in deflecting the fourth Crusade from Jerusalem and directing it against Constantinople. This was not a new idea. Soon after the first Crusade, that is at the beginning of the twelfth century, it became apparent that the interests of the Crusaders and of the Byzantine Imperial House were not in harmony. In spite of all appearances to the contrary Constantinople proved to be a hindrance rather than a friendly base for these campaigns. The second Crusade of 1147–49 led by Conrad III of Germany and Louis VII of France foundered for this reason. The third crusade of 1189 led by Frederick I Barbarossa did not at first encounter many difficulties. This was due principally to the clever political manoeuvring of the German Emperor, who arranged the passage of his troops through Anatolia by treating not with Byzantium but with the Seljuk Turks who then ruled in Konya (Iconium). At that time the Byzantine Emperor wrote to Sultan Saladin, the conqueror of Jerusalem, expressing regret that he was not powerful enough to prevent the passage of the Crusaders. Under these circumstances it is not surprising that in the West the idea of by-passing Byzantium in order to keep open the land route to Jerusalem was considered. This was recommended by Bernard de Clairvaux and Abbé Suger of St. Denis in the middle of the twelfth century, but not until 1204 was this plan put into operation by the driving force of Doge Dandolo who is buried in Aya Sofia. The Latin kingdom under Baldwin of Flanders replaced the Byzantine empire.

The Seljuks of Rum ruling in Konya took advantage of this situation. Between 1207 and 1214, in a series of lightning campaigns, they conquered Antalya on the south coast of Asia Minor and Sinope on the north, and obtained access hitherto denied them by Byzantium to the Mediterranean and to the Black Sea. Thus began during the next few decades the brilliant but brief period of the Seljuks of Rum whose power is still evident in the monumental caravanserai along the great overland routes. Venice took this into account and in 1220 concluded a commercial treaty with the Sultan of Konya which contributed materially to the outstanding commercial success of the Seljuk empire during the first six decades of the thirteenth century.

The great carpets (Figs. 23–28 and 106) found sixty years ago in the Alaeddin Mosque in Konya were probably made in the thirteenth century. Today these are the most precious possessions of the Türk ve Islam Eserleri Museum in Istanbul, and are among the oldest knotted carpets in the world (Fig. 106; and see pp. 41 ff).

We do not know whether carpets were exported at that time. Certainly there is no piece from such an early period extant outside Anatolia. The trade in carpets must have been started at the latest in the early fourteenth century and everything indicates that Venice played an important part in it from the start. The most notable imports were carpets with figural ornament in square fields which probably were woven in the Bergama district of North-west Anatolia. Naturally few pieces are preserved and the best known, a yellow-ground carpet (Fig. 1) with a dragon and phoenix in combat, today in the Berlin Museums, came from a church in Central Italy. Another piece with two stylized birds beside a tree (Fig. 4) in the Statens Historiska Museum in Stockholm, was found in a church in Gotland, a good proof of how far trade relations extended even in the early fifteenth century. Smaller fragments of this type have come to light in Old Cairo.

The main source of information for the Anatolian carpet production of the fourteenth and fifteenth centuries is not these few originals, which have survived the centuries, but the numerous portrayals of such rugs in the paintings of all Italian schools of that time (cf. Figs 2 and 3).

Rugs in pictures were still popular in the sixteenth century and remained an important source for carpet studies. The manner of their use in pictures changes for, although in earlier centuries carpets lay before the throne of the Madonna, later they were represented more like genre pieces which certainly corresponded to their actual use. Instead of being precious possessions which only a few could afford and which were specially displayed in churches at festivals, carpets had become furnishings of the middle class home. It would be interesting, and a fascinating task for an art historian, to determine the extent to which Oriental carpets have influenced the colours used by Titian, Tintoretto and Veronese.

A carpet is draped picturesquely over the balustrade of a balcony in Carlo Crivelli's *Annunciation* (Fig. 108) in the National Gallery in London, and another is used as a table cover in the portrait of Domenico Morone (Fig. 109) by Andrea Solario in the Brera in Milan. It was a popular custom in Venice to hang carpets out of windows as shown by a delightful Mansueti in the Accademia in Venice. Vittore Carpaccio introduced a wealth of carpets into his pictures, especially into the St. Ursula cycle which is also in the Accademia.

106. Anatolia (Konya), thirteenth century.

107. Altar painting by Lorenzo Lotto.

There is another interesting picture by this master in the Jacqemart André Museum in Paris, in which the carpet, combining large and small motifs, departs from the norm where the design consists of uniform rows of figures of the same size. Such grouped designs have survived only occasionally in originals.

The wealth of Oriental carpets in Venice at the turn of the fifteenth to sixteenth centuries is not to be seen in pictures alone. Numerous inventories demonstrate the same profusion and give an even better idea of it. The following are a few examples:

In a will of 18th August 1483 is mentioned

'sei tapedi ala damaschina, sei tapedi belli e dodici chandelieri ala damaschina. . . .'

In another will of 6th April 1495 it says:

'Item dimitto ecclesie corporis Cristi duos tapetes equales novos laboratas ala damaschina. . . .'

The estate inventory of the silk manufacturer Andreas Benedictus, dated 21st January 1478, records:

'in una cassa con le arme ed altre picture un tapedo grande in do pezze, sei tappedi, quattro tappedi tristi. . . .'

In another estate inventory of 3rd January 1511:

'do tapedi damaschini novi . . . , un tapedo tavolo grande . . . nove tapedi tra grande e pizoli de piue sorte vecchi';

and in another inventory of the same year:

'tapedi tre turcheschi et rodioti de piu usadi e vecchi';

another inventory names:

'quattro tapedi damaschini . . . quattro tapedi rodioti et turcheschi';

and

'Uno tapedo da tavola usado . . . quattordici tapedi di piu sorte tra vecchi et strazadi . . . sette tapedi usadi';

VI. Persia (Isfahan), seventeenth century.

108. Anatolian carpet in a painting by Carlo Crivelli.

109. Anatolian carpet in a painting by Andrea Solario.

and

'Do tapedi grandi vecchi da terra – tapedi sei usadi turcheschi tra grande e mezani e uno tapedo damaschino vecchio da desco';

and finally in an estate inventory of 22nd April 1512:

'due tapedi da terra da camera in quattro pezzi . . . uno tapedo barbarescho finissima da cassa . . . sei damaschini da capo usadi'.

That is only a small selection. The archives of Venice contain hundreds, if not thousands of documents which have not yet been evaluated.

As shown by the above examples, most of which date from the year 1511, it was not unusual at the beginning of the sixteenth century to own ten or more Oriental rugs. One differentiated between 'tapedi turcheschi' that is Turkish carpets in general, 'tapedi barbareschi' by which perhaps carpets from North Africa are meant and 'tapedi rodioti' the meaning of

which is not yet known. Since it is unlikely that carpets were made in Rhodes at that time the name perhaps refers to carpets which were exported from there.

The 'tapedi damaschini' previously translated as 'Damascus Carpets' were listed most frequently. Neither in Damascus nor anywhere else in Syria have knotted carpets ever been made. As it lacked direct access to the sea Damascus cannot even be considered as a point of export, which Rhodes eventually became. Perhaps, as Kühnel has suggested, 'damaschini' means 'damascened', and Damascus carpets were 'shimmering' carpets. This would fit well those many examples of the late fifteenth and early sixteenth century where the small-pattern, geometric designs often in only three colours (carmine red, moss green and light blue) gave a shimmering effect to the surface. It is now known that these carpets were made in Cairo, at first for the court of the Mamluk sultans and later for export, especially to Europe. The term 'damaschino' disappeared from Venetian archives during the sixteenth century, and is replaced by the

Most carpets known from inventories and pictures came from districts under Turkish domination, from the Cairene workshops of Egypt and those of Ushak and Bergama in Western Asia Minor. It was easy to trade with the centres under Turkish rule but more difficult to deal with Persia, the second great carpet-producing area. One could only make contact in a round-about way through diplomatic channels. These became necessary to Europe also in the case of the mighty Ottoman Empire, the full menace of which became only too evident when Sultan Suleiman the Magnificent appeared before Vienna in 1529. Venice had realized the danger as early as 1453 when the Turks conquered Constantinople.

With considerable astuteness the Signory aligned herself with the new power, but when in 1463 the Turkoman Sultan Uzun Hassan emerged as an opponent in Persia they established relations with him and embassies were exchanged. One of these delegations is reported to have brought back the beautiful turquoise bowl now in the Treasury of St. Mark's. No carpets are mentioned but possibly some were included among the presents.

110. Persia (Kashan or Isfahan), seventeenth century.

term 'tapedi cagiarini', which can only be translated as 'carpets from Cairo'. Many originals of this type which must have been imported into Europe from the end of the fifteenth century and throughout the sixteenth have been preserved (Pl. IV). After the conquest of the city by the Ottomans in 1517, the Cairo workshops continued production at first in the old style of the Mamluk carpets, then in a new Ottoman style. The shape of the carpets proves that they were often made for export. Square carpets were not used in the Orient. Round or even cross-shaped carpets could only have been intended as table carpets and must, therefore, have been woven for Europe (Figs. 251–253).

Such uses are confirmed by the inventories. Floor carpets, 'tapedi da terra', are rare; table carpets, 'tapedi da desco' or 'tapedi de tavola', are mentioned more frequently. Along with these are 'tapedi da cassa' meant for the cassapancas, the chests used in Venetian houses. During the sixteenth century documentary proof becomes rare.

111. Persia (Kashan or Isfahan), seventeenth century.

In any case the Venetian Ambassadors at the court of Tabriz, especially Barbaro and Contarini, have left interesting accounts about court life of the Persian princes, in which they describe in great detail the wealth of carpets in the palaces and tents. After the death of Uzun Hassan, Venice, having backed the wrong horse, at once negotiated again with the Ottomans.

These negotiations were restarted by Venice and other European powers, when, with the rise of the Safavids at the beginning of the sixteenth century, conditions in Persia became stabilized. The aim was to involve the Ottoman adversary in a war on two fronts by concluding a treaty with Persia. This was never realized in spite of the exchange of many embassies.

One of these was led by Fethi Bey, who came to Venice in 1603 on behalf of his master Shah Abbas the Great. Among the gifts which he presented was a silk carpet worked in gold and silver. This, as Fethi Bey explained, was sent by the Shah to the Signory in order to display on it the world-famous treasures of St. Mark's which, he had heard, were shown to the people once a year.

113. Persia, sixteenth century.

112. Persia (Kashan or Isfahan), seventeenth century.

Of the five Persian silk carpets, which are still preserved in the Treasury of St. Mark's, the one with the central medallion (Fig. 110) is, according to the measurements given in the inventory, the piece that was presented in 1603. The four others came to Venice with an embassy in 1622. One of these shows a design of ribbon-like scrolls in spiral arrangement, two originate from the same cartoon and have rows of blossoms (Fig.111) and the fourth, of poor design, shows a cartouche pattern (Fig. 112), Carpets like these are always of silk, often richly brocaded in gold and silver and have been preserved in great numbers. The five carpets in St. Mark's are not the best of their kind for there are others which are larger, richer and more finely worked. It is remarkable, however, that though most Shah Abbas carpets are identical or closely related in design, four of the five St. Mark's carpets are unique.

In 1636 a Persian embassy again brought 'tre tappeti tessuti con seta et oro'. A total of eight silk carpets, therefore, came to Venice at the beginning of the seventeenth century, of which five are still in the Treasury of St. Mark's. The other three are not there, but the Correr Museum has two of this type. The inventories do not show when they were acquired, but it would not be too daring to connect these with the gift of 1636 so that, in fact, only one of the eight carpets has disappeared.

Added to the seven carpets in the Treasury of St. Mark's and in the Correr Museum, those in the Ca d'Oro, which are not especially important pieces, bring the total in Venice to just under a dozen. In public collections that is all that remains of the wealth of carpets once in the possession of the city. Other

Italian cities have fared no better. In the Poldi Pezzoli Museum in Milan two of the six carpets exhibited are important pieces (Fig. 207) and before the war there were two pieces in the Castello Sforzesco. The Civico Museum in Turin has a top quality East Persian fragment. The two Shah Abbas carpets in the Museo degli Argenti in Florence may come from the Medicis, but the Persian prayer rug is of too late a date for that. In the Bargello, as well as the magnificent fragment of a Persian Animal carpet (Fig. 113) of the best period, there are a large Holbein and a Lotto carpet. The richest collection is contained in the Bardini Museum which is exceptional since it houses the collections of one of the greatest Italian art dealers. (See the carpet in Fig. 232.) In Rome in the Castello St. Angelo are three small Turkish carpets and perhaps other pieces, like the cross-shaped Ottoman carpet (Fig. 253) in the Civico Museum in San Gimigniano, may still be hidden in other Italian provincial museums. Without doubt Italy was, between the fourteenth and sixteenth centuries, the greatest carpet importing country in Europe. It was also, and too little notice is taken of this, the greatest exporting country during the second half of the nineteenth century when the antique carpet was being 'discovered'.

A few of the hundreds of examples will exemplify this:

The famous silk Hunting carpet until recently in the possession of the Rothschilds in Paris once beonged to the Marchese Torrigiani in Florence, who is reputed to have sold it to Bardini for 150 francs. The white-ground Animal carpet (Fig. 151) in Berlin, which was burned during the war, formerly lay in the Synagogue in Genoa. The Berlin Dragon carpet (Pl. VII) came from a church in Burano. The silk Kashan carpet (Fig. 68) in the Gulbenkian collection in Lisbon was acquired in Milan. Two Persian Animal carpets (Fig. 114) in the Metropolitan Museum in New York came from the Palazzo Capponi in Florence and four Ottoman carpets all in one design (Fig. 230) from the Palazzo Corsi. The four Lotto carpets with the impaled arms of the Genoese families Centurione and Doria (Fig. 144) are no longer in Italy.

Doubtless the Italian museums in the sixties and seventies of the last century did not take full advantage of their opportunities and it is difficult to judge whether the supply of carpets in Italy is now exhausted. This of course can never be established. Only recently a roll of carpet was found in a greenhouse in a villa in Tuscany. It proved to be a six-metre long Mamluk rug from about 1500. It was in bad condition because it had long been in use to keep the sun off the greenhouse.

There can be no doubt that even today the Italian carpet trade has better material available than that of any other country but outstanding pieces no longer seem to come to light there. They are however still to be found in London or New York. On investigation they almost always prove to be pieces already known for decades. In my experience fresh stocks of medium quality, by which is meant large Turkish or Caucasian rugs of the sixteenth and seventeenth centuries, appear more

114. Persia, end of the sixteenth century.

VII. Caucasus, *c.* 1600.

often in the Italian trade than in the English, French or American and not at all in the German. All this implies that these pieces come mostly from Italian private possession.

In 1961–62 when visiting palaces in Florence, some of which, although no longer inhabited today, are still furnished and kept in repair, it was astonishing to see how many antique and semi-antique carpets lay on the floors. If these were cleaned, repaired and cared for, the contents of a single palace would not cause a sensation on the international carpet market, but would undoubtedly stimulate it.

Carpets in Turkish Mosques

In contrast to the mosques in Egypt, Syria and for the most part also in Persia, those of Turkey, both large and small, always have carpets on the floor. In such buildings in large cities like Istanbul, Edirne (Adrianople) or Ankara these furnishings sometimes harmonize with the decorations and, if specially made for the building, are of recent date. Usually the effect is colourful and prayer rugs predominate, but they are not obligatory. Some of these which are wider than they are long have several niches woven side by side. Though popular in former centuries these multi-niche prayer rugs are uncommon today. It is incorrect to call them 'family prayer rugs' for it is unthinkable that men and women should pray next to each other either in the home or even in a mosque. Any type of carpet can be used for prayer, even kilims, skins and plaited straw mats.

Naturally the picture varies. The carpet furnishings of a mosque in Bursa in West Anatolia look different from those of a mosque in Sinope in North Anatolia or in Erzerum in East Anatolia. Certain types are to be found everywhere, but local rugs predominate. The carpet furnishings of a mosque, of course, reflect the degree of prosperity of a place and to some extent also the piety of the community. A thorough study of the subject is needed. So far there is only one book devoted to carpets by a Turkish author: *Eski ve Yeni Türk Haliciliği* by Kazim Dirik (Istanbul, 1938).

115. West Anatolia, eighteenth century.

116. Anatolia, eighteenth century.

118. Anatolia (Ushak district), *c*. 1700.

117. West Anatolia, eighteenth century.

Antique carpets are rare. The 'Campaign Evkaf' (see p. 105) during which rugs were brought in from the mosques for safe keeping in the museum has, with few exceptions, done its work thoroughly (Figs. 115–119). Attractive pieces from the end of the eighteenth century and the beginning of the nineteenth century are still frequent in mosques. They are really too good for ordinary use and should also be put into provincial museums.

Once, in an out-of-the-way place, we came across a mosque which still contained over a hundred carpets of which about fifty were antique. Among them was a perfectly preserved Dragon carpet of the early sixteenth century which would do credit to the Metropolitan Museum in New York. There were also a blue-ground Medallion Ushak of large size, Caucasian floral carpets up to eight metres in length, a Persian Medallion carpet of the early seventeenth century, a seven-metre-long East Perisan carpet of the same period and many others. I said to the Hoja (the teacher at the mosque) that these pieces should really be in Istanbul. 'Yes,' he replied 'I know that, but you see, there they disappear into the depot where nobody can see them and here we have pleasure in them'. On my undertaking not to mention the matter he promised to safeguard those pieces which were specially valuable.

Sixty years ago such collections certainly existed in many

Turkish mosques and more than one valuable piece has been sold by a less scrupulous Hoja to a buyer commissioned by a merchant in Istanbul through whom it has found its way to Europe or America. Hans-Hermann Graf von Schweinitz writes in his very readable book *In Kleinasien – Ein Reitausflug durch das Innere Kleinasiens im Jahre 1905* (*Berlin, 1906*). 'There are several old carpets in the mosques [of Niğde] especially in the Pasha Mosque. The beadle told us that the most beautiful carpet of Niğde and probably of all Asia Minor was no longer in the mosque but in the safe keeping of a government official because a European consul in Konya had cast covetous eyes upon it. He had offered 160 Turkish lira for this carpet and some Greek merchants had succeeded in getting it. However, word of this reached Constantinople and an order was telegraphed that the carpet, which was already on its way to Konya, should be stopped and returned to Niğde.' That government official, how-ever, seems to have been lacking in vigilance because the carpet, an unusually beautiful Caucasian piece, appeared a few years later in Istanbul and finally reached the Metropolitan Museum in New York.

This is no longer possible today. I recall an incident in Beyshehir. In large mosques there is often a corner with a pile of carpet fragments which are no longer usable. My companion

119. Central Anatolia (Konya?), eighteenth century.

discovered amongst these the remains of an old kilim whose colours so charmed him that he offered quite a good new kilim in exchange. The Hoja, although he saw that this would be to the advantage of the mosque, would not agree to it.

Even more telling is another story. One of my assistants in Istanbul who wrote her thesis on Caucasian carpets, discovered by chance the fragment of an antique rug under the more modern uninteresting pieces in a mosque and since then, on our excursions we have always turned up the rugs to see what was underneath. The inhabitants of the place were sometimes horrified but usually they took part in this curious hunt in a friendly and often enthusiastic way. The results were remarkable, especially in eastern Anatolia. In Erzerum, for instance, we found four fragments which belonged to a Dragon carpet of the sixteenth century. That afternoon we were invited to call on the Vali (governor). My assistant, who was obsessed with carpets – her name was Sherare (the Spark) – begged one of the fragments as a memento of her work and this was immediately granted. The Vali, however, had reckoned without the Hoja. In spite of his personal intervention the four fragments disappeared again under the protective layer of newer carpets, where they probably still are today.

This change in attitude to old rugs in mosques seems to have occurred about 1907 when a number of carpets and carpet fragments (Figs. 23–27 and 106) which undoubtedly date from the thirteenth century, were found in the great Alaeddin mosque, the old Seljuk capital of Konya (see pp. 41–46). The risk of leaving valuable antique carpets in mosques became apparent and when 'Campaign Evkaf' started, the Konya carpets (Figs. 23–27) were the first to be taken to Istanbul where today they form the most valuable possessions of the Türk ve Islam Eserleri Museum.

A similar discovery, though not so important, was that made by R. M. Riefstahl at the beginning of the twenties in the Eshrefoğlu Mosque in Beyshehir (see pp. 43–46). Three of the four thirteenth- and fourteenth-century fragments described by Riefstahl are now preserved in the Mevlana Museum in Konya.

The Türk ve Islam Museum in Istanbul

The largest collection of carpets in the world is also the youngest. The Evkaf Museum (the Museum of the Administration of Pious Foundations) in Istanbul was opened in 1914. Today it is called the Türk ve Islam Eserleri Müzesi (Museum of Turkish and Islamic Art). For a long time Turkish authorities were concerned that works of art of great historic interest used in mosques were insufficiently protected. This applied particularly to antique carpets still existing in great numbers but which were becoming badly worn through daily use. In the years before the first world war the Administration of Pious Foundations brought together in Istanbul all such artistic objects, especially Koran manuscripts and other valuables, which were housed in a building belonging to the mosque of Sultan Suleiman the Magnificent. During the war when there was a threat to the Eastern provinces this activity was intensified and additions to the collections continued subsequently. In 1914 there were about 700 carpets, in 1936 almost 950 and today there are more than 1,000.

1,000 carpets! A nightmare for a museum director. No museum in the world would be in a position to exhibit such a number. The majority must be stored and carpets are much more difficult to store than textiles or manuscripts. It presents an almost impossible task to make 800 carpets accessible in a depot. The position in Istanbul was further complicated by the fact that most of the mosque rugs arrived in a dirty and often damaged condition. It would have cost thousands to wash and repair them and would have taken many years even if dozens of restorers had been employed. This was impossible. There remained nothing for it but to store them as they were and protect them against moth. In 1936 only a small selection – 219 out of the 946 – could be exhibited. Today the position is even worse, for the rearrangement of the museum after the last war resulted in even less room being available. Only fifteen per cent of the rugs can be shown – the rest are in storage.

Most of the carpets exhibited (Figs. 120–125) are Turkish. As the majority of rugs reaching Europe since the fourteenth century came from Turkey we are particularly well informed about them. Many of these untold thousands have survived and today this stream has still not dried up but there is good reason why even this number is insufficient to answer all questions concerning Turkish carpets exported to Europe. Only certain groups, those which accorded with the buyers' tastes, were in fact exported and therefore the material available for carpet studies is limited to such groups and within the groups to certain designs. It is rare to find a carpet that does not fall into one of these categories. Therefore, the material in the West, in spite of its richness, does not include all the types made in the

East, many of which obviously were never exported. It can be readily understood that the earlier examples of a type are almost completely lacking. A new type would not be exported until it had become popular which means that it must first have been produced locally for some time. Those types not suitable for export and the early pieces of each group which were later exported can now only be found in Turkey, notably in Istanbul in the Türk ve Islam Eserleri Museum. Some are exhibited, but only a few, because it is not the task of a museum to show problem pieces. Among the many types in storage what is there that no European has seen? This is a question which becomes ever more acute for all who are concerned with the Turkish rug. One is tempted to say that the uninvestigated store-rooms of the museum in Istanbul hang, like the sword of Damocles, over the Turkish branch of carpet studies.

In 1936 I was sent to Istanbul for the purpose of gaining access to the depots. It was evident that this would not be easy. I decided to become familiar with the museum at first as an ordinary visitor. It is a sixteenth-century building, originally a kitchen for the poor, one of the many religious foundations which belong to the mosque of Suleiman. The courtyard with its ancient plane trees is surrounded by a cloister-like colonnade

120. Anatolia (Bergama district), sixteenth to seventeenth century.

I occupied the first few days by looking equally closely at the carpets and at the labels. The museum had few visitors and the attendants sat in the sun in the courtyard. When I arrived one of them got up, followed me into the hall and remained suspiciously at my side, probably inwardly cursing the visitor who for hours deprived him of the sun. On the third day I risked going a little further and produced a notebook which immediately brought the injunction 'Yasak' (forbidden). My knowledge of Turkish did not amount to more than ten words, but in the Orient one can always make oneself understood by gestures. After I had made it clear to him how large the museum was and how small my head he despatched a colleague who returned with an Assistant Director who spoke a little French and gave permission to make notes and from then on I was no longer incognito. Later a small grey-haired gentleman appeared, who pointed to the 'Polish' carpet in front of which I happened to be standing and said 'Polski, Polski'. I tried to explain to him that this was a Persian carpet but my knowledge of the language was insufficient. Soon after the Assistant Director reappeared, 'The Director would like to know . . .' Heavens!

121. Anatolia, sixteenth to eighteenth century.

122. Anatolia (Bergama district), seventeenth to eighteenth century.

which gives access to six large halls, where the poor of the neighbourhood were provided with food at the expense of the Sultan. Halls with mighty vaulting and an arsa of some 1,000 square metres are not our idea of a soup kitchen. In these rooms about 200 carpets were exhibited along with other objects. It was a startling and magnificent collection, and what was even more astonishing was that, as the labels proved, the man who had arranged this exhibition knew a lot about carpets. This could only have been the Director Abd-el-Kader, who, according to rumour, had even forbidden the museum to the eminent Friedrich Sarre. Such was the man with whom I had to deal.

The grey-haired gentleman was the much to be feared Abd-el-Kader, whom I had not treated very politely. He returned and, helped by the Assistant Director as interpreter, we managed to understand each other. He listened with interest to my explanations as to how the 'Polish' carpets had acquired their ridiculous name (see. p. 37). Today the carpet is still labelled 'Polish work' which proves that, in the Orient, explanations are not highly valued. We went on to the next carpet and at the third the Director made the attendant hold his cap in front of the label and asked me to tell him what was on it. For a moment I was nonplussed, but I remembered my mission and took part in this unusual game with good grace. I now profited from having studied the carpets and the labels for three days, incognito. I was able to tell him what was on his labels. Because of the language difficulty I only expressed a difference of opinion when I thought it would be understood. Finally we reached a carpet where I did not recall what was on the label. After some hesitation I shrugged my shoulders and said 'Anadolu' (Anatolian). The cap disappeared and the label revealed 'Anadolu'. Abd-el-Kader clapped his hands and beamed. 'Anadolu,

124. West Anatolia, eighteenth century.

123. West Anatolia, seventeenth to eighteenth century.

Anadolu' he said, happy that I knew no better than he did.

From then on we were friends. Each morning when he arrived an attendant came to take me to his office where I had to drink a cup of coffee with him, a rather silent occasion because he did not speak a single word of any European language and my own knowledge of Turkish only increased slowly. This done, I went back to work under very different conditions. I was no longer supervised. On the contrary, the hall in which I worked was closed to other visitors and so I could examine at leisure the carpets which were exhibited.

After six weeks this was done and the critical point was reached. When I appeared for morning coffee in company with the Director of the German Archaeological Institute who acted as interpreter, Abd-el-Kader said 'I do not know whether I had a German among my ancestors or he had a Turk, but in any case I like him.'; but, when the word 'depot' was mentioned he became reticent. It still took weeks till the point was reached when I became the first European to see the hidden treasures.

Our plan, which was prepared in detail, was to issue a large publication on the carpets of the museum, but after my departure the project came to nothing in spite of the interest shown in it in Turkish circles.

125. Anatolia (Ushak district), *c.* 1700.

From 1951–58, when I was professor at the University of Istanbul, I never again succeeded in entering the depot but, by assigning essays on specific groups of carpets to my students, examples of these types became accessible. They were brought out and spread in the 'cloisters'. During this time the museum had to be closed, mountains of naphthalene converted the scene into a snowy landscape and the staff worked at top pressure. The difficulties of caring for 800 Oriental carpets, all more or less in need of repair, were obvious.

The real significance of the collection in the Türk ve Islam Eserleri Museum lies in the number of its pieces, even though so few of them can be shown. Its importance is somewhat reduced because a good many of the unknown or rare types are in bad condition or exist only as fragments but this collection, brought together from mosques all over the country, gives a unique picture of Turkish possessions at the beginning of our century. The careful labelling of the pieces exhibited does not give the provenance and a new system of museum numbering makes it difficult to look them up in the inventory.

In spite of such limitations the collection is important even in its negative aspect, that is to say in what is not or is poorly

presented. It contains only a single Indian carpet and no Spanish, which is understandable since there is no reason for such carpets to find their way into Anatolian or Istanbul mosques. Persian carpets are also scarce and there is only one example of the not uncommon Shah Abbas carpets, which were made in Isfahan in the seventeenth century. We know from documentary sources that they reached the court of the Sultan, from where, even in Istanbul, they obviously did not find their way to the mosques. The equally numerous East Persian Isfahan carpets are represented by only two complete examples and a few fragments. On the other hand the museum possesses two important intact South Persian Vase carpets (Fig. 134) as well as some fragments, three large Garden carpets, two Medallion carpets and a fragment of a 'Portuguese' carpet, a type originally assigned to Goa in India, but which I am quite convinced comes from North Persia. These few rugs may not represent the original possessions; indeed one may assume that when carpets were sold secretly and in great numbers from the mosques

126. Anatolia (Ushak), seventeenth century.

VIII. Anatolia (Bergama district), sixteenth century.

between 1870 and 1910 these very types were in special demand. It is surprising that the museum possesses no Damascus (Mamluk) carpet, as it is known that these were plentiful in the seventeenth century in the Yeni Valide Mosque in Istanbul and in the Kara Mustapha Pasha Mosque in Gebze. The products of the Ottoman court manufactory are also poorly represented. Caucasian carpets (Fig. 131), however, are much more numerous and among these are some good Dragon carpets which later led to the Kubas and Shirvans. Nowhere else in the world can they be seen in such numbers and occasionally of such fine quality. These are mostly large pieces or fragments of large pieces from the eighteenth century, whereas there are not many of smaller size such as the Kazaks, Daghestans and Gendjes from the nineteenth century. A study of Caucasian rugs, which form one of the most attractive and interesting groups of Oriental carpets, must start with the examples in this museum. They are probably as numerous as all those in American and European collections put together.

128. Anatolia (Ushak), seventeenth century.

127. Anatolia (Ushak), seventeenth century.

Anatolian rugs naturally take pride of place. The most valuable possessions are the carpets and fragments of the thirteenth century from the Alaeddin Mosque in Konya. After these come several pieces which may be dated to the fourteenth and fifteenth centuries. The museum possesses no Anatolian Animal carpet of this period, of which two originals (Figs. 1 and 4) have survived in Europe where rugs in such designs are frequently represented in paintings; nor has it any of the fragments (Fig. 5) which came to light in Fostat (Old Cairo). It is also worth noting how the three groups of Holbein carpets are represented. The two of these types which I should like to assign to Ushak (cf. Figs 13; 56 and 144) are poorly represented. They are characterized respectively by the small-square design and by the yellow pattern on a red ground, today known as Lotto carpets. There is, however, a six-metre-long piece of the latter type in the museum and examples of the third type with a large-square pattern, which I assign to the Bergama district, are numerous. Among these are excellent older pieces and many transitional types. The latter lead to the later Bergamas and a wealth of variants which either do not occur in other collections or else only rarely. Occasionally 'Chanakkale', a name unknown

109

129. Anatolia (Ushak), eighteenth century.

130. Caucasus, eighteenth century.

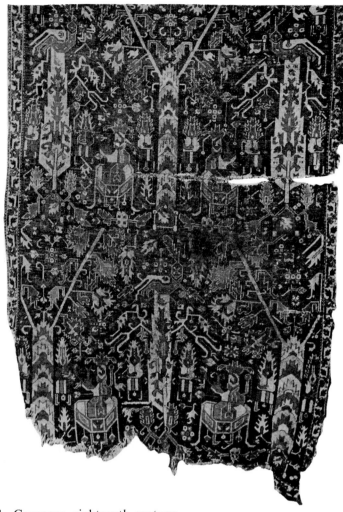

in Europe, occurs on the labels. There are good examples of both Star and Medallion Ushaks but none of the much-needed early examples which would throw light on their origin. On the other hand I have found a number of variants and derivatives (Figs. 126–131), which increase our knowledge. White-ground pieces, of which the museum in Konya possesses better examples, are rare, but there is a good Bird carpet. There is no white-ground Chintamani rug. In some pieces, however, the Chintamani is combined with other motifs in an unfamiliar way. There is a small group of white-ground prayer rugs, one of which is dated A.D. 1721/22 (A.H. 1134). Other examples exist in European collections. The museum possesses half a dozen carpets with designs like animal skins, which probably served as prayer rugs, but none is known outside Turkey.

There are innumerable prayer rugs of the Ghiordes, Ladik, Kula, Kirshehir, Mujur and other types, among them excellent pieces, but none is unusual, except perhaps in the Kirshehir group which has some amusing variants. Coarser but more uncommon pieces, obviously of nomadic origin, are labelled 'Yürük' in the museum.

131. Caucasus, eighteenth century.

111

Chinili Kiosk (Tile Pavilion) of the Saray. In 1953 on the 500th anniversary of the conquest of Constantinople it was decided that this building, which was erected in the time of Mehmet the Conqueror, should be converted into a museum in his honour. The beautiful building was restored and many later unsightly additions demolished, but regrettably the works of art which it contained were removed, stored and have not been shown since.

They had 'disappeared' as one would say in the Orient; but when Jan Kerametli, one of my pupils, became Director this collection was put on exhibition in the Türk ve Islam Eserleri Museum in 1963 and thus Istanbul regained its second Islamic collection.

The only representative carpet collection in Turkey therefore is that of the Evkaf, today the Türk ve Islam Eserleri Museum. The Top Kapi Saray Museum must be mentioned together with the Türk ve Islam Eserleri Museum. The Saray, a large area with many residential palaces and annexes much reconstructed, is now being restored. A considerable number of carpets, mostly badly worn, lay there thirty years ago when many of the rooms were inaccessible to the public. Among them were Ushaks, North-west Persian floral carpets (Fig. 135) and a large Medallion carpet with a cartouche design (Fig. 136), which I found nailed to the floor in one of the rooms of the harem. The Saray collection is of importance because it contains carpets which belonged to the Sultans, but the museum can show only a few.

134. South Persia, sixteenth century.

135. Caucasus – North-west Persia, c. 1800.

Six prayer rugs lying in the room with the relics of the Prophet belong to a group of some forty pieces of similar workmanship but different designs (Figs. 88–91) which are in store. These are all later Ottoman work of the type referred to in the chapter 'Persian Carpets of Turkish Provenence' (pp. 76–80).

136. North-west Persia, *c.* 1600.

Carpets in German Museums

An article which I wrote on this subject appeared in the *Zeitschrift der Deutschen Morgenländischen Gesellschaft* (*Leipzig* 1942, vol. 96, p. 393) where few people interested in the subject would come across it. The material for the article was collected in the years 1936 and 1937. On account of the war the carpets were no longer accessible when it was published and now some have disappeared. Nevertheless, it seems justifiable to deal briefly with the theme again since presumably readers will be interested even if not all the statements now apply. The fate of some of the pieces which have disappeared may become known as a result of this account.

In 1937 *Berlin* had the richest carpet collection in Germany, and it is described in detail in the next section of this book.

Munich occupied the second place because, apart from the Wittelsbach carpets (Pl. III) in the Residenz Museum, there were valuable carpets in the Bavarian National Museum, in the Völkerkunde Museum and in the Lenbachhaus. A Small Silk carpet made in Kashan in the first half of the sixteenth century is the most valuable in the National Museum. This is the only example in Germany of a group which today comprises fourteen pieces. There was a second example in the Kunstgewerbe Museum in Berlin which was sold when the Guelph Treasure

137. Persia (Isfahan), seventeenth century.

138. Egypt (Cairo), sixteenth century.

115

Turkish booty taken at the relief of Vienna in 1683.

The beautiful Shah Abbas carpet (Fig. 143) from the church of Edemissen in the Kestner Museum in *Hanover*, believed to have been destroyed during the war, was recovered in 1966. The Leibnizhaus had some interesting pieces among its seventeen fragments. I was told that these were acquired in Spain by Professor A. Haupt, together with a number of large carpets, which for lack of space were given to the Kestner Museum many years ago. Nothing was known of them there. After some searching I found a chest with eleven Anatolian prayer rugs, which could not possibly have come from Spain. The search continued and ended with a box in the cellar, the contents of which no one could remember. To everyone's surprise it contained three Isfahans, one Indo-Isfahan, four seventeenth-century North-Persian fragments, a blue-ground Dragon carpet, four Caucasian Flowering Plant fragments, a carpet in a textile design, a large Caucasian of quite unusual design with cartouches, trees and some animals in the field, two top-quality Ottoman fragments, a Medallion Ushak and several less important, smaller pieces. The storage room was too narrow to spread out the large pieces. Fortunately, this forgotten treasure was so dirty that the moths were obviously discouraged from attacking it. The restoration upon which I insisted was not effected before war broke out in 1939 and afterwards when the matter was raised again everything was said to have been destroyed and the collections were inaccessible because of the reconstruction of the museum. Eventually, however, the pieces were found and have now been restored and catalogued.

The *Halle* Stadtmuseum, apart from Ushak and Isfahan fragments, has pieces from the border of an enormous Chinese carpet, the large field of which was in a Berlin private collection and today is in the Museum in Cincinnati (see E. Kühnel, 'Mongolen Teppiche' *Cicerone* Leipzig, 1938, XX, pp. 1 ff).

The Grassi Museum in *Leipzig* had valuable carpets, amongst them an early Isfahan with particularly beautifully drawn arabesques, illustrated in colour in my article mentioned above, a North-Persian carpet with inscription, the fragment of a top-quality Ottoman and others.

The Kunstgewerbe Museum in *Dresden* provided the biggest surprise. Its carpets were quite unknown, though they were not hidden in the cellar like those in Hanover. Obviously these were so overshadowed by the world-famous collections of the city that nobody ever visited them. I noticed no less than fifty-one carpets and fragments, amongst which were the lower part of a Persian tapestry carpet (Fig. 225), the field of which is in the Kunstgewerbe Museum in Cologne, a large Mamluk carpet and five fragments of this group, an Ottoman, a beautiful Ushak with unusual design, eight other fragments, two Bird carpets, four Lottos, prayer rugs of good quality, three Spanish carpets and others. It is not known what was happened to them.

A New German Carpet Collection: Hamburg

One of the most important collections, that of the Kunst und Gewerbe Museum in Hamburg, has so far been omitted from the list of German museums possessing carpets.

Bode writes in his autobiography 'Dr. Justus Brinckmann, who built up the Hamburg Museum collection, happened to be present when a shipment of carpets had just arrived at the Berlin Museum. I asked him whether he did not intend to start collecting Oriental rugs. He turned this remark aside by saying that too many other departments of his museum still needed acquisitions. Not until 1st April 1900 at the earliest did he intend to start a collection of old rugs. At that time he assumed that there would be plenty available. My contention has been borne out by the facts that even if he were prepared to pay a lot of money then he would hardly be able to get one good antique rug.'

Indeed when Erich Meyer became director in 1947 the Hamburg Museum, so rich in all other respects, had only four carpets – the border of a seventeenth-century Persian tapestry carpet, one unimportant Lotto carpet and two indifferent Caucasians. In 1950 he could show six new acquisitions in the exhibition 'Orientalische Teppiche aus vier Jahrhunderten' which was held in the Museum on the occasion of his sixtieth birthday. In 1957 I was able to publish six more in the Festschrift and three more pieces have been added since. Within thirteen years the number of carpets in the Kunst und Gewerbe Museum in Hamburg had increased from four to nineteen.

The first six acquisitions were a large Lotto carpet, a weaver's sample (Fig. 235) known in Persia as a Wagireh, a Kula, a Dragon carpet, an East Anatolian nomad carpet of unusual design and a Samarkand.

The Lotto carpet (Fig. 144) is especially interesting since it bears in the upper right corner of the field a coat of arms which has been identified as that of the Genoese families Centurione and Doria. This carpet was probably made on the occasion of a marriage between these two families and it is interesting that a pattern for the arms was sent to Ushak. We know that carpets to European order were made there since Medallion Ushaks with Polish arms are known. The matter is rather more complicated in the case of this carpet which appeared at an auction in Hamburg and was bought cheaply. Originally two carpets of this kind with the same arms were known, one in a private collection in Leipzig, the other in the Silesian Museum of Art and Antiquities in Breslau (now Wroclaw). These two form a pair, in which the arms in the one are introduced into the upper right corner and in the other into the upper left. The newly acquired Hamburg piece is obviously somewhat later than the two others, as is evident from the design of the border. It must

therefore be a repeat order and furthermore its companion piece has been found and today is in the McMullan collection in New York.

The second group acquired between 1949 and 1957 contains a Beyshehir, the fragment of a big Ushak, a small Rosette Ushak, a Mamluk, a Shah Abbas and a large Medallion Ushak.

144. Anatolia (Ushak District), seventeenth century.

149. East Persia (?), beginning of the seventeenth century.

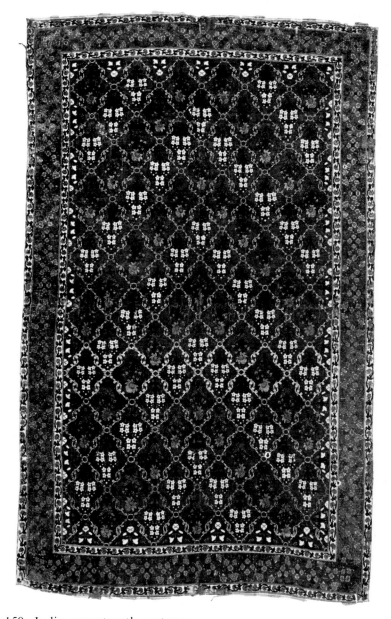

150. India, seventeenth century.

that gives the impression of velvet, to which the unusual grace of the pattern contributes. I recall how greatly Consul Bernheimer admired this carpet, though to me it lacks the

character of a carpet, but in that respect it is typical of Indian work and is therefore a valuable addition to the Hamburg collection.

THE BERLIN CARPET COLLECTION

THE BURNT CARPETS: PERSIA

(Figs. 151–160)

Fig. 151. Inv. Nr. I 1. White-ground carpet (604 × 365 cm.). North Persia, first half of the sixteenth century. Acquired about 1890 from a synagogue in Genoa by W. von Bode and exhibited in 1891 in Vienna, 1910 in Munich and 1931 in London. This piece formed the foundation of Bode's studies of carpets which resulted in the well-known handbook by Bode-Kühnel. The carpet, which at the time of its acquisition had already been shortened at both ends for the synagogue by cutting away the figures of angels in the corners, could be restored after the war to about a quarter of its original size. The intact pair to it is in the County Museum in Los Angeles.

Fig. 152. Inv. Nr. KGM 73, 1195. White-ground carpet (506 ×
256 cm.). North Persia, second half of the sixteenth century.
Acquired 1873 from a church in the Tyrol. Small fragments are
preserved. A carpet based on the same cartoon but less clearly
drawn and therefore probably a little later is in the possession
of Count Boucqoi in Vienna.

Fig. 153. Inv. Nr. I 1313. North Persian carpet (490 × 265 cm.),
first half of sixteenth century. Acquired 1909. This carpet was
one of the most important examples of the early Medallion
carpets, which are otherwise known only from fragmentary
examples. Small pieces are preserved.

Fig. 155. Inv. Nr. KGM 90,10. North Persian carpet (545 × 212 cm.), beginning of the seventeenth century. Acquired 1890. To my knowledge this carpet has never been published. It is a typical, but not especially fine, late example of the usual Medallion carpets in which the field is designed in scrolling tendrils. As large fragments were preserved, restoration to two-thirds of the original size was possible.

Fig. 154. Inv. Nr. KGM 88,330. Fragment of a carpet (350 × 260 cm.), probably from Central Persia, about 1600. Acquired 1888 in Bologna. It belongs to a group which I have ascribed to Kashan but differs in the pictorial arrangement of the animal combats. Small fragments are preserved.

X. Asia Minor (?), seventeenth century.

Fig. 156. Inv. Nr. I 5055. Persian carpet (306 × 230 cm.), sixteenth century. Acquired 1927. This carpet with its deep-blue arabesques and scrolling stems on a red ground was acquired as a large fragment and was one of the most impressive Persian pieces of the early sixteenth century. No other examples of the design, which is unusually well planned, are known. Because of its colour it is assigned to South Persia, but the provenance is disputed. Only very small fragments have survived.

Fig. 157. Inv. Nr. I 2656. South Persian carpet (540 × 235 cm.), first half of the sixteenth century. Acquired 1875 in Munich. Among the Vase carpets which are preserved in a series of examples, this piece was one of the earliest and most important on account of the precision of its drawings and the richness of its colours. Its almost total destruction is a great loss to the Berlin collection but fortunately for carpet studies a counterpart exists in an English private collection.

E.O.R.C.

Fig. 159. Inv. Nr. KGM 99,315. East Persian carpet (410 × 294 cm.), seventeenth century. Acquired 1899 in Paris. This unique fragmentary carpet represents a variant of the Herats, in which the influence of the Shah Abbas, formerly known as Polish carpets, can be seen. Only small pieces have survived.

Fig. 158. Inv. Nr. KGM 87,974. 'Portuguese' carpet (500 × 252 cm.), Persia, seventeenth century. Acquired 1887 in Paris. The Berlin piece was one of the most beautiful of the eight known examples of this group, which is something of a curiosity among seventeenth-century Persian carpets. It was completely destroyed.

Fig. 160. Inv. Nr. I 3089. Garden carpet (630 × 300 cm.), North-west Persia, eighteenth century. Acquired 1920, probably from a mosque in Iraq. Part of a larger piece. The carpet, which gives a bird's eye view of a garden, was one of the rare early examples known in a number of intact and fragmentary pieces.

THE BURNT CARPETS: CAUCASUS, TURKEY, SPAIN

(Figs. 161–170)

Fig. 162. Inv. Nr. KGM 81,1018. Dragon carpet (572 × 268 cm.), Caucasus, about 1600. Acquired 1881. This carpet was an excellent late example of the group in which strongly stylized blossoms predominate and is notable for its strength of colour and excellent preservation. It is doubtful whether the significance of the dragon motif was understood by the weavers.

Fig. 161. Inv. Nr. I 3. Dragon carpet (678 × 230 cm.), Caucasus, early sixteenth century. The carpet is reputed to have come from a mosque in Damascus and passed into the Graf collection in Vienna from which, in 1905, it was acquired for Berlin. Along with a carpet which has disappeared but which seventy years ago was in the hands of a dealer in Florence, it was the oldest of the Caucasian carpets which are still preserved in numerous examples. No other piece of this group achieved such richness in motifs, delicacy of drawing and harmony of colour. Its destruction is the greatest loss suffered by the Berlin collection. A fairly large piece has been put together from surviving fragments, but this only echoes the grandeur of the original carpet.

Fig. 163. Inv. Nr. I 13. Fragment of a Caucasian or North Persian carpet (228 × 228 cm.), seventeenth century. Acquired 1905 as a gift from Bode. A small number of these carpets, in which the field, between alternating shield and cross-shaped cartouches, is filled with stylized, flowering trees, has been preserved. The Berlin piece was only a fragment and probably belonged to the same carpet as that in the Williams Collection in Philadelphia.

Fig. 164. Inv. Nr. I 2840. Caucasian carpet (313 × 187 cm.), end of the eighteenth century. Acquired 1917. This carpet, which is interesting only because of a knotted but illegible inscription, would hardly have been of sufficient importance to store with the most valuable pieces. It is not known how it came to be in one of the rolls of carpets in the Mint.

Fig. 165. Inv. Nr. I 10. Ottoman carpet (290 × 217 cm.), Cairo about 1540–5.
Acquired 1905 as a gift from von Dirksen. Carpets of this sort, of course, are preserved
in great numbers, but the Berlin piece was the most beautiful. Mamluk details of design
which have persisted in the central medallion prove that it belonged to the earliest
examples of this group, which about 1540 replaced the Mamluk carpets made in Cairo
up to that time.

Fig. 166. Inv. Nr. I 30. Ottoman carpet (415 × 287 cm.), Cairo or Istanbul about 1600. Acquired 1905 as a gift from Bode. This was probably the most important piece of a group of later Ottoman carpets, still preserved in many intact and fragmentary examples. It was outstanding for its particularly fine design, warm colouring and excellent state of preservation. The elements of the design are known from other carpets but this particular arrangement occurs here only. Its complete destruction is a bitter loss.

Fig. 167. Inv. Nr. I 7. Ushak carpet (430 × 268 cm.), Asia Minor, sixteenth to seventeenth century. Acquired 1905 as a gift from Bode. Among the many surviving examples of the Ushak group, this piece occupies a special position and since no second example of the pattern is known its classification is difficult. This makes its loss doubly regrettable. Large fragments are preserved but restoration of the whole is not possible. After the war another smaller and later carpet appeared and this (Fig. 145) was acquired for the Kunst und Gewerbe Museum in Hamburg and, to some extent, is a substitute for the burnt piece.

VANISHED CARPETS

(Figs. 171–180)

Some of the smaller carpets had remained in the Pergamon Museum and therefore escaped the fire in the Mint. There were losses among them too but these may not be irretrievable. Seventeen carpets are listed as 'vanished'. One was a small Dragon carpet, a loan from the Cassirer estate, and another (Fig. 177) of the sixteen carpets was apparently stolen during the confusion at the end of the war. The remaining fifteen were removed for safe keeping by Russian troops. Though by 1958 the Soviet Union had returned to Berlin most of those works of art which it had placed in safety in 1945 and 1946, it is still possible that these fifteen carpets may be recovered. The list of losses cited is therefore provisional and will be confined to the ten most important pieces.

Fig. 172. Inv. Nr. KGM 05,120. Fragment, about one-third, of a Medallion carpet (167 × 167 cm.), North Persia, mid sixteenth century. Acquired 1905 in Rome. The field design of endless scrolling tendrils shows that it belongs to the second group of North Persian Medallion carpets, which were perhaps made in Tabriz. However this second group is almost always characterized by pastel colours, as in Fig. 173, while this fragment, which has brilliant yellow scrolls on a dark-red field, is in colouring more closely related to the first group of Medallion carpets (Fig. 153). It therefore occupies a special place in its group. The extremely accurate drawing of the scrolls suggests a relatively early origin, probably before the middle of the sixteenth century.

Fig. 171. Inv. Nr. KGM 73,1198. Fragment of an Animal carpet (155 × 161 cm.), North Persia, second half of the sixteenth century. Acquired 1873 for 28 talers at the Vienna World Exhibition. Green central medallion on a red field with fine scrolling tendrils ornamented with animals. A typical example of carpet art of the Safavid period at its peak. Strangely, there is no other known piece closely related to this. The drawing of the animals in the foliage is closest to that of the pair of carpets (Fig. 229) from the shrine of the Mosque in Ardebil. These have a marked colour contrast but no central medallion.

Fig. 173. Inv. Nr. I 32. Medallion carpet (402 × 180 cm.), North Persia, sixteenth century. Acquired 1906, as a gift from Count Welczek. A typical finely-designed example of the second group of Medallion carpets. The field is raspberry red and the rays of the star-shaped medallion are creamy yellow, pale cream and pink. The border is yellow with dark-blue arabesque bands.

Fig. 174. Inv. Nr. KGM 84,495. Silk carpet with gold and silver brocading (210 × 143 cm.), Central Persia, Isfahan, first half of the seventeenth century. Acquired 1884. Typical of the so-called Polish carpets – better called Shah Abbas carpets – which for the most part were produced in the court manufactory in Isfahan. In the West at some time the Berlin piece may have been cut to form a cope and when reassembled as a carpet some additions were necessary.

Fig. 175. Inv. Nr. I 33. So-called Isfahan carpet (265 × 180 cm.), East Persia (Herat?), about 1600. Acquired 1906. It is strange that the Berlin collection did not, and does not, possess an important piece of this type which was still prevalent in the sixteenth and seventeenth centuries. This carpet is relatively early and well preserved but not typical.

Fig. 176. Inv. Nr. I 25. So-called Tree carpet (197 × 130 cm.), North-west Persia about 1700. Acquired in 1906 as a gift from Bode. A small, not specially important example of a type known from perhaps as early as the end of the sixteenth century until the eighteenth century.

Fig. 177. Inv. Nr. I 11. Holbein carpet (242 × 137 cm.), Asia Minor, Ushak district, sixteenth century. Acquired 1906 as a gift from Bode. This is not the earliest but it is certainly the best known of the small-pattern Holbein carpets, of which a considerable number of intact or fragmentary examples are preserved. It is a classic which has often been illustrated and shows with great clarity the characteristics of the type.

Fig. 178. Inv. Nr. I 21. Holbein carpet (334 × 186 cm.), Asia Minor, Ushak district, sixteenth century. Acquired 1905 as a gift from Bode. The name Holbein carpet, justified in the case of Fig. 177, since Hans Holbein the Younger depicted a carpet of this type in his portrait of the Merchant Gisze, is meaningless here, because Holbein never painted this type of which many are still extant. Apparently they were made from the early sixteenth century until the middle of the eighteenth century. Among hundreds of examples the Berlin piece occupies a position in this group similar to that of Fig. 177 in its group. It is a characteristic and probably early example.

Fig. 179. Inv. Nr. KGM 83,571. Mamluk carpet (315 × 230 cm.), Cairo, early sixteenth century. Acquired 1883. In the Venetian inventories of about 1500 these were called Damascus carpets but, since they are now known to have been made in Cairo, they are referred to today as Mamluk. Much work has been done on this group in the last few decades. The carpet in Fig. 179 belongs to those important examples in which the design of a carpet of normal size, of which the Berlin collection still possesses a number (Pl. IV), is used in one of much larger size.

Fig. 180. Inv. Nr. KGM I 2239. Garden carpet (310 × 178 cm.), North-west Persia, eighteenth century. Acquired 1912 as a gift from Beccard. In the eighteenth century the design of the Garden carpets, which were originally large or even enormous in size, was used in smaller carpets. This adaptation was not always successful, but the Berlin piece was an acceptable compromise. The weaver, however, did not fully understand the design since instead of fish he depicted trees in the water channels.

The five remaining carpets in this list are of little importance: a Smyrna carpet (Inv. Nr. I 6), a late Caucasian version of an Animal carpet (Inv. Nr. I 2241), two Nomad carpets from the Ushak district (Inv. Nrs. I 5 and 35) and a Tekke Turkoman (Inv. Nr. I 6929).

Carpets in East Berlin at the End of the War

The Berlin carpet collection was not completely destroyed. Undoubtedly the war losses were extremely heavy but the Berlin collection was so rich that a good deal remains.

The original department on the Museum Island in East Berlin still possesses about fifty carpets and fragments, among which are ten small pieces from Old Cairo (Fostat), which were put away for safety and have been returned. Among the fifty there is only one large piece, a Medallion carpet (515 × 296 cm.), which owes its preservation to the fact that it was acquired during the war and not stored in the Mint. Among the small carpets are well-known and famous pieces such as:

Fig. 1. Inv. Nr. I 4. Carpet with Dragon and Phoenix (172 × 90 cm.), Asia Minor about 1400. Acquired 1886 in Rome, reputedly from a church in Central Italy. It was considered to be the oldest extant carpet until those of the thirteenth century from the mosque of Alaeddin in Konya became known. Carpets with this design have often been depicted in Italian paintings of the fifteenth century, and small fragments of such carpets have been found in Old Cairo. *page 17*

Fig. 15. Inv. Nr. I 24. Prayer rug with cloudband (180 × 120 cm.), Asia Minor, Ushak, early sixteenth century. Acquired in 1905 as a gift from Bode. This famous carpet is still outstanding because of its unique design. Pieces of the same design have proved to be imitations of a later date. *page 28*

Pl. IV. Inv. Nr. KGM 82,704. Mamluk carpet (207 × 133 cm.), Cairo about 1500. Acquired 1942 from the Berlin Textile College. This carpet was of special importance for those Egyptian rugs, formerly called Damascus carpets, which show in their design the typical Mamluk cup blazon repeated eight times.

facing page 84

Pl. V. Inv. Nr. I 2577. Silk Tapestry carpet (221 × 136 cm.), Persia, Kashan, seventeenth century, formerly at Schloss Friedrichshof and acquired 1914 from the Kaiserin Friedrich. The inscription 'Padishah' in the cartouches is evidence that it was made for the Shah. Two other pieces in the same design in Copenhagen and Washington lack this inscription.

facing page 92

Fig. 181. Inv. Nr. I 27. So-called Synagogue carpet (303 × 94 cm.), Spanish, fourteenth to fifteenth century. Acquired 1880 from a church in the Tyrol. This unique piece is probably the oldest Spanish carpet in existence. According to Sarre the design represents the Ark of the Law.

143

Fig. 185. Inv. Nr. I 29. Large-pattern Holbein carpet (170 × 113 cm.), Asia Minor, Bergama district, seventeenth century. Acquired 1905 from Bode. This carpet belongs to the classical examples of a much-illustrated group.

Fig. 184. Inv. Nr. I 6737. Small-pattern Holbein fragment, (159 × 89 cm.), Asia Minor, district of Ushak, fifteenth century. Formerly in the Municipal Collection, Düsseldorf. This is the only carpet of this group which, because of the border design, can probably be dated to the fifteenth century.

Fig. 186. Inv. Nr. I 9. Ushak carpet (294 × 165 cm.), Asia Minor, seventeenth century. Acquired 1905 by Bode. This carpet shows an unusual variant of the normal Ushak design not known in other examples. A much larger area of the same design can be seen in the Musée des Arts Décoratifs in Paris.

Fig. 187. Inv. Nr. KGM 89,156. Prayer Rug (172 × 127 cm.), Turkish court manufacture, Istanbul or Bursa, about 1600. Acquired 1889 in Istanbul. The Ottoman court manufactory was situated in Cairo, but at the end of the sixteenth century, eleven master weavers were ordered to Istanbul. Only recently has it been possible to distinguish between the work of Cairo and Bursa, where prayer rugs were an important part of the output.

Fig. 189. Inv. Nr. I 12. Fragment of carpet (396 × 298 cm.), with a large lozenge design. Caucasus, sixteenth to seventeenth century. Acquired 1906 as a gift from Bode. It is an example of a small group and, in spite of the lack of animal figures, must be regarded as a Dragon carpet. A similar fragment is in the Victoria and Albert Museum in London.

Fig. 188. Inv. Nr. KGM 91,26. Mamluk carpet (196 × 130 cm.), Cairo, beginning of the sixteenth century. Acquired 1891 in Munich. One of the most beautiful examples of that group, formerly known as Damascus carpets, which are characterized by specially rich colour.

In addition there have also been preserved the beautiful Ottoman carpet (Fig. 230) Inv. Nr. I 6355 and a small Bird carpet (Inv. Nr. KGM 90,150).

Carpets in West Berlin at the End of the War

During the course of the war the less important possessions of the Islamic Department were removed from the Pergamon Museum to the anti-aircraft tower in Friedrichshain. This was also burnt out but only after the boxes from the Islamic Department had been removed to the salt mine in Kaiserroda. As the carpets were also stored there, they, together with other objects, were returned to West Berlin through the American collecting point in Wiesbaden. That is why the West Berlin Department today possesses 140 carpets and carpet fragments. This number however is misleading. Most of these carpets, which are of recent date and little artistic value, were not originally in the collection but were sent to the museum later from a bank depot. Only about sixty-five pieces are of interest to scholars. Though it contains nothing of outstanding quality, anyone who knew the original collection will rejoice that some of the pieces have been preserved. Only those pieces which have been published, and are therefore known to a wider public, will be discussed.

Pl. VI. Inv. Nr. KGM 84, 929. Silk Shah Abbas carpet (190 × 140 cm.), Persia, Isfahan, seventeenth century. Acquired 1884. It is a good example, perhaps early, which has not been brocaded. The cartoon has been used frequently, so that a number of carpets of this design exist. *facing page 96*

Pl. VII. Inv. Nr. I 2. Dragon carpet (525 × 212 cm.), Caucasus, about 1600. Acquired in 1905 for 120 lire from a church in Burano near Venice. Gift from Bode. Of the middle period of the group, it still shows a great number of different motifs filling the lozenges, but is rather crudely drawn and does not bear comparison with the burnt piece (Fig. 161).
facing page 100

Pl. VIII Inv. Nr. I 5526. Holbein carpet (427 × 190 cm.), Asia Minor, Bergama district, sixteenth century. Acquired 1928 as gift from Dr. I. Goldschmidt. This is a variant of the usual large-pattern Holbein carpet (Fig. 185), in which large squares are not only arranged in rows but are grouped with smaller figures. Examples of this combination of large and small motifs are not unusual and in fact persisted in Bergamas and Kazaks into the nineteenth century. A second example in this large size has not come to light so far. *facing page 108*

Pl. IX. Inv. Nr. KGM 82, 707. Anatolian Arabesque carpet (381 × 210 cm.), called also Holbein or Lotto carpet, Asia Minor, Ushak district, seventeenth century. Acquired 1882. Such rugs, which are classed with the small-pattern Holbein carpets, were probably products of the same workshops and have survived in great numbers. They usually show a uniform yellow design on a brick-red ground. Occasionally large sizes are found. Colour variations, as in this piece in which some leaves are knotted in blue or green instead of yellow, are rare. *facing page 112*

Pl. X. Inv. Nr. I 14. Chess-board carpet (396 × 208 cm.), Asia Minor (?), seventeenth century. Acquired in 1905 as a gift from Bode. A considerable number of these carpets has been preserved. Until now examples of large size have been considered as variants of Mamluk carpets, formerly called Damascus, which show Anatolian influence and like the former were made in Cairo. Recent investigations have thrown doubt on this and a convincing provenance has not yet been established. *facing page 128*

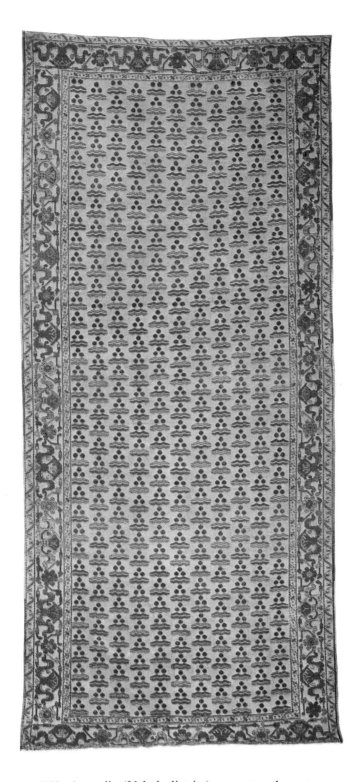

XII. Anatolia (Ushak district), seventeenth century.

Fig. 191. Inv. Nr. KGM 86, 1172. Fragment of a small-pattern Holbein carpet (226 × 230 cm.), Asia Minor, Ushak district, sixteenth century. Acquired 1886. It is a good example of this type of rug which is comparatively rare in a large size.

Fig. 190. Inv. Nr. I 15, 64. Prayer rug (183 × 122 cm.), of Turkish Court manufacture, Istanbul or Bursa, dated 1610–11. Acquired 1915 in Rome. The significance of this carpet has only recently been noticed. In the richness of its drawing and the delicacy of its colouring – the uniform field of the niche shows an olive-green of rare beauty – it is one of the best examples of the Cairene court manufactory which was established in either Istanbul or Bursa at the end of the sixteenth century. It is of special interest because of a chronogram (Fig. 210) which is knotted into its upper border and shows the date A.H. 1019 (equivalent to A.D. 1610/11). This therefore is the only known, dated Ottoman carpet and consequently is important for the dating of the whole group.

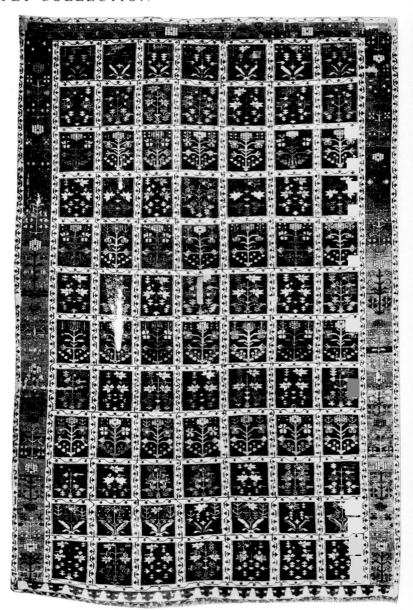

Fig. 193. Inv. Nr. KGM 82, 706. Garden carpet, North-west Persia, eighteenth century. Acquired 1882. This carpet, so pleasing in its colouring, exemplifies the last phase of stylization of the Garden design, in which the small-pattern squares finally prevailed (cf. Figs. 69 to 76 and Pl. I).

Fig. 192. Inv. Nr. I 4928. Medallion Ushak (350 × 190 cm.), Asia Minor about 1700. Acquired 1927. Typical example of a late, red-ground Medallion Ushak with thoroughly degenerate drawing. The piece is interesting on account of the European coat of arms in the upper border, which has been identified as that of the Polish family Wiesotowski. The pair to this is in the Wavel in Cracow. Both carpets were therefore woven in Ushak to the order of the Polish family.

Fig. 194. Inv. Nr. KGM 86, 602. Spanish carpet (427 × 195 cm.), fifteenth century. Acquired 1886. Such carpets with multiple borders, whose outer stripes show misunderstood Kufic script, and with small-pattern, geometric field design, are typical examples of fifteenth-century Spanish knotted carpets. They often have blazons in the field, mostly those of the Enriquez family.

The ten pieces illustrated in this chapter represent only a small part of the material which has been preserved in West Berlin. There are no Persian carpets except a few fragments and a late Isfahan, but there are a number of large Anatolian rugs with unusual designs, good fragments of Holbein, Mamluk and Ottoman carpets and an unusually rich collection of intact and fragmentary pieces of the fifteenth and sixteenth centuries.

151

197. Caucasus, end of the eighteenth century.

Berlin, 1936, 6, XII, p. 6, 'Sammlung Prof. Bichlmaier, Kiel'. – Hauswedel auction, 26.11.1956, Nr. 293. – K. Erdmann, *Oriental Carpets*.

It has long been customary to associate with the Mamluk carpets of Cairo those Holbein carpets in which large and small squares occur together, that is, where there is a grouping of motifs rather than rows. As proof early examples can be cited, especially a carpet in the Williams collection in the Museum of Art in Philadelphia, where cypresses and candelabra motifs arranged radially suggest an Egyptian connection. It was overlooked, however, that the radial arrangement of these motifs does not occur in true Mamluk carpets but only in that type characterized by small squares (Pl. X), which at one time was considered to be a late product of the Cairene workshops. Today they are classified as Anatolian, without however overlooking the close relationship with the main group of Mamluk carpets. The fragment illustrated in Fig. 198 appears to be a smaller and probably somewhat later counterpart of the piece in Philadelphia and, therefore, a West Anatolian work of the sixteenth century. A detailed examination shows that this carpet is closely connected with the Cairo group and, thereby, the discussion of the Cairene carpets is shifted onto new ground. It was imperative that Berlin, which as a result of the work of Sarre, Kühnel and myself had contributed so much to the clarification of the question, should secure this carpet. Through the generosity of Bernheimers it was given to the Islamic Department.

Classification: The piece, distinguished on account of its glowing colours, shows a field design which in early examples was infinitely extensible but here is centred in the middle of the field and is complete in itself. Both features, as well as the small size, indicate a late date. The little animal figures scattered in the field resemble similar ones in Caucasian carpets of the nineteenth century but this piece must be dated to the end of the eighteenth century on account of the drawing of the dragon which is still fairly correct. Closest to it is a carpet in the von Heyl Collection (Helbing auction 1930, Nr. 263). Similar pieces are in the Museum of Art in Philadelphia and in the Cassirer Collection.

Literature: K. Erdmann, 'Later Caucasian Dragon Carpets', *Appollo*, London, 1935, XXII, p. 24, fig. VI. – *Die Weltkunst*,

198. West Anatolia, sixteenth century.

The small prayer rugs with opposed niches are among the most charming pieces included in the large group of West-Anatolian carpets in multifarious designs known as Ushak carpets. Many examples are still extant. The Islamic Department possessed one piece (150 × 94 cm. Inv. Nr. I 17) which was presented in 1908 and stolen in 1918. No photograph exists but the main stripe of the border contained cloud bands. During the last war a late and poorly preserved example was acquired as a modest substitute. The carpet purchased recently (Fig. 199) is a good and typical example. Judging from the design of its border, it belongs to the early group datable to the second half of the sixteenth and the first half of the seventeenth century. Because of the filling of the spandrels with arabesques instead of cloud bands, which are probably earlier, it belongs among the later works of this early group. Usually these carpets show in the niches hanging motifs which may represent lamps. In this piece it is unusual that the hanging motif also extends like a pendant from the central medallion, an arrangement occurring only three times in seventy available photographs of the type.

199. Anatolia (Ushak), seventeenth century.

Fig. 199. Prayer carpet with opposed niches, Anatolia, Ushak district, seventeenth century.

Size: 185 × 118 cm.

Warp: Wool, Z2S, ivory and a little brownish.

Weft: Wool, Z spun, ×2, red.

Pile: Wool, Z spun, Turkish knot, *c.* 1,450 per sq. dm.

Colours: 7 (11); red (2 shades), blue (4 shades), brown, yellow, green, black, white.

Condition: Some small repairs.

Design: Red field with opposed, curving niches, whose arabesque filling is separated by an inner light-blue zone from an outer red one. In the middle of the field a yellow quatrefoil with red palmette blossoms and a shield-like pendant at the upper end. In the main stripe of the border, alternating rows of blossoms directed medially, the larger of which are framed by arabesque pairs in gable formation.

Classification: Two colours in the spandrels are rare in the group with the arabesque leaf border, but sometimes occur in the group, probably later, with the cloud border. This carpet is closest to the smaller and coarser piece which was exhibited in Hamburg in 1950 (Catalogue Nr. 39).

Literature: Coloured reproduction in the *Bilderbuch für Teppichsammler* by U. Schürmann, Munich, 1960, Pl. 5.

Multiple-niche prayer rugs which have their niches arranged in rows occur only occasionally in European collections. They were of little interest for the European market and, therefore, only rarely exported, but they are often to be found in the Orient. The Türk ve Islam Eserleri Museum in Istanbul possesses a number and the oldest pieces are probably fifteenth century. They are only occasionally found in mosques (as in the Bayazid mosque in Istanbul), all alike and therefore modern furnishings. The purpose of such carpets is to ensure the correct placing of the rows of worshippers. Probably the original idea was to leave the niche of the prayer rug free of decoration, but the Oriental delight in ornament soon led to the introduction of decorative elements even here. The effect of this carpet (Pl. XI) is the greater, therefore, because even in the spandrels all decoration has been dispensed with and the effect is dependent on the contrast between dark-blue and red. Only one other example of this type is known to me from a photograph supplied by Haim in Istanbul in 1937, but the whereabouts of the rug was unknown and it has never come to light. It is probable that these two fragments belonged to the same carpet, or more likely, to the carpet furnishings of the same mosque, probably a royal one. They were certainly produced in the Ushak or Ladik districts of Western Anatolia. The dating, however, is more difficult due to the lack of detail. The large reciprocal design, preserved in the main stripe of the Haim fragment border, precludes a dating later than the seventeenth century. At this period royal mosques were being built in Istanbul only, and, therefore, there are grounds for supposing that the Berlin fragment came from a mosque in the capital.

Pl. XI. Fragment of a multiple-niche Prayer carpet, Anatolia, Ushak district, seventeenth century. *(facing page 144.)*

Size: 329 × 128 cm. (size of the complete carpet unkown).

Warp: Wool, Z2S, ivory.

Weft: Wool, Z and 2Z, red, × 2.

Pile: Wool, 2Z, Turkish knot, *c.* 1,200 per sq. dm.

Colours: 5 (8); red, blue (4 shades), brownish-yellow, green, black.

Condition: The design is woven at right angles to the warps and the half niche is at the beginning of the work. At one end the border has been attached subsequently and the carpet may therefore have had additional niches here. Regular diagonal weaving-lines; some torn and repaired. Some larger repairs at the ends, otherwise uniformly worn. The border halved.

Design: Carmine field with a row of 5½ dark-blue curved spandrels, both without ornamentation. The inner guard has a reciprocal arrow-head design in brownish-yellow or red and light blue. The halved main border stripe shows a similar but larger reciprocal design in dark blue and yellowish brown.

Classification: This piece, which probably had additional niches, may not have had a border on the 'top', but may have had another row of niches there in order to fill a larger floor space.

Literature: Exhibition in Basle, 1934, Cat. Nr. 65. Exhibition in Hamburg 1950, Cat. Nr. 69, Fig. 17. – *Alte Teppiche des 16. bis 18. Jahrhunderts der Firma L. Bernheimer,* Munich, 1959, fig. 32.

The Berlin carpet collection owes its existence to the generous gifts of Wilhelm von Bode. It is not known why he retained the two white-ground Anatolian carpets (Fig. 94), which were both auctioned in 1929. The Islamic Department possessed only a modest, later Bird carpet of this large-sized type, which may also be ascribed to the Ushak district. The gap in the collection was filled with the purchase of an important example of the so-called Chintamani design, of which only a few pieces have been preserved.

Pl. XII. Anatolian carpet, Ushak district, seventeenth century. *(facing page 148.)*

Size: 386 × 168 cm.

Warp: Wool. Z2S and Z2Z, yellowish.

Weft: Wool Z spun, pale yellowish, × 2.

Pile: Wool, Z spun, Turkish knot, *c.* 1750 per sq. dm.

Colours: 6; white, carmine, light blue, light brown, brownish black.

Condition: Much, but evenly worn, restored edges, brownish-black eroded; but still important in its colour.

Design: Offset rows of spots arranged in triangles and pairs, alternating with pairs of wavy cloud-bands on a white ground. The spots are all brownish-black and the cloud pairs in two colours, without a definite rhythm. A border of cloud-bands in different colours, directed medially and alternating with rosettes, between guards with continuous tendrils. In the main stripe the tendril filling is not continuous, but always springs from the cloud-bands.

Classification: The colouring is in keeping with the small-pattern, repetitive design in rows. The same dull white is used for the field and all three border stripes, while pastel shades are used for the design. Carpets of this kind, of which only a few examples are known in such large size (Florence, Bardini Museum, Fig. 93; Vienna, Prince Schwarzenberg, Fig. 95; Konya, Mevlana Museum), differ from the customary colouring of Oriental rugs which is based on strong contrasts. The Chintamani rugs show the same colouring as the Bird carpets and both groups probably come from the Ushak workshops of Western Anatolia. The same design also occurs in textiles and ceramics. These carpets do not appear in paintings. Because of the type of border they can be dated to the seventeenth century.

Literature: Unpublished.

Like most museums, the Islamic Department in Berlin limited its collecting to carpets before 1800. Long before the war, however, Ernst Kühnel realized that in the long run this would have to be changed. It was planned to establish a study collection and afterwards to purchase good examples of nineteenth-century carpets in order to show how the artistic forms of the classical period persisted in our century as popular art. This plan could not be put into effect. When I became Director in 1958 I found a large number of late rugs which the Museum had acquired through a special transfer, but unfortunately there were few good pieces among them and the task still remains to be achieved.

A beginning was made with the purchase of a white-ground Anatolian prayer rug (Fig. 134, Pl. XI) known as a 'Kis Ghiordes', of a type still occasionally to be found, but they are usually smaller and rarely so colourful. They are wholly in the tradition of the white-ground carpets of the Ushak district, especially in the design of the border, but Ushak prayer rugs never have opposed niches. The older Kis Ghiordes may be from the end of the eighteenth century but most are from the first half of the nineteenth.

Pl. XIII. Prayer rug with opposed niches, Anatolia, Ushak district; so-called Kis Ghiordes, about 1800. *(facing page.)*

Size: 197 × 133 cm.

Warp: Wool, Z2S, natural white; orange end-dip; selvage warps dyed red throughout.

Weft: Cotton 2Z and Z2S, natural white, × 2.

Pile: Wool, Z spun, Turkish knot, about 1,250 per sq. dm.

Colours: 7 (10); white, black, dark green, blue (2 shades), red (2 shades), yellow (2 shades), dull brown.

Condition: Apart from small repairs in the niches, excellently preserved. Black, dark green and to a certain extent the dark blue are a little eroded, thus producing a relief effect.

Design: White ground with a design of small offset, diamond

XIII. Anatolia (Ushak district), *c*. 1800.

forms with black outline. Light-blue central medallion with dark-red outline and dull-brown centre. Floral pendants on the long axis. Dark-green spandrels with leaf filling. The three border stripes have a white ground and the guards continuous tendrils. The main border stripe, patterned like the field, shows triangles filled with blossoms, the inner ones on dark green and the outer on dark blue.

Classification: Opposed niches became popular in prayer rugs in the course of the seventeenth century. All details of the design, including those of the border, can be traced back to this time, but carpets of this type were not made before the eighteenth century and continue to the middle of the nineteenth.

Literature: Unpublished.

This completes the list of purchases made between 1959 and 1961, details of which, as I have already mentioned, were published in *Berliner Museen.* During 1962 and in the first month of the following year further purchases were made, and these are discussed here for the first time.

Some readers may know the fragment of a Persian multiple prayer-niche rug (Pl. XIV) which is included in the magnificent publication by Sarre and Trenkwald. This honour was well merited since, in spite of its poor state of preservation, its design and colouring exemplify the best in Persian carpets of the sixteenth century. Persian prayer rugs, or rather prayer rugs with patterns in the Persian style of the sixteenth and seventeenth centuries, exist in considerable numbers, but the majority are late Turkish imitations and cannot be compared with this fragment in fineness of drawing and delicacy of colouring. Two other fragments in the fine art trade, which were shown in the Persian Exhibition in London in 1931, and whose whereabouts are now unknown to me, were probably made in Persia in the sixteenth century. They were not of the same high quality as the piece (Pl. XIV, *facing p. 160*) which has now been acquired for Berlin and has been known to me for thirty-five years. It belonged to Friedrich Sarre, the first Director of the Islamic Department, and hung in his office in the Kaiser Friedrich Museum, where as his young assistant I often admired it. After the war it was in the possession of his widow in Switzerland, along with the few pieces of his collection which had survived. I acquired it for such a modest sum that it would be better regarded as a gift, and it is a great joy to Frau Maria Sarre and myself that, after twenty years, this piece has returned to Berlin.

The South Persian fragment (Fig. 200) was a gift from the same collection. This type is assumed to have been produced in Kerman and must have existed in great numbers. Besides the main group, the so-called Vase carpets, there are other designs, and in no other group of Persian carpets is the number of surviving fragments so great. There are still hundreds of such pieces. One reason for this is the extensive production of South Persia, where there must have been several workshops. During the sixteenth and seventeenth centuries their rugs rarely seem to have reached Europe. They were made for home consumption

200. South Persia, beginning of the seventeenth century.

and judging from their size probably first and foremost for mosques. They were, therefore, much more worn than the Isfahan and Shah Abbas carpets which were in part destined for Europe. Presumably, in spite of being very closely knotted, the method of weaving the Kerman carpets was not adequate to withstand so much use. Counts of more than 7,000 Persian knots per square decimetre are found. In this technique one leaf of warp almost overlies the other and gives a strong double foundation; but this has the disadvantage that, once the pile is much worn, the thin second wefts which are exposed on the surface are easily destroyed and the warps which they hold in place are set free. If the sturdy first and third wefts concealed between the two layers of warp are undamaged the rug will still be held together although extensive areas of warp may be unattached. If loose warps are visible in a photograph they may indicate that the piece belongs to this group. The loosening of the foundation and subsequent loss of knots resulting from the destruction of the second wefts is evident in the field of this fragment (Fig. 200) which, in the better preserved parts like the border, still exhibits a design of outstanding beauty and harmony of colour. Many Kerman fragments have survived, thanks to Martin, who bought them during his travels in the Orient. A

201. India, seventeenth century.

used for yet another, rather worn carpet, which was at one time in the Berlin art trade but has disappeared.

It is well known that the design of these 'Isfahan' carpets migrated to India. The Indian copies are relatively rare and Berlin did not possess an example. It was, therefore, gratifying that the Museum received the piece, illustrated in part in Fig. 201, as an anonymous gift. Its size is unusual (253 × 213 cm.) and suggests that it might have been commissioned by a European. It is more worn and not so brilliant in colour as that of Pl. XV. Red is the dominant tone and the small, almost fussy design is typical of the group. Cloud bands no longer occur and the lancet leaves are made up of a series of small blossoms, a form of design characteristic of India. Similar pieces are in the Metropolitan Museum in New York (Inv. Nr. 41. 190, 264) and in the Cleveland Museum of Art (Inv. Nr. 18, 410).

A well-known group of Anatolian carpets, the Medallion Ushaks, many of which are still extant, were made from the sixteenth to the eighteenth century. The design consists of offset and alternating rows of two types of medallion, those on the central axis being circular and on the side, star shaped. This design remained constant during the whole period of their production and even if the size of the field varies the size of the motifs in it did not change. The group is also uniform in colouring. The field in most pieces is red and its tendril ornamentation and medallions are dark blue. A few of these carpets have a dark-blue ground with red medallions on the central axis and pale-blue medallions at the side. The tendrils in these pieces,

number of such pieces in different museums are known to have been acquired from him and some excellent examples are still in his estate.

A happy acquisition was the 'Isfahan' (Pl. XV, *facing p. 164*), a type of carpet which is not uncommon. The production, in which a number of workshops participated, must have been extraordinarily large and exported at an early date. In North America and especially in Portugal examples, sometimes of enormous size, are found in all collections. Usually they are fairly worn and this along with their muted colours gives them a somewhat sad appearance. The Berlin piece, however, is unusually well preserved and is of remarkably rich and intense colour. It is a piece of medium size (470 × 250 cm.). Its small-pattern design consists of three floral scrolls in each quarter of the field, and the lack of emphasis on the cloud-bands as well as the stressing of the bi-coloured lancet leaves which predominate, especially in the design of the border, suggest that it was made early in the seventeenth century. This piece is therefore a little later than the one in the Metropolitan collection and somewhat earlier than that in the Kann collection. The same cartoon was

202. Anatolia (Ushak), sixteenth century.

203. Morocco, nineteenth century.

which are usually better designed than the red-ground ones, are a brilliant yellow. In more than a thousand pieces I had never come across an exception to this colour scheme. It was surprising, therefore, to find the fragment illustrated in Fig. 202 which is related to the blue-ground Medallion Ushaks. Judging from the design of the yellow tendrils this fragment is a specially good example, but the medallion on the central axis does not have a red ground: it is light yellow like the tendrils, an effect which is striking but not aesthetically satisfying. The arabesques in the medallion are a little lifeless, and certainly much slighter than the scrolls of the field. Presumably this is a unique but not quite successful experimental piece but, in spite of its fragmentary state, it was sufficiently interesting to be acquired by the Islamic Department of the Berlin Museum.

The last two acquisitions came from auctions. The carpet illustrated in Pl. XVI was impressive at the preview on account of its unusual design, brilliant colouring and good condition. It seemed vaguely familiar. Looking through the relevant section of my files I found that it had been in the Bode collection auctioned in 1929, a fact which fortunately went unnoticed, so that it could be bought for a modest sum. At the Bode auction it appeared in the catalogue as 'Caucasus about 1700' but now it was labelled 'Transylvanian', a type of carpet commonly believed to be woven in Anatolia. This surprising change in name was suggested by Heinrich Jacoby and is quite correct as proved by a close technical investigation. In fact this most interesting piece is one of those rare Anatolian copies of a Caucasian design. (Pl. XVI, *facing p. 172*.)

The second auction find (Fig. 203) (385 × 166 cm.) a large Moroccan carpet, probably not made before the end of the nineteenth century, was less sensational. Since the auctioneer and author of the catalogue had never seen such a piece and several details, for instance the tulips in the inner borders, pointed to Anatolia, he called it Ushak. None of the prospective buyers really knew what it was and, therefore, it was bought for very little for the Islamic Department of the Berlin Museum, which in this case did not acquire a great work of art but a sample of a type not previously in their possession. These rare rugs, of which I have not come across more than a dozen moderately well-preserved examples, are coarsely woven (450 knots per square dm.). The Berlin piece is in good condition and in its rather barbaric mixture of colours it reflects those Anatolian and Spanish-Moroccan elements characteristic of the group.

XIV. Persia, sixteenth century.

Verses in Carpets

A number of carpets exist whose borders, mainly in the principal stripe and occasionally also in the inner stripe, show cartouches with verses in flowing script (Fig. 204). It only occurs in Persian carpets and is not known in Turkish or Indian rugs; even in Persia this kind of decor was limited to certain manufactories, in particular those of Tabriz, and was mainly employed for specially rich and costly pieces which were made for the Shah's court, as can be seen from the inscriptions.

Some forty examples of this type are known and about half of them have been deciphered. The material has not yet been properly investigated because it needs the cooperation of an epigraphist, a literary historian and a carpet expert and such a team cannot easily be assembled. The result of such cooperation could be fruitful in various ways. Because the letters are not always clearly written, or rather knotted, the epigraphist would have most difficulty and would gain least new information from the inscriptions as they are written throughout in the ordinary Naskhi script. The literary historian would find more of interest because, although some inscriptions contain verses by well-known poets such as Hafiz, who is quoted by Maqsud of Kashan in the Ardebil carpet (Figs. 16, 17), others are by unknown authors and often composed for the carpet in question. The carpet expert might gain further knowledge of a piece from inscriptions because, as far as can be ascertained, such verses refer to carpets which they adorn even if only in a general and loose way.

204. Persia (Tabriz), second half of the sixteenth century.

205. Persia (Tabriz), sixteenth century.

Spring has come and it is time to drink from the rose.
The inclement season is ended and the time is come for the clouds
to shed the rain

is a verse appearing on a carpet in the Arab Museum in Cairo.

Of rosebuds the meadow shows a thousand green tents.
The new-born blossom gives up the wine, which it has, to the wind.
The tender cloud scatters every ruby which it finds
To them who fondly imagine the meadow like the roof of heaven.
Raise thine head and see the trees which at daybreak
Make their prayer for the Ruler of the World and entreat
That he may ever enjoy fame and might.

These verses in a carpet in Vienna (Pl. XVII) strike a new theme in the last line referring to the ruler. Whether this means that this carpet was made for the Shah must remain an open question, but the one in the Musée des Gobelins in Paris certainly was:

This carpet, trodden by the feet of the Lord of the World,
is highly honoured, since its dust promises happiness.
Regard it with veneration and awe,
for it is treated as a confident in the harems of the world.
You look upon the blossoming meadow whose gleam
is refreshing and beautiful as the garden of Paradise.
Its beauty is such that even the art of China pales before it,
For hundreds of tulips and other blossoms are blended in its
colours.
Turtle doves and nightingales sit in every tree so bemused by
the beauty of the carpet that they can hardly take flight.
There is perpetual spring in this scented garden and no harm
comes to it from autumn and winter storms.

In this verse the reference to the ruler is explicit and what was only hinted at in other verses is clearly expressed: the carpet is a garden, but not an earthly garden, menaced by autumn and winter, but a garden of eternal spring like the garden of Paradise.

This theme of Paradise is also expressed in another form as in a carpet (Fig. 206) in Dutch private possession and in the Tree carpet in the Poldi Pezzoli Museum in Milan, in whose inscriptions are mentioned houris (the servants who according to Islamic belief minister to the blessed in Paradise) and the same pieces states that *from the garden of the carpet a path leads to the source of life.*

It is also said of this carpet:

It has been knotted specially for the Darius of the world, which must be a reference to the Shah. A similar reference occurs in a verse in a carpet in Leningrad:

O thou, whose abode is the seat of justice,
for whom throne carpets are spread out on the path,

Several examples may be cited. The carpet reproduced in Fig. 205 bears the following poem:

O cup bearer! The clouds of spring have appeared, all is now green
and the rose is refreshed by the rain.
The dew has dropped its pearls into the tulip's cup. The tulip has
raised the banner of youth.
The narcissus has looked up towards the stars, and to the reveller
the night is as light as the morning.

Happy is he, who, like the tulip, raises his cup and greets the down
on the faces of his rosy-cheeked companions.

The verses are typical. Spring, wine and the love of beautiful youths are ever recurring themes.

XV. East Persia, *c.* 1600.

whose courtyard is swept with the eyelashes of his servant Zephyr,

whose constant companion is success and whose constant refuge is God,

While he holds court indulging in every pleasure and the fulfilment of every wish,

For whom Darius and Alexander and Feridun are among the meanest in his mighty army.

Thou possessest magnanimity and generosity and compassion

The peoples of this world and the next pray for thee.

Mayest thou reign forever.

May Sun and Moon revolve according to thy wish.

The verse on a carpet in the Rothschild Collection in Paris takes up the same theme:

Mayest thou be honoured in the world as one of the valiant and the wise.

May no unpropitious Heaven bring thee grief.

May no trouble afflict thy heart.

May the world do thy will and may fate be thy friend.

May the illustrious Heaven be thy protector.

May thy lodestar illumine the world

and may the sinking star of thine enemies be extinguished.

May thine every deed be successful.

and for thee may every year, every day be springtime.

Dated Carpets of the Sixteenth and Seventeenth Centuries

Reactions vary when an expert is questioned about carpets with dates because this touches on a fundamental problem in carpet studies.

The layman assumes that the majority of the great carpets of the classical period, most of which today are in museums, bear the date of making possibly also the name of the maker, the individual who commissioned it and the place for which it was destined. On the contrary it was not customary to date and sign carpets until the eighteenth century. This is remarkable when one considers how often even in early times in the Orient other

207. Persia (Tabriz), dated 1542/3.

shrine of the mosque in Qum, dated 1671, bears the signature of Nimatullah the Joshagani. Several silk carpets from the shrine are so closely related that the date and signature may be valid for the whole group but not for the large central woollen carpet (Fig. 255) also from this mosque.

In addition to directly dated carpets there are some indirectly dated, such as the silk kilims made in Kashan in 1601/2 for the Polish King Sigismund III, although of course only those which bear his arms (Fig. 261) can be assigned with certainty to this order. One of the rugs in the Treasury of St. Mark's in Venice (Figs. 110, 111, 112) which was presented by the Persian Ambassador in 1603 must have been made before then, but it is not known which of the five pieces in the Treasury it is. Three carpets of this type which came to light in the possessions of the Dukes of Holstein-Gottorp can be dated 'before 1639'. The Coronation Carpet (Fig. 104) of the Danish Royal House cannot have been woven later than 1665 since it was presented by the Dutch East India Company shortly before this date. The Shah Abbas carpet in the Moore Collection shows the date 1683 on the under surface just as do others taken as booty at the relief of Vienna in that year.

There is only one dated Indian carpet from the seventeenth century. It was completed in Lahore in 1632 for the Girdlers' Company in the City of London and bears the arms of Sir Robert Bell (Fig. 265). The pieces from the palace in Jaipur (Fig. 254) often have labels sewn to the under surface which state the year of acquisition, such as 1655, 1661 and 1689. If one assumes that the carpets were new when they were bought the labels indicate the approximate dates of production.

Turkish carpets with dates are also rare in the seventeenth century. An Ottoman prayer carpet in Berlin (Fig. 190) is an entertaining exception because it is dated 1610/11 by means of a chronogram (Fig. 210), a type of dating usually employed in buildings, which does not give figures but their value in script. This is the first case in which it has been established in a carpet. There may be other examples unrecognized up to now, since this possibility of dating has not previously been recognized. Towards the end of the seventeenth century dates which must be considered doubtful, because they are not in keeping with the style of the pieces occur in Anatolian prayer rugs. The figure three (٣) can easily be converted into a two (٢) by omitting and substituting a few knots. A more reliable source exists for those rugs from Transylvania which are inscribed on the back and often state that a particular carpet was donated for a church pew. Such dates only indicate the *termini ante quem* that is, the dates before which the carpets must have been woven.

The following seventeenth-century dates appear in Ushak carpets before 1646, 1658, 1690

Transylvanian carpets: before 1661, 1666, 1689, 1698

Ghiordes carpets: before 1687

Bird carpet: before 1646. The carpet (Fig. 263) with the arms of Archbishop Prochnicki of Lwow (Lemberg) made between 1614 and 1633 during his term of office should be added to this list of carpets.

European copies of Anatolian carpets often bear seventeenth-century dates (1603, 1690, 1614, 1649, 1672) but they hardly provide useful dating points for the originals.

The first two examples of dated carpets from the Caucasus are from the end of the seventeenth century. One of these, a piece signed in Armenian by a women called Gohar, played a large part in the controversy about the provenance of such rugs. The date of this carpet, which is equivalent to A.D. 1679, seems somewhat early and 1779 would be more plausible. It may be that the numeral of the hundreds has been tampered with. This could perhaps be established by examining the actual carpet but its present whereabouts are unknown. A second carpet (Fig. 211) which is in the Textile Museum in Washington is a Dragon carpet, which differs in some details from the normal pieces of this type still extant in large numbers. It is signed by a certain Hasan Beg and the woven inscription reads 'In the holy month of Muharram in the year 1101', which corresponds to October 1689. It is presumed to be a Kurdish copy of a typical Dragon carpet, which is plausible. It is interesting that the two oldest dated and signed Caucasian carpets were knotted by people who belonged to a minority ethnic group living in the region.

Dated Carpets of the Eighteenth and Nineteenth Centuries

During the course of the eighteenth century dated carpets become more frequent. In Persia in the sixteenth and seventeenth centuries it was customary to add the name of the weaver to the date, but in Caucasian and Turkish carpets usually the date only appears, sometimes symmetrically arranged so that the figures on the left are repeated in mirror image on the right. These dates cannot always be easily read since the figure four was written in different ways, probably because the weavers lacked skill and also may have been illiterate. Furthermore, it is questionable whether a date was intended since the impression is often given that date-like shapes were used as ornaments. It should not be forgotten that a weaver who put a date into a carpet had to know the year, always of course according to the Muslim calendar which is based on the Hijra, and this information was not as widespread as it is today. A simple Yürük woman could hardly be interested in the year in which she wove her carpet, because carpets with a definite date presuppose a certain level of civilization. The weaver of a Persian carpet, however, left a valuable document when he added his name to the date. To weave in the date only is odd and indeed contradicts the typically Oriental awareness of time. It is unlikely, therefore, that the date was included to fix the age of a piece since no Oriental values a carpet for that reason and the fact that a carpet was made fifty years ago would lower its value in his eyes. Forged dates do not occur before the end of the nineteenth century and may have been prompted by the European demand for old carpets. In some isolated instances false dates are found earlier but it is difficult to prove that they are forgeries. More frequently subsequent corrections occur in which the numeral denoting the hundreds was converted without much trouble from a three (٣) to a two (٢). Presumably this was only done when the piece was to be sold.

212. Persia, dated 1776/7.

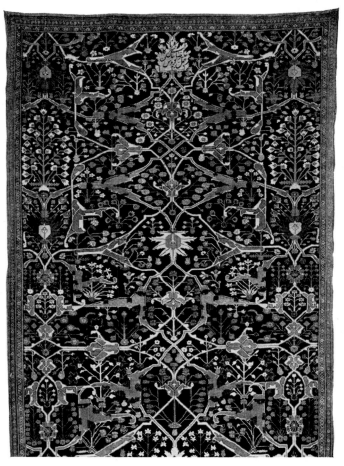

213. Persia, dated 1794.

214. Anatolia (Ushak district), dated 1721.

In Turkey dates on carpets were still rare at that time. The white-ground Prayer carpet (Fig. 214) in the Türk ve Islam Eserleri Museum in Istanbul is an exception. Dated examples, almost always prayer rugs, only become common towards the end of the century. Dates recorded in my file are: for Ladiks 1790, 1791, 1794 (Fig. 215), 1795, 1797, 1798 and 1799; for Ghiordes 1795 and 1796; and for a Bergama 1758.

Documentary and other indirect sources for dating, so valuable for Persian carpets of the seventeenth century, decline in the eighteenth. Such evidence is only preserved in the Turkish sphere of influence in the inscriptions on carpets in the Transylvanian churches. For the Transylvanian types dates are: before 1706, 1718, 1723, 1730, 1745, 1752, 1756 and 1778; for the Ghiordes: before 1710, 1719, 1727, 1733, 1736 (Fig. 216), 1746, 1751, 1752 and 1754.

These dates which cease during the first decade of the nineteenth century are only *termini ante quem*, but one can assume that these carpets were new when they were donated and

The eighteenth-century dates usually appear as four figures but in the nineteenth century the numeral denoting the thousands is omitted as is still done today in correspondence.

A Persian carpet belonging to the Princess Lichnowsky is a case in point. This bears the signature of Ali of Sarukh and the date A.H. 1184 (A.D. 1770). Jacoby, who illustrates it (*Eine Sammlung Orientalischer Teppiche*, Berlin, 1923, Fig. 17) does not suppose it to be so old, and since the inscription appears in mirror image assumes that the weaver copied it from the back of an older carpet. A large carpet with vases and birds woven by Riza the Kermani is dated 1725. Another (Fig. 212) in private possession in Belgrade, signed by Yusuf the Kermani, bears the date 1776 and one in London is signed by Hussein the Kermani and dated 1799. These pieces are of slight artistic value but the arabesque carpet (Fig. 213) in the McMullan Collection in New York is an excellent piece on account of its design, weave and colouring. It is signed by Ali Riza Khan of Garrus and dated 1794. These fully signed and dated Persian carpets continue a tradition that goes back to the sixteenth century.

The two oldest examples of dated carpets from the Caucasus (Fig. 211) show similar complete inscriptions. In the eighteenth century only the date is woven in; and it should be noted that we have here from that very region the first known series of dated carpets, mostly from the Kuba district. They bear the dates 1717, 1719, 1721, 1723, 1724, 1743, 1789.

215. Anatolia (Ladik), dated 1794.

XVI. Anatolia, seventeenth to eighteenth centuries.

inscribed. Such information should lead to the reliable dating of the Anatolian prayer rugs of the eighteenth century, but no one so far has troubled about this.

The picture does not change much in the nineteenth century although the number of extant dated carpets is much greater than in the preceding centuries. The information regarding dated pieces of the sixteenth, seventeenth and eighteenth centuries is based mainly on references and illustrations in documents. In contrast, however, the number of properly published carpets of the nineteenth century is small, considering the amount of material extant from this time and the many books published lately. Many entries in my file are based on brief notes often recorded subsequently from memory after a reception in Ankara, a cocktail party in New York or visits to dealers in Baghdad, Tehran or Cairo, and such occasions are not conducive to proper investigation. Photographs were hardly ever available. It would, therefore, be of the greatest value if collectors or dealers who possess dated carpets were to have these pieces and a detail of

217. Caucasus, dated 1913.

216. Anatolia (Ghiordes), dated 1736.

the date photographed. In this way a collection of several hundred photographs could be assembled in a few years, but this would present a new difficulty.

The omission of the numeral representing a thousand has already been mentioned. In the nineteenth century there occur dates of three figures which do not make sense when preceded by the numeral for a thousand. Obviously in this case, especially if it is a nought, indicated in Arabic script only by a dot, it has been omitted. The date 123 can therefore mean A.H. 1123 (A.D. 1711) but it could also be read A.H. 1230 (A.D. 1814). Dates in European characters sometimes occur, especially in pieces from the Caucasus which were probably made to Russian order. The Kazak (Fig. 217) is a curiosity since the dates 1331 and 1913 in Arabic characters are woven side by side into the middle stripe of the border. The year A.H. 1331 corresponds, of course, to A.D. 1913. This carpet, one of the latest dated pieces known to me, is especially attractive on account of its colouring and, therefore, without the inscription, would have been dated several decades earlier. Altogether a comparison of the dates from the end of the nineteenth and the beginning of the twentieth century will show that many carpets have been dated too early, in other words that even 70, 60 or 50 years ago carpets with excellent designs and colours were still made, especially in the Caucasus. The dating of carpets stopped with the first world war, and the date 1932 in a Daghestan in the Roseliushaus in Bremen is the sole exception which I have recorded.

219. Caucasus (Daghestan), dated 1867/8.

218. Caucasus (Daghestan), dated 1876/7.

In Persia, dated carpets contain as always the signatures of the weavers, especially those from Kerman, and examples are dated 1835, 1859, 1872, 1874, 1893, 1906, 1909. Since these pieces are related in design, the place of origin of the weaver (nisbeh) must be the same as the place of production of the rugs. Other dates are: Garrus 1823 and 1851; Ferraghan 1813 and 1870; Khorassan 1874; Hamadan 1870.

Dates are much more numerous in nineteenth-century Caucasian carpets: Kazaks: 1796, 1801, 1802, 1805, 1806, 1813, 1840, 1850, 1863, 1878, 1879, 1902, 1909, 1912, 1913 (Fig. 217), 1914, 1915, 1917; Shirvans: 1806, 1812, 1831, 1857, 1861, 1863, 1911; Karabaghs: 1841, 1848; Seichurs: 1863, 1887; Sumaks: 1868, 1872. The white-ground Daghestan prayer carpets are often dated: 1807, 1809, 1811, 1818, 1826, 1862, 1865, 1867 (Fig. 219), 1870, 1871, 1876, 1910, 1932. Those illustrated in Figs. 218 and 219 show how carpets so near in time can differ so much in quality.

In Anatolia dated carpets are not frequent even in the nineteenth century. I have recorded for Ladiks: 1804, 1807, 1831, 1836, 1843; for Bergamas 1845 and 1851.

Occasionally information concerning the owners is included. A Kashkai carpet dated 1832 belonged, according to its inscription, to Murteza Kuli Khan, and a Caucasian carpet of the year 1864 was the property of Abbas Ali.

As mentioned these are only pointers. Much rewarding work is still to be done because it may be assumed that a chronological survey of Oriental rugs of the nineteenth century can be established from such an investigation.

Carpet Fragments

It has already been mentioned that a beautiful fragment of a North Persian carpet (Fig. 82) was formerly in the collection of Baron Hatvany in Budapest. Another piece of the same carpet (Fig. 220) from the Yerkes Collection is in the Museum in Brooklyn, a gift of Mr. Herbert L. Pratt. It has been put together from seven pieces, one from the field of the carpet and five from the border. The biggest shows the remains of a field corner with four winged figures (Fig. 78), the houris who minister to the blessed in Paradise. It can be proved that these fragments all belong to the same carpet because the Budapest piece shows not only the centre medallion illustrated here, but also parts of the field and border. The Budapest and American fragments agree in so many particulars that one cannot doubt that they are from the same carpet, unless one assumes that they originate from two different carpets of the same design. This has been known to happen, but is hardly likely in a carpet of such unusual design. Another corner fragment of the border is in the Musée des Tissus in Lyons. A skilful draughtsman could reconstruct

221. India, sixteenth century.

220. Persia (Tabriz), sixteenth century.

222. India, sixteenth to seventeenth centuries.

the design of the whole carpet. The only difficulty would lie in recreating the pictorial form of the central medallion. Even the original size could be ascertained approximately; it was more than 7 metres long and about 4·25 metres wide. These are big measurements and this carpet was doubtless one of those important special orders of the Tabriz or Qazvin manufactory from the middle of the sixteenth century.

It is not unusual to find fragments of the same carpet in different collections. The best known and most often quoted example is the Animal carpet (Fig. 103) in the Musée des Arts Décoratifs in Paris, the other half of which is in the sacristy of Cracow Cathedral. The Paris piece was apparently obtained in Italy by Jules Maciet, its previous owner, who gave it to the museum. If this is the case there is still no explanation of how the carpet got to Italy.

Another North Persian Medallion carpet without figures has been divided between the Bardini Museum in Florence and a private collection in Hungary. It belongs to the same group as that illustrated in Fig. 153.

A piece of rare North Persian or Caucasian Cartouche carpet (Fig. 163) was formerly in the Berlin Museum and another came to the Philadelphia Museum of Art with the Williams Bequest. Parts of an Indian carpet (Fig. 140) with flowering plants in lozenges are in the Victoria and Albert Museum in London and the Städtische Kunstsammlungen in Düsseldorf. One fragment of a famous white-ground Vase carpet is in the Angewandte Kunst Museum in Vienna and another one in the Textile Museum in Washington. The latter shares the remains of a Persian Animal carpet of the sixteenth century with the Museum of Fine Arts in Boston. An interesting case is that of an Indian Tree carpet in the Musée des Tissus in Lyons, whose collection of carpets is too little known. It possessed a small fragment which had been acquired in 1871 from the Madrid painter Fortuny and in 1888 the Museum was able to acquire the larger part (Fig. 223) at the Paris auction of the estate of the painter Goupil.

Two long pieces (Pl. XVII, *facing p. 180*) formerly in the Hapsburg Collection belong to the group of sixteenth-century East Persian carpets. These show well-drawn animals and animal-combat groups in a scrolling design. One piece is in the Angewandte Kunst Museum in Vienna and its counterpart reached the Metropolitan Museum in New York through the Rockefeller-McCormack Collection. Carpets in these designs, though only extant today in fragments, must have been much more numerous in the sixteenth century. The pieces in the Musée des Arts Décoratifs in Paris and in the Museo Civico in Turin (formerly in the Yerkes Collection), probably belonged to the same carpet. The fragments in the Angewandte Kunst Museum in Vienna and in the Nordböhmisches Gewerbe Museum in Reichenberg belong to a similar piece.

At least a dozen fragments are known of an obviously very large Indian carpet with fantastic animals (Fig. 221). These pieces are in the Louvre, Paris; Museum of Fine Arts, Boston;

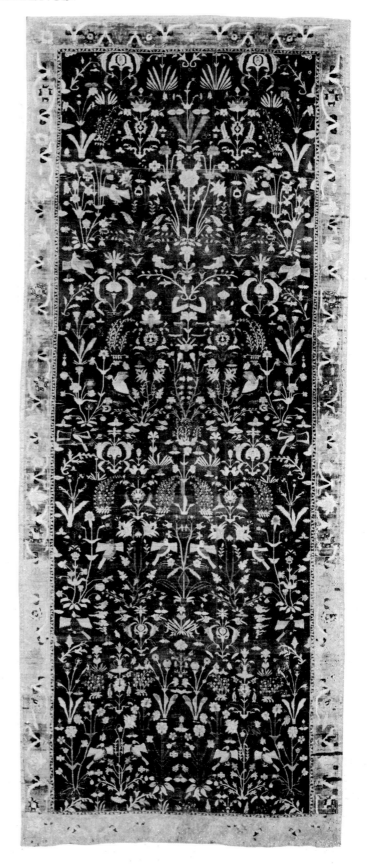

223. India, seventeenth century.

224. India, seventeenth century.

Textile Museum, Washington; Art Institute, Detroit; Burrell Collection, Glasgow; Palace of the Legion of Honour, San Francisco and the David Collection, Copenhagen. Other fragments whose whereabouts are unknown to me were exhibited in St. Louis in 1913 and in the Hermitage in Leningrad in 1935. Fragments of another Indian carpet are in the Musee des Arts Décoratifs, Paris, in the Museum of Fine Arts, Boston and in the Landesmuseum in Hanover. A piece of a border in similar design (Fig. 222) is in the Burrell Collection in Glasgow and a second in the National Museum in Stockholm. Some time ago I found a third in a private collection in Paris. These three fragments originally were probably in the possession of F. R. Martin, the Swedish collector and dealer.

One of the largest carpets in the world was formerly in the hall of the Forty Columns (Chihil Sutun Kiosk) of the Palace in Isfahan. In 1812 James Morier wrote in his travel journal as follows: 'The furnishings of the Chihil Sutun, consisting only of carpets, are still extant. These carpets are from the Shah Abbas period. They have large designs and are much better drawn and knotted than those which are made today.' Pascal

225. Persia (Kashan), c. 1600.

227. Egypt (Cairo), sixteenth to seventeenth centuries.

226. Egypt (Cairo), sixteenth to seventeenth centuries.

Coste illustrated the Chihil Sutun carpet in his *Monuments de la Perse* published in 1867. It appears to have measured 9 × 18 m., and this may be correct, because the border, some fragments of which are extant (Fig. 224), is 1·5 m. wide. This carpet was still preserved in part in 1887 and according to Sir Cecil Smith the tradition persisted at that time that it was brought to Isfahan 'from distant lands on two elephants'. There may be more than a grain of truth in this since the carpet is Indian work, probably commissioned in Lahore by Shah Abbas the Great. Today it has disappeared from Isfahan without trace and during our visit no one remembered it. Fragments, some quite large, are in the Victoria and Albert Museum in London and in the University Museum in Philadelphia. Some pieces turned up in the trade, in the Benguiat auction of 1925, that of Alphonse Kann of 1927 and at S. Haim in Istanbul.

Towards the end of the sixteenth and the beginning of the seventeenth century, silk tapestry carpets where old designs were used eclectically were made in Kashan. These are usually small. The only large piece is the Hunting carpet (Pl. III) from the Wittelsbach Collection now in the Residenz Museum in

179

228. Cairo or Istanbul, sixteenth to seventeenth centuries.

XVII. East Persia, sixteenth century.

Munich. The central portion of an apparently equally large carpet of this group is in the Kunstgewerbe Museum in Cologne. It does not have hunting scenes but a pointed oval central medallion filled with cloud-bands and surrounded by a bosky landscape with strange rocks. There are no figures but only the remains of shields which must have belonged to the corners of the field. Border stripes which could very well be from the same carpet are in the Kunst und Gewerbe Museums in Hamburg and Frankfurt. As the Cologne piece has no borders it was not possible to prove that the border fragments in Hamburg and Frankfurt were from the same carpet until I discovered the lower third in the Kunstgewerbe Museum in Dresden. When further pieces of the border appeared in private possession in Teplitz it became possible to reconstruct this carpet, though the upper third is lost. It is of larger size than the Munich piece which measures 230/240 cm. × 450/460 cm., and is, therefore, the most important carpet of this group. I found that in 1890 the original carpet, perhaps because the upper third had been damaged or lost, was cut up by a Dresden dealer and the pieces sold separately.

Such an occurrence is not unusual. In this instance the dis-covery of fragments led to the reconstruction of a hitherto unknown and important carpet of the classical period. Another case is that of an Ottoman carpet (Fig. 226) of the best period, which is in the Victoria and Albert Museum in London. Its square shape is unusual but is not improbable in carpets of this group. A second carpet (Fig. 227) in the same design and size is in the Musée des Arts Décoratifs in Paris. Both show pointed oval medallions and corner-pieces filled with arabesque leaves designed just as well as the scrolls of the field. These two carpets are undoubtedly genuine but their shape is the result of work by a clever dealer who apparently took the best parts of a large but damaged carpet and put them together as two smaller ones. Other museums – Stockholm, Berlin, Washington and Hanover – possess parts of carpets of this group which, however, have not been reassembled in the original form. The biggest piece (Fig. 228) is in the Angewandte Kunst Museum in Vienna. Judging from that the original carpet must have been 430 cm. wide. It still has to be established how long it was and whether all extant fragments belong to the same carpet.

A careful study of existing carpet fragments should yield valuable, perhaps even surprising, results.

expected more copies and in fact three examples of each are sometimes found. The majority, however, are preserved in pairs. If this is not chance, which is unlikely, because so many pieces are extant, it would point to the fact that these rugs also were made in pairs. These findings confirm that the estimate suggested previously of 1000:100:10 did not apply elsewhere and certainly not for certain Persian groups, and, therefore, a much more favourable relationship can be assumed between what was produced and what has survived.

Carpet Cartoons

In its first stage of evolution, the manufacture of the Oriental carpet was essentially a folk art. The second stage, during which carpets were produced in city workshops and manufactories, took place at different times and under different conditions in the various regions of the Near East. This process can best be observed in Persia.

In the second half of the fifteenth century, carpets depicted in miniatures show that the old designs were progressively replaced by new ones. Medallions, flowering scrolls and arabesque leaves were substituted for crosses, stars and rosettes and instead of rows of small patterns or squares, the middle of the field was emphasized by large compositions. This was a fundamental change. All the elements hitherto considered essential for the pattern of a carpet, that is, the geometric or predominantly geometric character of the single forms, their equal value in the design, their arrangement in infinitely extensible rows, disappeared to make room for new and mainly vegetal forms, arranged in apparently finite groupings around the centre of the field. The break with the past was decisive but perhaps did not occur abruptly. A number of carpets are illustrated in miniatures which show the attempt to create new designs better fitted to changed conditions. Quite possibly no less an artist than Bihzad, Persia's leading miniature painter, was concerned with this problem. It is not known, however, whether these new carpets were really made or whether they only existed in miniature paintings as attempts by these artists to effect a change in style. A break could not be prevented and the designs which became predominant by the end of the fifteenth century, no longer bore any relation to those of the past.

The sequence of events is quite clear: the traditional designs were quite unsuited to the new demands. Carpet weavers, who doubtless did not work from cartoons, could not be expected to develop new designs. Therefore the leading masters of book illustrations, miniaturists and limners, were commissioned to create new designs. They discharged this task by transferring their own art forms to carpet cartoons. The medallion and scroll designs which became dominant forms are typical of book art. Not content with that, the whole gay world of Persian miniature painting with its fantastic flowers, shrubs and trees, its clouds and cloud-bands, its animals and animal combats, hunting and Paradise scenes, all of which were borrowed from China during the time of the Mongol emperors, were transferred to carpet designs. A new field of activity was even found for calligraphy. All this amounts to the 'revolution in design' and indeed a Persian carpet from the year 1540 has nothing in common with one of the year 1440 except its technique.

The important feature of this change was a division of labour into two phases: the designing and the actual making of a carpet. This new situation has never been properly investigated, except perhaps by Pope, to whom we are indebted for the most extensive study of Persian carpets in 'The Art of Carpet Making' in *A Survey of Persian Art*, Oxford, New York, 1938, pp. 2257–2430. He touches on the problem by referring to 'large cartoons' probably made in the capital, which were subsequently sent to provincial workshops to be used as patterns. Many details, however, were left to the weavers, who did not always succeed in copying the cartoons satisfactorily. Sometimes earlier cartoons were imitated and occasionally several older cartoons from the workshop store were combined to form a new design.

Pope assumed original designs in the form of large cartoons which were transportable, sent on loan, put in store and occasionally used again. For all practical purposes the design of these large cartoons would be transferred to working cartoons, which, although Pope does not mention this specifically, were probably the size of the original, but of course it would not be necessary to transfer the whole carpet design. A quarter of it would be sufficient in centralized designs, a half in those with bilateral symmetry, and one repeat in repetitive designs. It would have been necessary, however, to prepare these working cartoons in a form which was suitable for use as a mirror-image design.

Such cartoons have not been preserved, nor do we have contemporary information about working methods. The richness of the design and precision of drawing of Persian carpets of the classical period presupposes such cartoons which would serve the weaver as patterns. For a long time I accepted this theory without seriously questioning it.

Shortly before the last war the Islamic Department of the Berlin Museum was presented with a small seventeenth-century Turkish carpet (Fig. 230) of Ottoman Court manufacture. Its design was well known since it occurred in three other carpets, one in the Victoria and Albert Museum in London, the second in the Jacqemart André Museum in Paris and the third in the Iparmüvészeti Museum in Budapest. All four carpets were formerly in the Palazzo Corsi in Florence, where at the end of the nineteenth century they were seen by Wilhelm von Bode. They therefore constituted a single purchase, and I used to think that it was probably a special order, but this has not proved correct because since then further examples in the same design but in different sizes have become known. There can be no doubt that the four pieces were made at or about the same time from the same cartoon. The width in three is between 132 and 133 cm.

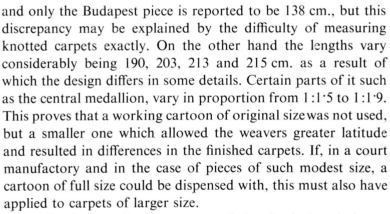

233. Persia (Kashan), sixteenth century.

234. North Persia, sixteenth century.

and only the Budapest piece is reported to be 138 cm., but this discrepancy may be explained by the difficulty of measuring knotted carpets exactly. On the other hand the lengths vary considerably being 190, 203, 213 and 215 cm. as a result of which the design differs in some details. Certain parts of it such as the central medallion, vary in proportion from 1:1·5 to 1:1·9. This proves that a working cartoon of original size was not used, but a smaller one which allowed the weavers greater latitude and resulted in differences in the finished carpets. If, in a court manufactory and in the case of pieces of such modest size, a cartoon of full size could be dispensed with, this must also have applied to carpets of larger size.

Another look at Persian carpets of the classical period confirms this. It is not even necessary to compare pairs since, for example, a Medallion carpet woven from a full-sized cartoon should, apart from small differences, agree in the drawing of each quarter. This is rarely the case. Even a poor illustration, providing the whole carpet is shown, proves this. It is only necessary to measure the distance from the middle of the medallion to the inner guard stripe at the ends to demonstrate that the

centre of the design is hardly ever in the centre of the field. The size of the two halves often differs considerably which of course implies that the drawing of these also differs. A comparison of the spandrels in the carpet (Fig. 206) from the von Pannwitz Collection shows that the corner designs at one end are mirror images and, therefore, are bilaterally symmetrical but differ from the corner designs at the other end, and the same can be said of the design of the field. This applies to a certain degree to almost all Persian carpets of this type. Carefully worked pieces, like the silk carpet (Fig. 102) from Warsaw Castle, show only slight differences, but even in a masterpiece like the famous Chelsea carpet (Fig. 231) in the Victoria and Albert Museum, differences can be observed, especially in the complicated design of the main border stripe.

On the whole the Persian carpet of the classical period which has a centrally based design shows only small differences bilaterally, unless it has been woven negligently. On the other hand the differences between the upper and lower halves are always noticeable and often pronounced. Usually the design is reproduced most correctly in the centre of the field. This is

XVIII. North Persia, seventeenth century.

understandable when one considers how a carpet is made. The weavers have the entire width before their eyes and can, therefore, without difficulty compare the right and left halves, but as work proceeds the finished lower part is rolled up. A comparison of the upper and lower parts is, therefore, still possible while work is going on the horizontal mid-line of the field, but this is no longer the case when the work approaches the upper end. The result is a more or less pronounced asymmetry in the design, which would not occur if a cartoon of full size had been available.

The work may have been carried out by a process similar to that described for modern rugs by Jacoby in his *How to know Oriental Carpets and Rugs*:

'If a Persian peasant or nomad wants to weave a carpet for his own use he sits down at the loom and starts. He may have a vague idea of the pattern but the details occur to him first as he works. He draws on tradition as does a gifted musician; both know how to improvise, one without notes the other without a model. It is otherwise in workshops. The ustad or master weaver who supervises three or four looms is furnished with the original cartoon. From this, rough details which are drawn on graph paper indicate the colour for each knot, but not detailed shading.'

It will probably never be known how carpet production was carried on in former centuries but the question of how differ-ences in the design are related to each other can be solved. It is only necessary to ascertain at which end the weaving began, and this can be done by feel, because the direction of the pile is always towards the end of the carpet at which the work was started. This cannot, of course, be ascertained from a photograph and strangely enough writers on carpets have so far not found it necessary to give this information with their illustrations.

Pope, though not correct in his assumption about working cartoons, is certainly right about the different uses of the designs. A few examples may suffice: in the Small Silk carpets of Kashan the same design has been used in different ways, as far as one can judge from existing material. A carpet (Fig. 62) in the Altman Collection in the Metropolitan Museum repeats, with slight variation, one (Fig. 63) which Edsel Ford gave to the Art Institute in Detroit. A third piece, with a different border design, was formerly in the Aynard Collection in Lyons. A fourth piece (Fig. 233) in the Louvre shows only a section of the original design. The well-known Chelsea carpet (Fig. 231) in the Victoria and Albert Museum has served as a model for the half carpet (Fig. 232) in the Bardini Museum in Florence, which was probably woven several decades later. The famous Tree carpet (Fig. 234) in the Poldi Pezzoli Museum in Milan combines two different models, a tree design and a scroll design in the manner of Herat carpets. At the junctions above and below the central medallion definite gaps occur between the two designs.

Wagirehs

By 1950 I had written a certain amount about Oriental carpets but I still did not know what a wagireh was. During the preparations for the carpet exhibition in the Kunst und Gewerbe Museum in Hamburg a curious piece (Fig. 235) turned up; it resembled the embroidered sample cloths known from many districts. I had never seen knotted models and, therefore, sent a photograph of the piece to Heinrich Jacoby who on 17th June 1950 replied:

'... you yourself know how difficult it is to arrive at a definite opinion about a piece from a photograph only. Bearing this in mind, I am reasonably certain what this piece is – a so-called wagireh from either the Sultanabad or Hamadan district, and I

agree with you about its age. Certain indications in this piece make me think that the carpet was made by Zieglers in Sultanabad. . . .'

A second wagireh (Fig. 236) was in the Hamburg exhibition, but less important because of its design, which showed strong European influences, and because of its painfully harsh colouring so typical of the dyes of the early aniline period. The piece had a certain rarity value since carpets of that period, the seventies of the nineteenth century, hardly exist today, because as a result of the fading of the aniline dyes most of them have 'passed away'.

Literature on the subject provides little information. In G.

235. Persia (Sultanabad or Hamadan), c. 1900.

236. Anatolia (?), c. 1870.

Griffin Lewis's *Practical Book of Oriental Rugs* a Bijar wagireh (Fig. 237) is illustrated and he says: 'Sample corners are mats about two feet square and are woven for the purpose of showing the variation of border, colour and design to some wealthy ruler who wishes a carpet woven. They are afterwards used in the weaver's family and seldom reach the market.'

The 'wealthy ruler' sounds somewhat odd; more interesting is the statement that these 'sample corners' (the term 'wagireh' is not used) do not often come onto the market, since the weavers keep them and use them in their homes.

W. Grote-Hasenbalg illustrates a Heriz wagireh (Fig. 238) and says: 'Wagirehs, which occasionally reach Europe, serve as models for the manufacture of large carpets in those districts of the Orient which work for the European market. Our illustration shows the design for the medallion and corner, the filling between these, the main border stripe and the guards.'

According to this statement wagirehs, therefore, are common only in commercial establishments which work for the European market and this means that they were not made before the middle of the nineteenth century, mainly in Persia but also in Turkey.

A second Bijar wagireh (Fig. 239) is illustrated by Dilley, who says: 'Among the most interesting and delightful of small rugs is the Bijar Vagireh or Orinak, which displays sections of numerous patterns artistically combined. The purpose of the weaving was to produce models of craftsmanship and color combination for use in the creation of carpets. Some Vagirehs contain as many as five incipient carpet designs. An ulterior purpose undoubtedly was the preservation of pattern and color, generation after generation. These records should not be neglected; genuine art treasure is found among them.'

Dilley emphasizes, therefore, that wagirehs occur with patterns for several carpets, that they serve as models not only for the drawing but also for the colours, and were of special importance as a record of design and colour for future generations; and he hints at their artistic worth. In 1949 Jacoby writes

237. Persia (Bijar), end of the nineteenth or beginning of the twentieth century.

238. Persia (Heriz), end of the nineteenth century.

191

239. Persia (Bijar), nineteenth century.

240. Persia, end of the nineteenth or beginning of the twentieth century.

under 'Wagireh' in his *ABC des echten Teppichs*: 'In Persia before a new design is woven a small sample piece, a wagireh, is made from which the final appearance of the field and border colours in wool can be judged. It is sufficient if such wagirehs show a piece of the border and a section of the design without reproducing the whole.'

Henri Hildebrand gives most information in his little known book *The Persian carpet and its Homeland*. He illustrates a Herati wagireh (Fig. 240) and writes: 'The wagireh, that is the knotted pattern, has probably been in use for centuries. Skilled weavers produce a small carpet from a design on graph paper, and this serves for years as a durable pattern whereas the paper patterns soon disintegrate. The weaver counts the knots on the back of the wagireh and uses the same number in his carpet. It is possible that the origin of the wagirehs lies in the distant past and that the designer who created the pattern and knotted the wagireh in this way perpetuated his ideas among the weavers for a long period. Nomads still use wagirehs and so do villagers in Central Iran. Forty years ago weavers in the Sultanabad and Hamadan districts worked almost exclusively from such models.

Wagirehs, commonly used by women, give the weavers a chance to use their initiative. Patterns are often employed in which neither the measurements nor the colour agree with the carpet as ordered. It is left to the skill of the weavers to make the necessary adjustments and they usually succeed very well, though in the case of village and nomad women it is often beyond their skill to complete a carpet harmoniously. Such changes in colour combinations and the design of the guard stripes are typical of certain villages and can serve as means of identification. Some weavers incorporate primitive motifs, especially domestic animals such as chickens, horses and goats, which do not exist in the wagirehs, and some of the best known designs are produced without models by skilful women who have known the designs from early childhood.'

He emphasizes that the wagireh is more durable than a cartoon and supposes that 'the origin of the wagireh lies in the distant past' without being able to bring proofs for that. Contrary to Grote-Hasenbalg, Hildebrand says that wagirehs are much used by nomads.

According to information from Heiner Jacoby, the present

XIX. Persia (Tabriz), sixteenth century.

241. Persia, beginning of the twentieth century.

director of Petag, this firm has always used wagirehs in the manufacture of its large Persian carpets. Unfortunately they were destroyed in the war. The sole surviving wagireh (Fig. 241) is obviously based on a carpet (Fig. 242) found about forty years ago in the shrine of the mosque at Qum. One of the set to which this carpet belongs is dated 1670–71. The wagireh was used to weave a carpet of similar design. These wagirehs not only served as workshop models but also may have been used to test the colour combinations before placing the order, and the surviving piece shows two versions of the border design. It was popular to make them in a size which, after their use as samples, would serve for other purposes, such as covers.

Once their existence had been recognized further examples were found. Two were given to the study collection of the Islamic department of the Berlin Museums. One (Fig. 243) came from the bazaar in Istanbul and its abominable jumble of motifs and combination of colours make it difficult to imagine how a carpet could have been woven from it. Perhaps it was a reservoir of designs for several carpets. The second (Fig. 245) given from the Bernheimer Collection was considered by them

242. Persia, seventeenth century.

to be a fragment but is probably a wagireh for a Caucasian carpet of the Karabagh district.

The piece illustrated in Fig. 244, known to me only from photographs, was in the Rhineland art trade twenty years ago, and that illustrated in Fig. 246 was exhibited in the National Museum in Stockholm in 1946. Without knowledge of the originals classification is difficult. Jacoby considered the one illustrated in Fig. 246 to be a Heriz but could it be a wagireh for a Medallion Ushak? An interesting piece (Fig. 247) was shown

in the exhibition of Caucasian carpets in Frankfurt. Though it has no borders it seems to be a wagireh, obviously for a carpet of the Seichur district. If this is correct it is probably more than a hundred years old.

A Persian wagireh (Fig. 248) in the collection of the late O. Sundt in Florence provides evidence that, as Hildebrand supposed, wagirehs were made before the time when Europe became active in the Persian carpet industry. This excellently preserved piece shows soft-red tendrils with strongly drawn

243. Anatolia (?), end of the nineteenth century.

244. North Persia, nineteenth to twentieth centuries.

arabesque leaves in dark blue and red on a cream ground. The narrow border is original and proves that this is indeed a wagireh but an unusually large one (176 × 162 cm.). Its design is closely connected with that of the carpet (Fig. 213) in the McMullan Collection in New York which bears the date 1794 and the signature of Ali Riza Khan of Gerus. Fig. 249 shows a detail of this carpet. At first glance this wagireh seems to be the model for the carpet in New York, and only a closer inspection reveals differences which exclude this direct link. The wagireh is stiffer and less richly drawn than the New York piece dated 1794. and may be later in date, although probably not much later than 1800. In spite of being complicated, the design was very popular in the nineteenth century and is found in about half-a-dozen carpets most of which are considerably later than the wagireh. Nearest in design is a carpet illustrated in the book by Hangeldian. It seems, therefore, that wagirehs were not so uncommon but were not, until recently, recognized as such or, like Fig. 238 and 246, were taken for fragments.

245. Caucasus (Karabagh district), eighteenth to nineteenth centuries.

246. Anatolia (Ushak?), nineteenth century.

247. Caucasus (Kuba), nineteenth century.

248. Persia (Gerus?), c. 1800.

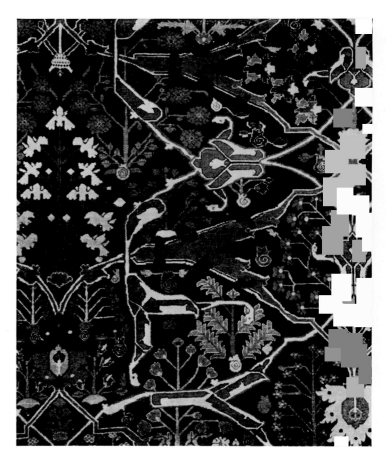

249. Persia, dated 1794.

Recently photographs of seven pieces in American possession were sent to me by Charles Grant Ellis. Three of these seem to be wagirehs while the other four, as Ellis points out, could be samples for European customers. This ought to be investigated because no such 'samples' by Oriental producers can be found in the literature. A further problem is posed by ten wagireh-like pieces, to which Dr. Zick has drawn my attention. They are in the Al-Manial Palace Museum in Cairo, and apparently show well-drawn Persian arabesque scrolls. Unfortunately I have not seen them nor have I got photographs.

Carpets of Unusual Shape

Carpets are generally rectangular, the relationship of width to length being variable. Runners may be several times as long as they are wide. In normal rugs the proportion of width to length is rarely less than 1:1·5, and the reason for this is easily understood. Carpets are nearly always woven on an upright loom. Such a loom is a rectangular frame on which the threads of the warp are stretched vertically. Usually this frame itself has a high rectangular shape and the upper and lower beams are removable. When the loom is set up the warp is rolled onto the upper or 'warp' beam and as the work proceeds the knotted part of the carpet is periodically rolled on to the lower or 'cloth' beam. In practice there are, of course, many variations of this process, but one condition holds for all – though a carpet can be of any length its width can only be that of the loom. In large manufactories large looms can be erected. The famous Ardebil carpet (Fig. 16) is over 5 m. wide but it is also 11·5 m. long. It would be not only costly but foolish to weave a carpet beginning at other than the narrow end and, therefore, the usual shape is that of a rectangle, having longer warps than wefts.

One half per cent of all carpets are woven in unusual shapes and some of these are broad in form, that is, they have shorter warps than wefts. Since few of these are represented in European and American collections not many people know of their existence. They were, however, known to Heinrich Jacoby who illustrated a piece of this kind from the Petag Collection in his *Eine Sammlung Orientalischer Teppiche* (Berlin, 1923, Plate 35) but they are not mentioned in his *How to know Oriental Carpets and Rugs*. In the Orient they are still common and a number (see Fig. 127) some of which date from the fifteenth century are in the Türk ve Islam Eserleri Museum in Istanbul. Later pieces, the majority probably from the nineteenth century, can be found in mosques and several decades ago the Bayazid, one of the principal mosques in Istanbul, was furnished throughout with recently manufactured carpets of this shape. These are the so-called multiple prayer rugs (Fig. 250) in which a series of niches are knotted side by side resulting in a large broad carpet. Such carpets were made for use in mosques and ensured that the worshippers aligned themselves in straight rows. Each took his place on one of the niches where even the places for the feet were sometimes indicated in the weaving. Such multiple prayer rugs are also found among Persian and 'Samarkand' carpets but examples from India are unknown to me.

These carpets are always wide in proportion to their lengths and the niches are woven side by side, sometimes in two rows one above the other. The shape results from the ritual requirements of Islam which demands of the Faithful to assemble for prayer five times a day. One may wonder why fewer niches, but with more rows one above the other, were not made resulting in a carpet of the usual long shape. Prayer is offered before that wall of the mosque which is defined by a centrally placed mihrab or prayer niche, indicating the direction of Mecca, the Holy City of Islam. The most coveted place is in the front of the mihrab and if this is already occupied the rows of worshippers extend sideways parallel to the wall. An arrangement of the

250. Anatolia (Bergama district), sixteenth century.

197

251. Egypt (Cairo), sixteenth century.

worshippers in depth in front of the mihrab rarely extends to more than three or four rows and those unable to find a place there stand at the side in order to be closer to Mecca. Though these multiple prayer rugs appear to be broad in shape they are in fact woven from the narrow end so that when on the loom the niche lies sideways and at right angles to the direction of the warp.

In Cairo carpets have been knotted since the fifteenth century. The manufactories were established by the Mamluk Sultans with the prime intention of exporting to Europe and continued to work even after the country was conquered by the Ottomans in 1517. From about 1530 to 1540 some of these workshops started to produce carpets for the Court in Istanbul, and, therefore, during the first half of the sixteenth century they became an Ottoman Court manufactory. During the past few decades these events have been studied by carpet experts and the results achieved are much more satisfactory than those arrived at in the study of the carpets of Ushak, Tabriz, Kashan and Isfahan. This success is due to the many extant carpets and documents, the latter mostly European, which so complement each other that a vivid picture of the evolution of the group can be given. Such sources established firmly the special position of these Cairene carpets in which two main groups, the Mamluk and the Ottomans, formerly called Damascus and Turkish Court carpets, are distinguished. No other type of Oriental carpet is so closely connected with Europe and there is much evidence that the idea of exporting to Europe was an important factor in the establish-

ment of this Mamluk manufactory. Even after the fall of the Mamluks in 1517, the workshops continued to produce for Europe and the Ottoman ruler made no changes. Considering all this it is not surprising to find unusual shapes among Cairene carpets.

Next to the carpets of the usual long shape, square carpets (Fig. 251) which would find no place in an Oriental house, are often found in the Mamluk and Ottoman pieces. In European and especially Venetian inventories of the fifteenth and sixteenth centuries, 'tapedi da desco' and 'tapedi da tavola', that is to say 'table carpets' are mentioned, where a square shape would be plausible. The correspondence between Albrecht Dürer and Willibald Pirkheimer definitely mentions square carpets, probably intended for table covers, which are so often depicted in paintings of the sixteenth and seventeenth centuries.

The 1596 inventory of Archbishop Ferdinand of Austria mentions a 'grossen runden teppich' and under Nr. 288 is the following entry 'zween schöne Alkheyrische teppiche so der obrist von Genua heergeben, mit allerlei farben und gelb haressen fransen, auf rundtafflen gehörig'. The inventory of the Marquis de Removille of 1632 mentions 'un tapis de Turquie rond le fond rouge avec des fleurs de diverses couleurs'. According to this evidence, round carpets seem to have been popular in Europe and were used as covers for round tables. An Ottoman piece made in Cairo in the middle of the sixteenth century,

252. Egypt (Cairo), sixteenth century.

198

belongs to the Corcoran Gallery of Art in Washington. A second, unknown to me in the original, is said to be in the Archbishop's palace in Kremsier, and a third one in a Mamluk design (Fig. 252) is in the Barbieri Collection in Genoa. Cruciform carpets must appear strange to Orientals. The best-known example is in the Victoria and Albert Museum in London and a second piece (Fig. 253) is in the Museum of San Gimignano. This piece has a European blazon, still unidentified, repeated four times in the border and I recently found a fragment of a third piece in this unusual shape in the Berlin Museum's depot. All three were made in Cairo in the sixteenth century. Such cruciform carpets are woven in one piece and when finished the foundation threads in the angles of the flaps, left without knots during weaving, are cut away. The result consists of a square field without border in the style of Ottoman carpets, and four rectangular flaps showing small sections of field in a geometric design and broad borders in Ottoman style (Fig. 253). The square field covers the table and the four flaps hang down at the sides. Pieces of this kind are curiosities, and blazons in the San Gimignano piece indicate that they were probably made to special European order. The difficulty, however, remains that the three extant examples were separated by decades and, therefore, cannot have been ordered at the same time. All these examples of square, round and cruciform carpets were made in Cairo for the European market and enjoyed some popularity even in Cairo.

254. India, seventeenth century.

253. Egypt (Cairo), sixteenth century.

Only occasionally are carpets of unusual shape found in the Near East. Round carpets were made in India in the seventeenth century, probably in the workshops of Lahore, and show a radial design of flowering shrubs whose naturalistic style is characteristic for Indian carpets of this period. Others, woven with one side in the shape of an arc (Fig. 254) may have been arranged on the floor around a dais, a throne or even a fountain of hexagonal or octagonal shape. Neither shape can have resulted from foreign demand. but were made for special use in India. The same holds for some Chinese carpets where, apart from circular and cope-like shapes, the best known are the pillar carpets.

Even more interesting are Persian carpets of unusual shape. The National Museum in Tehran possesses a large Vase carpet (Fig. 255) of the sixteenth century in the shape of a cross although the arms are only weakly indicated. As in the case of the Ottoman carpets discussed above to which it is in no way related, it is woven all in one piece and the surplus foundation threads at the corner have subsequently been cut away. It is supposed to have come from the Shi'ite shrine at Qum. Since it is too large for a table cover, local circumstances may have determined its shape as they did in the case of the small silk carpets in a tree design (Fig. 256).

The large twelve-sided silk carpet (Fig. 257) from the tomb of Shah Abbas II which is over eight metres in diameter comes from the same shrine. Although this was not justified on artistic grounds it caused a great stir when it was exhibited at the

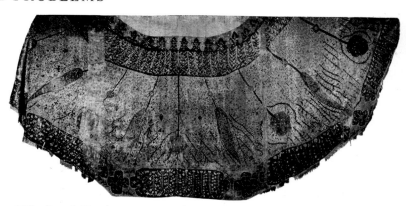

257. South Persia, seventeenth century.

255. Persia (Kerman), sixteenth century.

258. South Persia, seventeenth century.

256. South Persia, one of a set dated 1671.

International Exhibition of Persian Art in London in 1931. In 1958 I saw it in the shrine of the mosque of Qum where it lay on a cupboard bundled together and full of dust.

Octagonal carpets were also used to some extent in Persia in the seventeenth and eighteenth centuries. One of the oldest examples (Fig. 267) is in the Bernheimer Collection in Munich but has unfortunately lost its original blazon which must have been European. Other pieces in the National Museum in Tehran, in Washington, in the McMullan Collection and in other places are only fragments. A good example from the Satterwhite estate is the piece in Fig. 258.

One unusual type of carpet remains to be mentioned. The traditional arrangement of rugs in a Persian reception room consists of four pieces, one of which is placed horizontally at the head of the room. The largest carpet is arranged at right angles to it down the centre and is flanked by runners which take most of the traffic. All four rugs woven together in one piece (Fig. 259) are occasionally seen in recently made Persian carpets. In the American trade these are called 'Triclinium rugs'.

259. Persia, nineteenth century.

EUROPEAN PRODUCTION

Carpets with European Blazons

Carpets which came to Europe from the fifteenth to the eighteenth centuries either as booty or through diplomatic channels have already been discussed; they were probably more numerous than can be ascertained today, but their total number must have been small compared with those which reached Europe by way of trade. I have already discussed (pp. 182–186) how far this export of carpets from the Orient took into account the needs and the taste of the recipients. Sometimes the European buyers commissioned pieces which can be recognized today by their blazons and, although it is difficult to assess the number of such orders, carpets with coats of arms are more numerous than is generally realized. Three groups can be distinguished:

1. In Spain a large number of fifteenth-century carpets exists, usually bearing the blazon of the Enriquez family (cf. Pl. XX). These pieces are rooted in the tradition of the country where the weaving of carpets seems to go back to the twelfth century. They are, therefore, products of the Mudejar style – that is they were made to the order of Christians by craftsmen who were Muslims or of Muslim descent.
2. In Poland knotted carpets, only remotely connected with Oriental design, were made in the seventeenth century and they often show the blazons of Polish families.
3. In England, as in other European countries, the patterns of Oriental, usually Anatolian carpets, were often copied and these pieces usually show the blazon of the client. Three examples are the Star Ushak carpets, two of which bear the dates 1584 and 1585 respectively, with the arms of the Montagu family. Undoubtedly these are European, perhaps Flemish copies of Ushak carpets (Fig. 262).

260. Persia (Kashan or Isfahan), seventeenth century.

261. Persia (Kashan), datable 1601–2.

'Polish' carpet still persists. The Czartoryski carpet had not been exhibited since 1878 and I searched for it in vain in all the Polish museums only to come across it again in 1957 in the Metropolitan Museum in New York. It was on exhibition as a Rockefeller loan and has now been presented to the Museum. The blazons in it are not those of the Czartoryski and probably are not even Polish, but they have not yet been identified.

The position is simpler in the case of the two silk tapestry carpets with the arms of the Vasa, today in the Residenz Museum in Munich, and in the possession of the Wittelsbachs (Fig. 261). They were made in Kashan in 1602 to the order of the Polish King Sigismund Vasa and passed to the Wittelsbachs in 1642 as a dowry. A document exists in the Warsaw archives which obviously refers to these carpets. It states that in 1601 an Armenian, Sefer Muratowicz, was sent to Kashan in Persia by King Sigismund III, and on 12th September 1602 he presented the following account to the Polish Treasury:

262. England or Flanders, c. 1585.

3. Anatolia (Ushak), beginning of the seventeenth century.

This chapter however is concerned with Oriental pieces showing European coats of arms. The client supplied the workshop with the designs, but from the point of view of heraldry these were usually woven incorrectly.

The most important example is the Shah Abbas carpet from the Czartoryski family (Fig. 260), which embodies the same blazon five times. This carpet has had a chequered history. It was exhibited at the Paris Exhibition of 1878 when it was assumed that, as it came from the Czartoryski family, the arms must be those of the Czartoryski. The assumption was incorrect, as was the conclusion that these silk carpets enriched with gold and silver were Polish work. There was soon no doubt of the Persian provenance of such pieces but the meaningless label

Price of the objects which I bought in Persia in the city of Kashan for his Majesty our gracious King.

2 tents	360 crowns
2 pairs of carpets at 40 crowns, together	160 crowns
2 carpets at 41 crowns, together	82 crowns
For the execution of the royal arms extra	5 crowns
2 carpets at 39 crowns, together	78 crowns
(other items follow)	

These eight carpets are probably the ones which are today in the Residenz Museum in Munich. They cost, inclusive of the extra charge for the blazons, 325 crowns to which must be added a further 324 crowns as travel costs and custom dues. Mankowski established that in 1602 one crown would buy 250 pounds (continental) of wheat and therefore the cost of the carpets equalled the cost of about 81 hundredweights of wheat.

Such Persian orders were rather expensive because of the

265. India (Lahore), datable 1631–2.

additional cost of a long journey and the custom dues which had to be paid at four different places. It was preferable, therefore, to place orders in the more easily accessible workshops of Turkey, especially in the manufactories of Ushak. The 1596 inventory of the Archduke Ferdinand of Austria lists under Nrs. 167–168 'Türggische Teppich, darunter ain grosser, runder mit dem Oesterreichischen Schild', which probably means a carpet ornamented with arms. The piece has not survived. An Ushak carpet with the arms of the Countess of Shrewsbury of Hardwick Hall, mentioned in the 1601 inventory, has disappeared. Two later Medallion Ushaks in Berlin (Fig. 192) and in Cracow bear the arms of a Polish family.

264. Polish, seventeenth century.

266. India, seventeenth century.

267. South Persia, seventeenth to eighteenth centuries.

The four Lotto carpets with the arms of the Genoese families Centurione and Doria (Fig. 144), probably ordered on the occasion of a marriage, are mentioned in the chapter 'A New German Carpet Collection: Hamburg'. A Bird carpet (Fig. 263) from the Ushak district, with the blazon of Johannes Andreas Prochnicki who was the Latin Archbishop of Lemberg (Lwow) from 1614 to 1633, is in private possession in Sweden. In 1603 his predecessor Jan Zamojski ordered from Istanbul twenty carpets with his coat of arms. These were intended to adorn the Cathedral in Lwow, but unfortunately none has survived.

Occasionally orders were placed in the Cairo workshops. The church of San Gimignano has a cruciform carpet (Fig. 253) with an unidentified coat of arms. The well-known carpet (Fig. 264) with the arms of the Polish families Kretkowski and Güldenstern in the Bavarian National Museum in Munich is probably a Western, possibly Polish, copy of an Ottoman carpet made in Cairo.

Carpets with English blazons came from India. In 1630 Sir Robert Bell, Master of the Girdlers' Company, ordered in Lahore a carpet with the Company arms on it (Fig. 265). An Indian Animal carpet (Fig. 266) displays, in the border, the coat of arms of the Fremlins who, in the seventeenth century, were closely connected with the East India Company. An octagonal South Persian carpet (Fig. 267), belonging to Bernheimers in Munich, has in the middle of the field two heraldic lions drawn in the European manner, which must have flanked a coat of arms now unfortunately cut out and replaced by a flower.

Twenty carpets with European blazons are known today, ten from Ushak, two from Cairo, six from Persia and two from India. Seventeen of the arms can be identified, eight Polish, five English and four Italian. Polish arms are found in carpets from Ushak, Cairo and Persia; English in Ushak and Indian carpets; and Italian only in Ushaks.

XX. Spain (Alcaraz), early fifteenth century.

Spanish Carpets

Spain, although a European country, was under Muslim rule for several centuries, but existing Spanish pile carpets were not made until the fifteenth century, by which time the country had been reconquered by the Christians. These early carpets may have been made by the Mudejares, as the Muslim craftsmen were called, but later the production was taken over by Christians and raises the question whether such carpets can be regarded as European products. The later editions of Bode-Kühnel do not discuss them, and in my book *Oriental Carpets* they are treated as a peripheral problem. In order to get information on all aspects

268. Spain (Alcaraz), fifteenth century.

269. Spain (Alcaraz), fifteenth century.

pointing Kufic script with a filling of rosettes or small figures (Pl. XX, *facing p. 208*). In better preserved pieces an extra band is woven across the ends with trees, wild men and animals in a truly European style (Fig. 268). The fields may bear arms, often those of the Enriquez family. These rugs can, therefore, be dated to the first half of the fifteenth century and may have been made in Alcaraz or Letur.

The early pieces of another large group may also have been made in Alcaraz in the fifteenth century. Such carpets (Fig. 170) show large squares with an octagon filling which relates them to

270. Spain (Alcaraz or Cuenca), sixteenth century.

of the subject it is necessary to consult specialist literature such as *Catalogo de la Exposición de Alfombras Antiguas Espãnolas* by José Ferrandis Torres (Madrid, 1933) or Kühnel-Bellinger's *Catalogue of Spanish Rugs in the Textile Museum* (Washington, 1953).

The oldest surviving Spanish carpets, with the exception of the 'Synagogue Carpet' in Berlin (Fig. 181), which dates from the fourteenth century, go back to the beginning of the fifteenth. They have a small-pattern geometric design with fairly wide borders, whose outer stripes have a strongly stylized, inward-

271. Spain (Alcaraz), fifteenth century.

the large-pattern Anatolian Holbein carpets. Later examples of this group contain two or three rows of adjoining squares (Fig. 269). The crystal-like ornamentation and the arrangement and design of the motifs distinguish them from Anatolian carpets. At the beginning of the sixteenth century European elements were introduced and the octagons became wreaths (Fig. 270), a motif familiar from the Italian Renaissance, as can be seen in the tondos of the della Robbias.

The small Holbein pattern (Fig. 13) was also used in Alcaraz (Fig. 271) but more rarely, whereas Spanish carpets (Fig. 272)

273. Miniature from the third quarter of the fifteenth century.

related to the Lotto design (Fig. 52) of Anatolia are preserved in greater numbers. Torres and Kühnel assigned these pieces to Cuenca and dated them to the seventeenth century, which may be correct in some cases. The group, however, goes back to the fifteenth century as can be seen from a carpet of this kind in the dedication picture (Fig. 273) of a manuscript of the Theseide in Vienna from the third quarter of the century. A type preserved in many examples (Fig. 274) based on Italian textiles of the Renaissance, can be dated to the sixteenth and seventeenth centuries.

The evident relationship of the Spanish designs with those of the Turkish Holbein groups has led to the view that the Spanish production of the fifteenth century was linked to that of Anatolia and because of the influence of the Italian Renaissance during the course of the sixteenth century Spanish carpet designs became Europeanized. The gradual transformation from an Oriental to a European style is certainly true but the question arises whether the early motifs were actually borrowed directly from Anatolia.

Muslim authors of the twelfth century mention Spanish carpets from Chinchilla and those from Andalusia were known at the court of the Fatimid Caliphs in Cairo in 1124. This is confirmed by the finding of carpet fragments in Old Cairo, some of which from their technique must have been made in Spain.

As Spanish carpets are knotted around a single warp thread instead of around two as is common in other Oriental rugs, a further problem arises. Among the fragments of the third to the sixth centuries A.D. found in Central Asia by Sir Aurel Stein some pieces are supposed to be knotted in the Spanish manner

272. Spain (Alcaraz?), sixteenth century.

and not with Persian or Turkish knots. They are, therefore, knotted around one warp thread but it has not been satisfactorily proved that single warp knots actually occur in the Central Asian fragments and it seems unlikely that there was any contact between Spain and Turfan in Central Asia. Therefore, everything points to the fact that Spain learned the knotting technique from the Near East. The following hypothesis may solve this problem.

275. Old Cairo, ninth to eleventh centuries.

274. Spain (Alcaraz?), sixteenth century.

Among the fragments from Cairo are some which Lamm considers to be ninth-century Abbasid. It is immaterial whether or not they are so old. What matters is that these fragments are not true knotted carpets, but are in a U-loop technique, in which an additional weft is so introduced that it forms a loop on the surface. When these loops are cut the free ends form a pile resembling that of a knotted carpet; but as the loops are only held in place by the warps and wefts of the foundation, they can easily be pulled out. If it is assumed that such pseudo-

same small-pattern geometric design (Fig. 275) as the early Spanish Armorial rugs (Pl. XX, *facing p. 208*).

There is also documentary proof that Spanish carpets were made as early as the eleventh or twelfth century and a true invention may have marked their beginnings, the single-warp knot superseding the U-loop of the Eastern examples.

If such a long evolution is assumed for Spanish carpets it should be determined whether their later patterns were really

276. Spain (Cuenca), *c*. 1700.

277. Spain (Cuenca), *c*. 1700.

knotted carpets were known in Spain in the tenth and eleventh centuries, attempts at imitation by knotting would fail because the U-loop is not tied but results from the cutting of the additional wefts. Is it unreasonable to suppose that in Spain, where at that time the technique of true knots attached to two warps was not yet known, the idea arose of fastening the knots to a single warp in an attempt to achieve the same effect as that seen in the Abbasid carpet? There is some evidence for this, for certain Abbasid carpets, woven in the U-loop technique, show the

213

278. Spain (Madrid, Santa Barbara), end of the eighteenth century.

derived from the Anatolian or whether there was an independent parallel development because it cannot be proved that these designs existed in Asia Minor at such an early period.

Spanish carpets woven in the Turkish knot first occur in the seventeenth century and these are copies of Anatolian prayer rugs (Fig. 276) and Medallion Ushaks (Fig. 277) and in the eighteenth century commercially produced carpets were made in the contemporary French and English styles (Fig. 278).

European Peasant Rugs

The attentive reader may have noticed that, in the chapter on Spanish carpets, Alpujarra rugs which occur relatively often are not discussed. They have been omitted, firstly, because they are not true knotted carpets, and secondly, because they lead into the realm of European folk art where, however, rugs played a considerable role. It seems that at one point in their development all groups of European peasant rugs have been related to and influenced by the Oriental carpet. The arrangement in which the design is separated into inner field and border and the latter into main stripe and narrow inner and outer guards is typical of the Oriental carpet and unlikely to have been reinvented in European folk art. Although the lay-out is Oriental the designs of field and border are only occasionally taken from Oriental models.

The Alpujarra carpets of Spain are not knotted carpets but are in the genuine U-loop technique. It would be tempting to associate this late occurrence of the U-loop with the hypothesis mentioned above, that the Spanish single-warp knot is related to the U-loop or pseudo-knot as used in the eleventh and twelfth centuries. The distance in time however is probably too great. The Alpujarra designs are not connected with those of the early Spanish carpets, but have European designs which occasionally recall those of Cuenca carpets. These, in their turn, used Oriental design in a strongly Europeanized form. Latin inscrip-

279. Spain (Alpujarra), eighteenth century.

280. Poland, eighteenth century.

tions, usually indicating the owners, occur. The piece reproduced in Fig. 279 is inscribed ANTONIO CAYO; one in Madrid: SOY PROPYA DE OBDULLA ZURDO; and one in the Iparmüvészeti Museum in Budapest: DONA ROSALIO BLAVO. Another in the Alexander Moore Collection bears the legend: NUESTRA SIGNORA DIA ASUMCION DE LA SENORA SANTA ANA; and in a piece whose whereabouts is not known, the meaning of the inscription: VIVA MIAMO BIVA MIAMO is obscure.

Kühnel considers that the Alpujarras, which average 150 × 200 cm., were mostly made in the nineteenth century and because of their coarse weave (800 knots per square cm.) they were not suitable for floor covers. Their production, however, must go back to the eighteenth century for I find in my files

282. Finland, eighteenth or early nineteenth century.

281. Poland, end of the seventeenth century.

photographs of pieces dated 1766, 1788 and 1799 but only one dated 1830. Compared with other groups of European peasant carpets these Alpujarras occupy a special position, because undoubtedly they look Spanish and are a late example of carpet production of that country. They are more closely, or rather more organically connected with the Oriental carpet than other groups, although Oriental elements are never so evident in them as for instance in the Masurian carpets of East Prussia.

I have already explained that the Oriental silk carpets known as 'Polish' were not in fact made in Poland (see p. 37). The confusion over their provenance was settled in 1894, when Riegl explained that the silk carpets were Persian work and that carpets made in Poland were of wool and looked entirely different. Some of the latter are still extant and a few have dates such as 1698 and 1752 or show Polish blazons such as Sierakowski, Potocki and Mriszech. Many are based on Oriental designs, usually Turkish, but occasionally also Persian, and these are more or less altered in the drawing (Fig. 280). A piece

283. East Prussia, dated 1792.

in the Statens Historiska Museum in Stockholm proves that Oriental carpets had reached the Baltic in the fifteenth century.

There is no foundation for the assumption that the East Prussian knotted carpets, known as Masurian carpets, were connected with the Rya. They are covers as opposed to floor-coverings, are somewhat larger and denser, have a more closely clipped pile and often have dates knotted into them. Even though European designs predominate, others derived from Oriental models are found (Figs. 283 and 284).

Between the two world wars knotted carpets were still being made in Pomerania, in the district of Prerow, but unfortunately I cannot recall whether they showed Oriental influences.

Little research has been done on the Italian peasant knotted carpets, which have striped designs with European motifs and only occasionally hark back to Oriental designs (Fig. 285). It is uncertain whether a unique piece (Fig. 286) from the Bernheimer Collection belongs to this group. The carpet, which unfortunately has been cut along the sides, was exhibited in Hamburg in 1950 and I described it in the catalogue as follows: 'This is a unique piece and difficult to place since it gives the impression of a late date but shows motifs which go back to the fourteenth century. The dragon shapes (cf. [catalogue plate 40] No. 111) which predominate in the field can still be seen in a similar form in the Silé flat-weave carpets of the Caucasus where they are combined with smaller figures similar to the birds in the carpet under discussion. The design of the border,

284. East Prussia, dated 1818.

(Fig. 264) in the Bavarian National Museum in Munich is of special interest because it is a copy of an Ottoman carpet and, since it has the impaled arms of the Kretkowski and Güldenstern woven into it, must have been made in Poland. Others are Oriental only in the way they are woven but have European designs (Figs. 281 and 282). Some of these pieces are large and runner-like in form and were meant for the floor and not for use as covers as was usual with most European work.

Knotted carpets from the Baltic are numerous and such Rya were made in Finland, Sweden and Norway. They were small in size with a shaggy pile and intended for use as covers. The oldest reference to them is found in a document of 1495. The many hundred extant pieces, mainly from the eighteenth and early nineteenth centuries, are often dated and display numerous indigenous folk art motifs. Oriental influences are seen only occasionally and it is quite possible that the knotting technique did not come from the Orient but evolved locally, though the Anatolian carpet (Fig. 4) from the village church in Marby, now

especially at the ends, can only be explained as Kufic script and is related to that in the famous fourteenth-century carpets from the mosque of Alaeddin in Konya, today in the Türk ve Islam Eserleri Museum in Istanbul (Fig. 27). A survival of these forms beyond the fifteenth century cannot be proved in Anatolian rugs and, therefore, there is no possibility of connecting this carpet (Fig. 286) with either the later Silés or their predecessors. That such prototypes existed is proved by a carpet probably from the seventeenth century formerly in the Davis Collection (Ill. Exhib. New York, 1910, Nr. 6) in which less stylized dragons are depicted in rows in similar form (later addition). The establishment of this design in a traditional form must have occurred in the West, and similar dragons are found several times in Italian paintings of the fifteenth century. Some of these carpets were made in Italy in Oriental style, as appears from contemporary literary sources (cf. K. Erdmann "Orientalische Tierteppiche auf Bildern des XIV und XV Jahrhunderts" *Jahrbuch der preussischen Kunstammlungen*, Berlin, 1929, L, pp. 261–298, especially

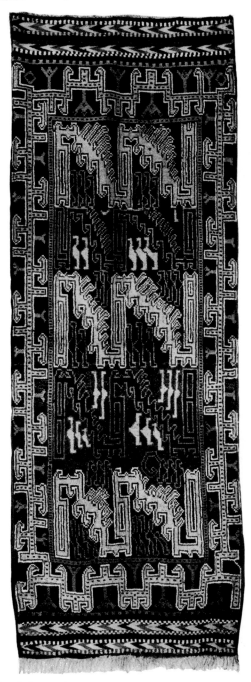

286. Italy(?), eighteenth century.

285. Italy, probably nineteenth century.

pp. 291 ff., Fig. 38a–c). This piece, which cannot be exactly dated, and whose antecedents cannot at present be established, comes from a Western tradition of carpet knotting which had been split off from the Oriental original in the fifteenth century.'

Rumanian carpets, which are all kilims, do not belong to this group. In contrast to the Oriental kilims the patterns are divided into field and borders and only occasionally recall Oriental knotted carpets.

Oriental carpets have influenced European art forms in other and fascinating ways, as in the case of the carpet with the dragon and phoenix combat in Berlin (Fig. 1) which has been copied in a Norwegian cushion cover. And Holbein carpet motifs reappear in Swiss and Alsatian embroideries.

Illustrations, Literature and Notes
Abbreviated Reference to Books Most Frequently Mentioned

BODE-KÜHNEL: Wilhelm von Bode and Ernst Kühnel, *Vorderasiatische Knüpfteppiche aus alter Zeit*, 4th edn., Brunswick, 1955. Translated by Charles Grant Ellis as *Antique Rugs from the Near East*, Brunswick and Berlin, 1958.

K. ERDMANN *Oriental Carpets*: Kurt Erdmann, *Oriental Carpets, An Account of Their History*, translated by Charles Grant Ellis, London, 1962.

K. ERDAMNN *Orientteppiche*: Kurt Erdmann *Orientteppiche*, Bilderhefte der Islamischen Abteilung, Vol. 3, Berlin, 1935.

SARRE-TRENKWALD: Friedrich Sarre and Hermann Trenkwald, *Old Oriental Carpets*, translated by A. F. Kendrick, Vol. I, Vienna/Leipzig. 1926, Vol. II, Vienna/Leipzig, 1929.

A. U. POPE *Survey*: Arthur Upham Pope and Phyllis Ackermann, *A Survey of Persian Art*, Oxford/London/New York, 1939. Vols I–VI (only Vol. VI is referred to in this book).

COLOUR PLATES

D = Detail   *F* = Fragment

The numbers within square brackets at the end of each caption are the corresponding numbers in the German edition. References to monochrome illustrations in *this* work are shown thus: Fig. . . .; references to monochrome illustrations in all *other* works are shown as: fig. . . .

Pl. I. Woollen knotted carpet, 'Garden' carpet (187 × 151 cm.). Persia, 17th C. Vienna, Angewandte Kunst Museum. [Pl. XV; Fig. 193.]
Lit. Sarre-Trenkwald, II, Pl. 12 in colour.

Pl. II. Woollen knotted carpet (88 × 80 cm.). *F*, India, 17th C. Formerly Sarre Collection, now Washington, Textile Museum. [Pl. XVI., Fig. 204.]

Pl. III. Silk tapestry carpet with hunting scene, flowering trees and genii (peris), (389 × 152 cm.) *D*, side borders missing. Persia, Kashan, *c.* 1600. Formerly Wittelsbach possession. Munich, Treasury of the Residenz. [Pl. I; Fig. 24.]
Lit. Sarre-Trenkwald, II, Pls. 47–49 (in colour); T. Mánkowski, 'Note on the Cost of Kashan Carpets at the Beginning of the Seventeenth Century', *Bulletin of the American Institute for Persian Art and Archaeology*, New York, 1936, VI, pp. 152 ff. For another detail of this carpet see Fig. 80.

Pl. IV. Woollen knotted carpet (207 × 133 cm.). *D*, Cairo *c.* 1500. Mamluk carpet. Berlin Museums Inv. Nr. KGM 82, 704. [Pl. II; Fig. 35.]
Lit. K. Erdmann, 'Kairener Teppiche, I. Europäische und islamische Quellen des 15–18 Jahr. II. Mamluken und Osmanen Teppiche', *Ars Islamica*, Ann Arbor 1938, V, pp. 179 ff. and 1940, VII, pp. 55 ff.

Pl. V. Silk tapestry carpet (221 × 136 cm.). Persia, Kashan, 17th C. Berlin Museums Inv. Nr. I 2577. [Pl. III; Fig. 109.]
Lit. K. Erdmann, *Orientteppiche*, Nr. 16, in colour; Sarre-Trenkwald, II, Pl. 45.

Pl. VI. Silk knotted carpet, 'Polish' carpet (190 × 140 cm.). Persia, Isfahan, 17th C. Berlin Museums Inv. Nr. KGM 84, 929. [Pl. IV; Fig. 117.]
Lit. K. Erdmann, *Europa und der Orientteppich*, Berlin-Mainz, 1962, fig. 43.

Pl. VII. Woollen knotted carpet, 'Dragon' carpet (525 × 212 cm.). *D*, Caucasus *c.* 1600. Berlin Museums Inv. Nr. I 2. [Pl. V; Fig. 118.]
Lit. K. Erdmann, *Orientteppiche*, Nr. 23; Sarre-Trenkwald, II, Pl. 4.

Pl. VIII. Woollen knotted carpet, 'Holbein' carpet, (427 × 190 cm.). *D*, Asia Minor, Bergama district, 16th C. Berlin Museums Inv. Nr. I 5526. [Pl. VI; Fig. 120.]
Lit. K. Erdmann, *Orientteppiche*, Nr. 29; idem, *Oriental Carpets*, fig. 36.

Pl. IX. (inadvertently reversed) Woollen knotted carpet (381 × 210 cm.). *D*, *F*, Anatolia, Ushak district, 17th C. Berlin Museums Inv. Nr. 82, 707. For the evolution of the design see K. Erdmann, *Oriental Carpets*, p. 25. [Pl. VII; Fig. 122.]

Pl. X. Woollen knotted carpet, 'Chess-board' carpet (396 × 208 cm.). *D*, Asia Minor?, 17th C. Berlin Museums Inv. Nr. I 14. [Pl. VIII; Fig. 124.]
Lit. E. Kühnel and L. Bellinger, *Catalogue of Cairene Rugs and Others Technically Related*, Textile Museum, Washington, 1957.

Pl. XI. Woollen knotted carpet, multiple-niche prayer rug (329 × 128 cm.). *F*, West Anatolia, Ushak, 17th C. Berlin Museums Inv. Nr. 25/61. [Pl. IX; Fig. 132.]

Pl. XII. Woollen knotted carpet (386 × 168 cm.). West Anatolia, Ushak, 17th C. Berlin Museums Inv. Nr. I 37/59. [Pl. X; Fig. 133.]
Lit. K. Erdmann, 'Teppicherwerbungen der Islamischen Abteilung', *Berliner Museen*, 1962, XII, fig. 6. I am indebted to Mr. L. Reidemeister for drawing my attention to this piece, which was in the Swiss art trade; Cf. Fig. 93.

Pl. XIII. Woollen knotted carpet, 'Kis-Ghiördes' (197 × 133 cm.). Anatolia, Ushak district, *c.* 1800. Berlin Museums Inv. Nr. I 1/61. [Pl. XI; Fig. 134.]
Lit. K. Erdmann, 'Teppicherwerbungen der Islamischen Abteilung', *Berliner Museen*, 1962, XII, fig. 7.

Pl. XIV. Woollen knotted carpet, multiple-niche prayer rug (274 × 122 cm.). *F*, Persia, 16th C. Formerly Sarre Collection. Berlin Museums Inv. Nr. I 66/62. [Pl. XII; Fig. 135.]
Lit. Sarre-Trenkwald, II, Pl. 50.

Pl. XV. Woollen knotted carpet (470 × 250 cm.). East Persia, *c.* 1600. Berlin Museums Inv. Nr. I 69/63. Cf. the carpet in the Metropolitan Museum in K. Erdmann's *Oriental Carpets*, fig. 81 and the carpet in the Kann Collection, ibid., fig. 87. [Pl. XIII; Fig. 137.]

Pl. XVI. Woollen knotted carpet (232 × 123 cm.). Anatolia, 17th–18th century. Berlin Museums Inv. Nr. I 39/63. Formerly Bode Collection. [Pl. XIV; Fig. 140.]
Lit. Auction Catalogue of the Bode Collection, 1929, Nr. 73, Pl. XXII.

Pl. XVII. Woollen knotted carpet, on silk foundation, (760 × 325 cm.). *D*, Persia, Herat, 16th C. Vienna, Angewandte Kunst Museum. [Pl. XVII; Fig. 223.]
Lit. Sarre-Trenkwald, I, Pls. 6, 7.

Pl. XVIII. Woollen knotted carpet (700 × 230 cm.). *D*, North Persia, 17th C. Formerly in the possession of the Hapsburg Royal House. Acquired in 1931 by Eugen Strauch and bought in London by Dr. Ulrich Schürmann, Cologne, to whom I am indebted for the colour plate. [Pl. XVIII; Fig. 247.]

Lit. H. Trenkwald, *Ein persische Teppich aus dem ehemaligen Besitz des Österreichischen Kaiserhauses*, Vienna, 1933; cf. the pair in the Kunst und Industrie Museum, Sarre-Trenkwald, I, Pls. 17, 18; a further example (526 × 216 cm.) with a more richly drawn border is in the collection of Baroness von Essen, Skokloster, Sweden (see F. R. Martin, *A History of Oriental Carpets before 1800*, Vienna, 1908, Pl. XXII).

Pl. XIX. Woollen knotted carpet with cartouche design (800 × 400 cm.). *D*, Persia, Tabriz, 16th C. Lyons, Musée des Tissus, Inv. Nr. 25, 423. [Pl. XIX; Fig. 248.]
Lit. F. R. Martin, *A History of Oriental Carpets before 1800*, Vienna, 1908, fig. 96; cf. the fragmentary counterpart in the Metropolitan Museum, New York (Bode-Kühnel, fig. 90); K. Erdmann, *Oriental Carpets*, fig. 58; Sarre-Trenkwald, II, Pl. 14.

Pl. XX. Woollen knotted carpet with the arms of the Admiral Enriquez (396 × 223 cm.). *F*, Spain, Alcaraz, early 15th C. Washington, the Textile Museum. [Pl. XX; Fig. 288.]
Lit. E. Kühnel and L. Bellinger, *Catalogue of Spanish Rugs, 12th to 19th Century*, Washington, 1953, Pls. IV, V. Cf. K. Erdmann, *Oriental Carpets*, fig. 174; J. Ferrandis Torres, *Exposición de Alfombras Antiguas Españolas*, Madrid, 1933, Pl. I.

MONOCHROME ILLUSTRATIONS

D = Detail   *F* = Fragment

The number within square brackets at the end of each caption gives the corresponding Fig. number in the German edition.
Figs. 1–22 retain the same numbering in both editions.

References to monochrome illustrations in *this* work are shown thus: Fig. . . . .; references to monochrome illustrations in all *other* works are shown as: fig. . . . .

1 Woollen knotted carpet (172 × 90 cm.). Anatolia, *c.* 1400. From a church in Central Italy, Berlin Museums Inv. Nr. I 4.
   Lit. K. Erdmann, 'Orientalische Tierteppiche auf Bildern des XIV und XV Jahrhunderts', *Jahrbuch der preussischen Kunstsammlungen*, Berlin, 1929, L, pp. 261 ff.; idem, 'Neue Tierteppiche auf abendländischen Bildern des XIV und XV Jahrhunderts', *Jahrbuch der preussischen Kunstsammlungen*, Berlin, 1941, LXIII, pp. 121 ff.; idem, 'Zur Frage der ältesten orientalischen Teppiche', *Cicerone*, Leipzig, 1930, XXII, pp. 152 ff.; Sarre-Trenkwald, II, Pl. 1 (colour); W. v. Bode, 'Ein altpersischer Teppich im Besitz der königlichen Museen zu Berlin', *Jahrbuch der preussischen Kunstsammlungen*, Berlin, 1892, XIII, pp. 43 ff, fig. 7. H. Jacoby insisted that this carpet was of a much later date (*How to know Oriental Carpets and Rugs*, London, 1952, pp. 98 ff.). Cf. another fragment of this carpet type in K. Erdmann's 'Zu einem anatolischen Teppichfragment aus Fostat', *Istanbuler Mitteilungen*, Istanbul, 1955, VI, pp. 42 ff. Another fragment was found recently in the Völkerkunde Museum in Basle.

2 Portrayal of an Anatolian Animal carpet of the 15th C. in a fresco of 1440–4 by Domenico di Bartolo in the hospital of Santa Maria della Scala in Siena.
   Lit. Bode-Kühnel, p. 26, fig. 5; cf. other carpets in paintings by Baldovinetti (*Art in America*, New York, II, p. 236, *Cicerone*, Leipzig, 1912, pp. 132 ff.), by Domenico Morone (K. Erdmann, *Oriental Carpets*, fig. 12), by Hans Memling, *Bathsheba in the Bath* in the Stuttgart Art Gallery (K. Voll, *Hans Memling*, fig.

158), by Pisanello, *The Annunciation*, in San Fermo, Verona (illustrated by A. Calabi and G. Cormaggia in *Pisanello*, Milan, 1928) and by Jacopo Bellini, *The Annunciation*, in S. Alessandro, Brescia (illustrated in A. Ugoletti, *Brescia*, Bergamo, 1909, p. 117.).

3 Anatolian carpet with stylized birds flanking a tree in a painting *The Betrothal of the Virgin* by Sano di Pietro, Rome, Vatican Collections. Cf. R. Ettinghausen, 'New Light on Early Animal Carpets' (*Aus der Welt der islamischen Kunst*. Publication in honour of Ernst Kühnel on his 75th birthday, Berlin, 1959, pp. 93 ff., figs. 4–6.).

4 Woollen knotted carpet (145 × 109 cm.). Anatolia, beginning 15th C. From the village church of Marby in Jämtland. Stockholm, Statens Historiska Museum Inv. Nr. 17786.
   Lit. Sarre-Trenkwald, Vol. II, Pl. 2; C. J. Lamm, 'The Marby Rug and some Fragments of Carpets found in Egypt', *Svenska Orientsällskapets*, Årsbok, 1937, pp. 51 ff.

5 Woollen knotted carpet fragment (25·5 × 18 cm.). *F*. Anatolia, 14th C. From Old Cairo (Fostat). New York, Metropolitan Museum of Art .
   Lit. K. Erdmann, *Oriental Carpets*, fig. 11. Cf. this with carpet with stylized cocks in a picture *The Betrothal of the Virgin* by Niccola da Buonaccorso, 1348–88, London, National Gallery.

6 Anatolian Animal carpet of the 14th C. in a picture *The Annunciation*, *D*, Siena. Formerly Schlossmuseum, Berlin.

7 Anatolian Animal carpet in a painting *Visit of Saint Catherine of Siena to the Pope in Avignon* c. 1440 by Giovanni di Paolo. Brussels, Stoclet Collection.

> *Lit.* E. de Lorey, 'Le Tapis d'Avignon', *Gazette des Beaux-Arts*, Paris, 1932, pp. 195 ff.

8 Persian silk carpet in *The Marriage at Cana*, D, by Paolo Veronese, 1562–3. Paris, Louvre.

9 Woollen knotted carpet (400 × 215 cm.). Anatolia, Ushak, 'Bird' carpet, 17th C. Formerly Berlin, private possession.

> *Lit.* K. Erdmann, *Oriental Carpets*, fig. 148. The name of this group was based on a mistaken interpretation of the motifs as birds, which was realized 35 years ago. (R. M. Riefstahl, 'Turkish Bird Rugs and their Design', *The Art Bulletin*, Providence, U.S.A., 1925, VII, pp. 91 ff.) In spite of this they are still called 'Bird' carpets.

10 'Bird' carpet in a picture of the Clouet School, probably 1560–1570. Madrid, Lazaro Collection.

11 Carpet with geometric field pattern in a Persian miniature of c. 1420. Baysunghur manuscript, Shiraz. Berlin Museums.

12 Drawing of a carpet design after a Persian miniature of 1485. London, British Museum. Cf. the similarity of this design with that of the 'Holbein' carpet, Fig. 13. See also the excellent study by A. Briggs, 'Timurid Carpets', *Ars Islamica*, Ann Arbor, 1940, VII, pp. 20 ff. and 1946, XI–XIII, pp. 146 ff.

13 Woollen knotted carpet (410 × 200 cm.). D, Anatolia, Ushak, 'Holbein' carpet, 16th C. Genoa, Barbieri Collection.

14 Medallion carpet in a Persian miniature, *Royal Audience*, 1525, School of Tabriz. New York, Metropolitan Museum of Art.

15 Woollen knotted prayer rug (180 × 120 cm.). Anatolia, Ushak, beginning of 16th C. Berlin Museums Inv. Nr. I 24.

> *Lit.* K. Erdmann, *Oriental Carpets*, fig. 158. Wilhelm von Bode, *Mein Leben* I, Berlin, 1930, p. 124.

16 Woollen knotted carpet (1152 × 534 cm.). D, The 'Ardebil' carpet from the mosque of Ardebil, North-west Persia, Tabriz, dated 1539–40. London, Victoria and Albert Museum Inv. Nr. 272–1893.

> *Lit.* C. Purdon Clarke, *Oriental Carpets*; V. J. Robinson, *Near Eastern Carpets*, London, 1882, 1893; W. R. Holmes, *Sketches on the Shores of the Caspian*, London, 1845; E. Stebbing, *The Holy Carpet of the Mosque at Ardebil*, London, 1893; Sarre-Trenkwald, II, Pls. 18, 19, 20 (details, in colour); A. U. Pope, *Survey*, Pl. 1134. The Ardebil carpet is one of a type existing in pairs. See chapter on 'Carpet Pairs'.

17 Detail of Fig. 16.

18 Detail of Fig. 16 showing the inscription. Translated by Sebastian Beck in Sarre-Trenkwald, II, Pl. 18.

19 Woollen knotted carpet, dated 1539–40. North-west Persia, Tabriz. Medallion carpet, pair to the Ardebil (Fig. 16), Los Angeles, County Museum.

20 Exhibition in Stockholm, 1892, Martin Collection.

21 Arrangement of the Islamic Department in the Kaiser Friedrich Museum, Berlin, c. 1910.

22 Arrangement of the Islamic Department in the Pergamon Museum, Berlin, 1932.

23 Woollen knotted carpet (608 × 266 cm.). Central Anatolia, 13th C. Istanbul, Türk ve Islam Eserleri Museum Inv. Nr. 689. From the Alaeddin Mosque in Konya. [142]

> *Lit.* F. Sarre, 'Mittelalterliche Knüpfteppiche kleinasiatischer und spanischer Herkunft', *Kunst und Kunsthandwerk*, Vienna, 1907, X, pp. 503 ff; F. R. Martin, *A History of Oriental Carpets before 1800*, Vienna, 1908, Pl. XXX. See also W. v. Bode, *Monatshefte für Kunstwissenschaft*, Berlin, 1908, p. 925; F. Sarre, *Erzeugnisse islamischer Kunst*, part II, *Seldjukische Kleinkunst*, Leipzig, 1909, p. 51. note 2; Bode-Kühnel, *Vorderasiatische Knüpfteppiche*. 2nd ed. pp. 105 ff, fig. 55–7; *Türkische Kunst*', exhibition catalogue. Darmstadt, 1965, Nr. 2.

24 Woollen knotted carpet (320 × 240 cm.). D, Central Anatolia, 13th C. Istanbul, Türk ve Islam Eserleri Museum Inv. Nr. 685. From the Alaeddin Mosque in Konya. [143]

> *Lit.* See 23 above; *Türkische Kunst*, exhibition catalogue, Darmstadt, 1965, Nr. 4.

25 Woollen knotted carpet (520 × 285 cm.). D, F, Central Anatolia, 13th C. Istanbul, Türk ve Islam Eserleri Museum Inv. Nr. 681. From the Alaeddin Mosque in Konya. [144]

> *Lit.* See 23 above. O. Aslanapa, *Turkish Arts*, Istanbul, n.d. (1960) in colour. *Türkische Kunst*, exhibition catalogue, Darmstadt, 1965, Nr. 1.

26 Woollen knotted carpet (183 × 130 cm.). D, F, Central Anatolia, 13th C. Istanbul, Türk ve Islam Eserleri Museum Inv. Nr. 688. From the Alaeddin Mosque in Konya. [145]

> *Lit.* *Splendeur de l'Art Turc*, exhibition catalogue, Musée des Arts Décoratifs. Paris 1953; K. Erdmann, *Oriental Carpets*, fig. 3.

27 Woollen knotted carpet (91 × 74 cm.), Central Anatolia, 13th C. Istanbul, Türk ve Islam Eserleri Museum Inv. Nr. 684. From the Alaeddin Mosque in Konya. [146]

> *Lit.* *Türkische Kunst aus sieben Jahrhunderten*, exhibition catalogue. Vienna, 1932, Nr. 155. O. Aslanapa, *Turkish Arts*, Istanbul, n.d. (1960) Pl. VI; Exhibition *Türkische Kunst*, exhibition catalogue, Darmstadt, 1965, Nr. 5.

28 Woollen knotted carpet (254 × 170 cm.). F, Central Anatolia, 13th C. Konya, Mevlana Museum. From the Eshrefoğlu Mosque in Beyshehir. [147]

> *Lit.* O. Aslanapa, *Turkish Arts*, Istanbul, n.d. (1960), Pl. IX. See also R. M. Riefstahl, 'Primitive Rugs of the Konya Type in the Mosque of Beyshehir', *The Art Bulletin*, Providence, U.S.A., 1931, XIII, fig. 3; C. J. Lamm, 'The Marby Rug and some Fragments of Carpets found in Egypt', *Svenska Orientsällskapets*, Årsbok, 1937, pp. 51 ff.

29 Woollen knotted carpet, Central Anatolia, D, 13th C. From the Eshrefoğlu Mosque in Beyshehir. Present location unknown. [148]

30 Border of the carpet, D, Fig. 29. [149]

31 Saint Nicholas buys a carpet from a poor man. Fresco in the church of Boiana near Sofia, dated 1259 (after A. Grabar, *La peinture religieuse en Bulgarie*, Paris, 1928, Pl. XVIII). [150]

> The fresco in Boiana raises the question whether instead of copying Byzantine textiles these 'Anatolian Animal' carpets were not modelled on Byzantine carpets. This would simplify the problem of their origin. The legend mentions a carpet but this need not have been knotted. As represented in the fresco

the rug is a long narrow runner which, from the appearance of the border and the manner in which the roundels are cut off at the ends, is reminiscent of a knotted carpet. However, the drawing of the roundels and the animals enclosed by them lacks that stylization of design associated with carpet knotting and familiar from representations of carpets in early paintings. Floor carpets were known in Byzantium (see Jean Ebersolt, *Les arts somptuaires de Byzance*, Paris, 1923). According to Byzantine sources, in the tenth century, Danilis, a noblewoman from the Peloponnesus, ordered a large soft carpet (de grands tapis moelleux) for the Palace chapel in Byzantium (Istanbul). Perhaps these carpets were similar in appearance to the fragments with birds in roundels which Ettinghausen described in 1959 in the publication in honour of Ernst Kühnel. He dated these fragments ninth to tenth century and assigned them to Egypt or Iraq. Neither example is a knotted carpet. They are woven in ancient techniques which, in spite of similarities in appearance, has nothing to do with true knotting. It is possible that the carpet in the Boiana fresco was woven in the loop technique. It may be that the Turks who had invaded Asia Minor actually imitated the Byzantine loop-woven carpets in the customary knotting technique. This, however, resulted in greater stylization and a restricted colour range.

32 Drawing of the carpet in the fresco in Fig. 31. [151]

33 Figure in Byzantine court dress of the 11th C. Miniature from the Chrysostom Codex of Nicephorus Botaniates (after O. v. Falke, *Kunstgeschichte der Seidenweberei*, Berlin, 1913, II, p. 6, Fig. 222). [152]

34 Embroidered cope in Anagni. Cyprus before 1295 (after O. v. Falke, *Kunstgeschichte der Seidenweberei*, Tübingen, 4th ed., fig. 206). [153]

35 Carpet with quadrupeds in a painting *Madonna Enthroned* by Ambrogio Lorenzetti. Formerly in Baer Collection, Munich. [154]
   Lit. K. Erdmann, 'Orientalische Tierteppiche auf Bildern des XIV und XV Jahrh.', *Jahrbuch der preussischen Kunstsammlungen*, Berlin, 1929, 50, pp. 261–98, and 'Neue orientalische Tierteppiche auf abendländischen Bildern des XIV and XV Jahrh.', ibid, 1941, 63, pp. 121–6. The other pictures which have been mentioned are: Carpet (?) with two-headed eagles in octagons in a picture of the *Madonna Enthroned*, Florence, middle 14th century, Berlin Museums (A. von Marle, *Italian Schools of Painting*, 1924, III, p. 270); Carpet with heraldic eagles in a picture from the Legend of Saint Lucianus, Siena, 14th C. Rome, Vatican Collections (D'Acchiardi *I Quadri primitivi della Pinacoteca Vaticana*, Rome, 1929, Pl. LXXIa); Carpet with two addorsed birds flanking a tree in a picture *The Betrothal of the Virgin* by Sano di Pietro (1406–81) Rome, Vatican Collections (D'Acchiardi, see above, Pl. LXXXVI).

36 Carpet with horned quadrupeds and hexagons. Drawing of a fragment from Old Cairo, Anatolia, *c*. 1400. Formerly C. J. Lamm Collection, Upsala (after C. J. Lamm, 'The Marby Rug and some Fragments of Carpets found in Egypt', *Svenska Orientsällskapets*, Årsbok, 1937, p. 93, fig. 13.). [155]

37 Carpet with stylized birds by a tree. Drawing of a fragment from Old Cairo, Anatolia, beginning 15th C. Formerly C. J. Lamm Collection, Upsala. (After C. J. Lamm, see above, 36, fig. 14.) [156]

38 Carpet with stylized cocks in a picture *Betrothal of the Virgin*, D, by Niccolo da Buonaccorso (1348–88) in the National Gallery, London. [157]

39 Carpet with birds in a picture *Madonna Enthroned*, by the Spanish painter Jaume Huguet (†1437/8), Museum of Catalonian Art, Barcelona. [158]

40 Woollen knotted carpet of the type illustrated in Fig. 39. Anatolia, 15th C. Konya, Mevlana Museum. [159]
   Lit. R. Ettinghausen, 'New Light on Early Animal Carpets' from *Aus der Welt der islamischen Kunst* (Publication in honour of Ernst Kühnel on his 75th birthday), Berlin, 1959, pp. 93 ff.

41 Woven cushion cover with Dragon and Phoenix combat. Norway. 15th–16th C. Stockholm, Nordiska Museum, after a carpet of the type illustrated in Fig. 1. [160]

42 *Madonna with Saints*, D, by Raffaellino del Garbo, Florence, end 15th C. Berlin Museums (destroyed during the war). Cf. Fig. 107; and the picture by Piero della Francesca, dated 1451. (H. Graber, *Piero della Francesca*, Basle, 1920, Pl. 9); Mantegna's altarpiece (F. Knapp, *Andrea Mantegna*, Stuttgart, 1910, Pl. 79); and the miniature by Fra Carnevale (Rome, Bibliotheca Vaticana, *Codex Urbinensis* lat. 508). The spread of these carpet designs in Europe is reflected in an embroidery with Swiss blazons dated 1532 and in imitations in English embroideries of the 16th C. (see F.R. Martin, *A History of Oriental Carpets before 1800*, Vienna, 1908, fig. 306 and 310). [161]

43 Drawing of a woollen knotted carpet fragment from Old Cairo (40·5 × 40 cm.). Anatolia, 2nd half 15th C. Röhss Museum, Gothenburg Inv. Nr. 322/1935. (After C. J. Lamm, see above, 36, fig. 24.) [162]

44 Woollen knotted carpet, D, F, Anatolia, early 15th C. Konya, Mevlana Museum. From the Mosque in Beyshehir. [163].
   Lit. R. M. Riefstahl 'Primitive Rugs of the Konya Type in the Mosque of Beyshehir', *The Art Bulletin*, Providence, U.S.A., 1931, XIII, pp. 10 ff. The flower motif in the inner guard-stripe of the border is identical with that in a fragment from Old Cairo (C. J. Lamm, see 36 above, fig. 27, Nr. 28).

45 Woollen knotted carpet. Tekke Turkoman (255 × 155 cm.). Turkestan, 19th C. Formerly Berlin art trade. In these late carpets the octagons, which lie on the intersections of the lines forming the squares, are divided into four equal parts by these lines. This cannot have been in accordance with the original design. [164]

46 Woollen knotted carpet, 'Holbein' carpet (191 × 100 cm.). D, F, Anatolia, beginning 16th C. Istanbul, Türk ve Islam Eserleri Museum Inv. Nr. 303. [165]
   For the discussion of the origin of this design see K. Erdmann, *Oriental Carpets*, p. 23 – in favour of the priority of the 'first form' (Fig. 46) is the fact that alternation of two different motifs arranged in offset rows occurs at an early period (e.g. Fig. 43). As evidence for priority of the 'second form' is the Beyshehir fragment (Fig. 44), the occurrence of a design of squares in the field due to alternation of colours which is to be found in carpets in early 15th–century Persian miniatures K.) Erdmann, *Oriental Carpets*, p. 23) and the obvious squaring of the field in Turkoman carpets (Fig. 45).

47 Woollen knotted carpet with colour change in the field, 'Holbein' carpet (285 × 255 cm.). D, F, Anatolia, beginning 16th C. Formerly Baron von Tucher Collection. [166]

48 Woollen knotted carpet, 'Holbein' carpet with abnormal octagons (185 × 115 cm.). Anatolia, 16th C. Formerly von Dirksen Collection. [167]
Lit. Lepke Auction, 28/29.4.1931, Nr. 517.

49 Woollen knotted carpet (pieces of a carpet of the type illustrated in fig. 48), Anatolia, 16th C. Munich, L. Bernheimer, Ltd. [168]
Lit. O. Bernheimer, Alte Teppiche des 16 bis 18 Jahrhunderts der Firma L. Bernheimer, Munich, 1959, Nr. 143.

50 Woollen knotted carpet, 'Holbein' carpet with unusual border (220 × 166 cm.). Anatolia, 2nd half 16th C. Berlin Museums Inv. Nr. I 26. [169]
Lit. Bode-Kühnel, Pl. I in colour. Cf. with a carpet in the University Museum of Philadelphia (Williams Collection) and with another in the Iparművészeti Museum in Budapest.

51 Woollen knotted carpet (158 × 114 cm.). Anatolia, 17th C. Berlin Museums Inv. Nr. KGM 88, 29. Variation of a 'Holbein' carpet design. [170]

52 Woollen knotted carpet, 'Lotto' carpet, Anatolia, 16th C. St. Louis, City Art Museum. Cf. K. Erdmann, Oriental Carpets, p. 25; for the Lotto carpets with European arms, Fig. 144; European arms in Anatolian carpets occur only in those from the Ushak district (Fig. 192). This supports the view that the Lotto carpets were made in this region. The Lotto design in a miniature of the 15th C., illustrated in Fig. 273, is insufficient evidence to date the Spanish group, and especially its Anatolian forerunners so early, since the latter do not appear in Italian paintings of the 15th century. [171]

53 Design of a 'Lotto' carpet. [172]

54 Palmette blossoms (a) in a Lotto carpet; (b) in a Medallion Ushak. [173]

55 Paired arabesque leaves (a) in a Lotto carpet; (b) in a Medallion Ushak.
Lit. K. Erdmann, Oriental Carpets, pp. 27 f. [174]

56 Woollen knotted carpet, 'Lotto' carpet (518 × 275 cm.). D, Anatolia, 17th C. Istanbul, Türk ve Islam Eserleri Museum Inv. Nr. 702. [175]

57 Woollen knotted carpet, 'Lotto' carpet (148 × 113 cm.). Anatolia, late 17th C. Formerly in the Dr. O. Jäger Collection, Chemnitz. [176]

58 Woollen knotted carpet, 'Lotto' carpet in atypical colouring. D. Anatolia, 17th C. Formerly Bode Collection. Cf. a small carpet formerly in the collection of Baron Hatvany, Budapest which shows the design in blue-green on a red ground; the Lotto carpet in this atypical colouring, represented in the tapestry in the Residenz Museum in Munich and another in the portrait of a lady by Sebastiano del Piombo in the Huldschinsky Collection, Pantheon, Munich, 1928, I, p. 28. A similar design in a Lotto carpet is in the Museum in Izmir. [177]

59 Woollen knotted carpet, 'Lotto' carpet. End 17th C. The design shows degeneration adjoining the side borders. Present whereabouts unknown. [178]

60 Silk knotted carpet (250 × 150 cm.). Persia, Kashan, 16th C. Paris, Gobelins Museum. [179]
Lit. K. Erdmann, 'Die kleinen Seidenteppiche Kaschans', Pantheon, Munich, 1961, XIX, p. 159 ff. Cf. R. M. Riefstahl, 'Oriental Carpets in American Collections; Part I Three silk rugs in the Altman Collection', Art in America, New York, 1926, IV, pp. 147–161; Sarre-Trenkwald, II, Pl. 41, 42; A. U. Pope, Survey, Pl. 1201.

61 Silk knotted carpet (266·5 × 156·5 cm.). Persia, Kashan, 16th C. Munich, Bavarian National Museum. [180]
Lit. A. U. Pope, Survey, Pl. 1202.

62 Silk knotted carpet with pictorially arranged animals and animal combats (238 × 178 cm.). Central Persia, Kashan, mid-16th C. New York, Metropolitan Museum, Altman Collection. [181]
Lit. K. Erdmann, Oriental Carpets, fig. 68; Sarre-Trenkwald, II, Pl. 39, in colour. The counterpart of this carpet is in the Aynard Collection (illustrated in the Auction Catalogue, G. Petit, Paris, 1–4.12.1913, Nr. 344; further illustrations in G. Migeon, Les Arts des Tissus, Paris, 1909, p. 354).

63 Silk knotted carpet (232 × 175 cm.). D, Persia, Kashan, 16th C. Detroit, Art Institute. Edsel Ford gift, 1925, Inv. Nr. 25.23. [182]
Lit. K. Erdmann, 'Tappeti Persiani', Dedalo, Milan, 1932, XII, p. 721; Bulletin of the Detroit Institute of Art, 1925, VI, April, pp. 70–1.

64 Silk knotted carpet (245 × 168 cm.). Persia, Kashan, 16th C. Amsterdam, Portuguese-Israelite Community. I am indebted to the former for permission to publish the carpet and to Dr. Louise Erkelens of the Rijksmuseum, Amsterdam for drawing my attention to it and for the photograph. [183]

65 Silk knotted carpet (247·5 × 165 cm.). Persia, Kashan, 16th C. New York, Metropolitan Museum. I am indebted to the Museum for permission to publish and to Dr. E. Grube, Curator, Department of Islamic Art, for information and photographs. [184]

66 Silk carpet (232 × 175 cm.). Persia, Kashan, end 16th or beginning 17th C. Vienna, Angewandte Kunst Museum. Clarice de Rothschild gift. I am indebted to Dr. Dora Heinz for permission to publish photographs and information. Cf. the pointed oval central medallion with those of the contemporary tapestry carpet in K. Erdmann, 'Persische Wirkteppiche der Safawidenzeit', Pantheon, Munich, 1932, pp. 227 ff. A closely related tapestry carpet was formerly in the Comtesse Béarn Collection in Paris (F. R. Martin, A History of Oriental Carpets before 1800, Vienna, 1908, fig. 159). A similar design occurs also in one of the five Shah Abbas carpets in the Treasury of St. Mark's in Venice (A. U. Pope, Survey, Pl. 1245). [185]

67 Silk knotted carpet (241 × 165 cm.). Persia, Kashan, 16th C. Washington, National Gallery, Widener Collection. [186]
Lit. A. U. Pope, Survey, Pl. 1197.

68 Silk knotted carpet (230 × 180 cm.). D, Persia, Kashan, 16th C. Lisbon, Gulbenkian Collection. The only carpet of the group which has no counterpart, but a similar border design appears in the Animal carpets in the Altman Collection and in Detroit. A woollen copy of this carpet also exists, a fragment of which from the Homberg Collection, is in the Musée des Arts Décoratifs in Paris. Sarre-Trenkwald, II, Pl. 40, in colour. [187]

69 Woollen knotted carpet, 'Tree' carpet (470 × 200 cm.). *D*, North Persia, 18th C. Munich, L. Bernheimer, Ltd. [188]

70 Woollen knotted carpet, 'Garden' carpet (925 × 357 cm.). *D*, North Persia, 18th C. England, private collection. [189]
Lit. K. Erdmann, *Oriental Carpets*, fig. 123.

71 Woollen knotted carpet, 'Garden' carpet (870 × 285 cm.). *D*, North Persia, 18th C. New York, Kevorkian Foundation (by kind permission of Mrs. Marjorie Kevorkian). [190]
Lit. M. S. Dimand, *The Kevorkian Foundation Collection of Rare and Magnificient Oriental Rugs*, New York, 1966, Nr. 13.

72 Plan of an Oriental garden. [191]

73 Woollen knotted carpet, 'Garden' carpet, North Persia, 18th C. Formerly Berlin private collection. [192]

74 Woollen knotted carpet, 'Garden' carpet (527 × 425 cm.). North Persia, beg. 18th C. Glasgow Art Gallery, Burrell Collection. [194]

75 Woollen knotted carpet, 'Garden' carpet (840 × 370 cm.). Centre *D*, South Persia, before 1632. India, Jaipur Museum. [195]
Lit. M. S. Dimand, 'A Persian Garden Carpet in the Jaipur Museum', *Ars Islamica*, Ann Arbor, 1940, VII, pp. 93 ff.

76 Flower bed in the field of the carpet in Fig. 75. [196]

77 Detail from the Vienna 'Hunting' carpet, cf. Fig. 99. [197]

78 Detail from the border of the Vienna 'Hunting' carpet. [198]

79 Silk knotted carpet, 'Hunting' carpet (555 × 285 cm.). *D*, Persia, Kashan, end 16th C. Stockholm, Royal Palace. [199]
Lit. F. R. Martin, *A History of Oriental Carpets before 1800*, Vienna, 1908, Pl. IV and V; A. U. Pope, *Survey, Pl.* 1193.

80 Silk tapestry carpet, *D*. See Plate III. [200]

81 Woollen knotted carpet (485 × 268 cm.). *D*, Persia, Kashan, end 16th C. Lyons, Musée des Tissus. [201]

82 Woollen knotted carpet (194 × 149 cm.). *D, F*, Persia, Tabriz, 16th C. Formerly Budapest, Baron Hatvany Collection. [202]
Lit. A. U. Pope, *Survey, Pl.* 1141 in colour; for another fragment of the same carpet see Fig. 220. The pictorial character is still more marked in a carpet ornamented with scenes from Nizami's stories which is in the Musée des Arts Décoratifs (F. Sarre, *Altorientalische Teppiche*, Leipzig, 1908, Pl. 16).

83 Woollen knotted carpet, scenic carpet (423 × 151 cm.). India, 17th C. Boston, Museum of Fine Arts. [203]
Lit. Sarre-Trenkwald, II, Pl. 59 in colour.

84 Woollen knotted carpet, 'Portuguese' carpet (677 × 372 cm.). *D*, North Persia ?, *c*. 1600. Vienna, Angewandte Kunst Museum. Further examples in the Berlin Museums, Fig. 158 (war loss), in the Musée des Tissus, Lyons, the Rijksmuseum, Amsterdam, the Metropolitan Museum, New York and in several private collections. According to Ettinghausen, the swimmer in this carpet could be a legendary sea creature (insan al-ma) sometimes depicted in Islamic art (G. B. Guest and R. Ettinghausen, 'The Iconography of a Kashan Luster plate', *Ars Islamica*, 1942, IX). [205]

85 Woollen knotted carpet in the Persian style of the 16th C. (232 × 165 cm.). Turkey, 19th C. Formerly Salting Collection. London, Victoria and Albert Museum. [206]

Lit. Edouard Lièvre, *Musée Graphique, 1880–1883* in colour. At that time the carpet was in the possession of Marks-Durlacher Frères in London; R. Koechlin and G. Migeon, *Cent Planches d'Art Musulman*, Paris, n.d.; F. R. Martin, *A History of Oriental Carpets before 1800*, Vienna, 1908, p. 50; A. F. Kendrick, *Guide to the Collection of Carpets*, 1931, London, Victoria and Albert Museum, pp. 14 ff. (in the editions of 1915 and 1920 this carpet was referred to as 'Persian, probably 16th century'). See also the same group in Bode-Kühnel, 3rd ed. figs. 6–7; F. R. Martin considered that it was 'too well preserved' (*A History of Oriental carpets before 1800*, Vienna, 1908, p. 49, fig. 117). Sarre also thought that this carpet was 'a more recent copy made in a Turkish Court Manufactory' (*Pantheon*, Munich, 1936, IX, p. 161); cf. also the carpet in the Czartoryski Museum, Cracow (illustrated with others in *Meisterwerke muhammedanischer Kunst*, Munich, 1912, Pl. 47).

86 Woollen knotted carpet in the Persian style of the 16th C. (360 × 183 cm.). Turkey, 19th C. Formerly Marquand Collection, Philadelphia, Museum of Art. [207]
Lit. A. U. Pope, *Survey*, Pl. 1152. Cf. carpet in Metropolitan Museum, New York (A. U. Pope, *Survey*, Pl. 1153); a similar carpet in the American trade (*Survey*, Pl. 1161); Auction V. and L. Benguiat, 23.IV.1932, Nr. 16, present whereabouts unknown; the carpet in the Goupil Collection, Lyons (*Survey*, Pl. 1160B); carpet in the Aly Bey Ibrahim Collection, Cairo (*Survey*, Pl. 1159); carpet in the Topkapi Palace Museum, Istanbul (*Survey*, Pl. 1160A). For the whole group, K. Erdmann, 'The Art of Carpet Making', *Ars Islamica*, Ann Arbor, 1941, VIII, pp. 164 ff.

87 Woollen knotted carpet, Prayer carpet (161·5 × 107 cm.). Turkey, 19th C. New York, Metropolitan Museum, Fletcher Collection. [208]
Lit. Sarre-Trenkwald, II, Pl. 51.

88 Woollen knotted carpet. Turkey, 19th C. Istanbul, Topkapi Palace Museum. [209]

89 Woollen knotted carpet, Turkey (Hereke?). 19th C. Istanbul, Topkapi Palace Museum. [210]

90 Woollen knotted carpet, (165 × 105 cm.) Turkey (Hereke?), 19th C. Istanbul, Topkapi Palace Museum. Inv. Nr. 2100. [211]
Lit. Türkische Kunst, exhibition catalogue Darmstadt, 1965, Nr. 54.

91 Woollen knotted carpet, Turkey (Hereke?), 19th C. Istanbul, Topkapi Palace Museum. [212]

92 Woollen knotted carpet, 'Chintamani' carpet (294 × 170 cm.). Forgery from the end of the 19th or beginning of the 20th C. Said to be from the Prince Schwarzenberg Collection. London, Victoria and Albert Museum. [213]
Faked carpets are more numerous than the author realized in 1964, and from technical investigations it is possible that the carpets illustrated in Figs. 144 and 145 and Pl. XII are of this group.

93 Woollen knotted carpet, 'Chintamani' carpet (392 × 220 cm.). Anatolia, Ushak, 17th C. Florence, Bardini Museum. [214]
Lit. K. Erdmann, *Oriental Carpets*, fig. 147; M. and V. Viale, *Arazzi e Tappeti Antichi*, p. 242, Pl. 168. A small but attractive carpet with the Chintamani design is in the City Art Museum in St. Louis. In another white-ground piece in the

Philadelphia Museum of Art the 'lightning' stripes have taken the form of lozenges and the spots are sometimes arranged inside small circles. A similar carpet, Nr. 568 in the catalogue of 1912 of the van Stolk Museum in Haarlem, was exhibited in Munich in 1910, catalogue Nr. 150. A large carpet of this group in the Mevlana Museum in Konya was shown in Europe for the first time in the exhibition 'Türkische Kunst', Darmstadt, 1965. The Chintamani design does not occur in white-ground carpets only. A large red-ground carpet, four metres in width, with a typical Ushak border, which has yellow lightning stripes and blue-green and black spots is in Istanbul, Türk ve Islam Eserleri Museum, Inv. Nr. 696/697a. A small red-ground Chintamani carpet is illustrated in colour, Pl. 41, in Otto Bernheimer's *Alte Teppiche des 16 bis 18 Jahrhunderts*. The carpet from Central Anatolia (Fig. 119 below) a late piece from the 18th C., has a brown-black field with blue stripes enclosing red and yellow, and white spots enclosing red and yellow. In an even later carpet in the Mevlana Museum the stripes have become horizontal red and blue leaves and the spots white lozenges with red centres.

94 Woollen knotted carpet, 'Chintamani' carpet (310 × 195 cm.). Anatolia, Ushak, 17th C. Formerly Bode Collection. For some time in the trade (see *International Studio*, London, July 1930, p. 60). [215]

95 Woollen knotted carpet, 'Chintamani' carpet (408 × 243 cm.). D, Anatolia, Ushak, 17th C. Formerly Prince Schwarzenberg Collection. [216]
   Lit. Vienna catalogue 1891, Nr. 353; Munich catalogue, 1910, Nr. 144.

96 Woollen knotted carpet, Armenian carpet. Forgery from the end of the 19th or beginning of the 20th century. Formerly in the trade in Hermannstadt. In his forthcoming book on Dragon carpets Charles Grant Ellis will present interesting material on this subject. [217]

97 Woollen knotted 'Dragon' carpet, of the Tuduc group of forgeries, formerly Bielz Collection, Hermannstadt (Sibiu). [218]

98 Woollen knotted carpet, 'Dragon' carpet. Formerly Süssmann Collection. Copy after fig. 5, Neugebauer-Orendi, *Handbuch der orientalischen Teppichkunde*, Leipzig, 1909. [219]

99 Silk knotted carpet (693 × 323 cm.). D, the Vienna 'Hunting' carpet, Persia, Kashan. 1st half 16th C. Vienna, Angewandte Kunst Museum. [23]
   Lit. A. Riegl, 'Ältere orientalische Teppiche aus dem Besitz des Allerhöchsten Kaiserhauses', *Jahrbuch der Kunsthistorischen Sammlungen Wien*, Vienna, 1892, XIII, pp. 267 ff.; C. Purdon Clarke, *Oriental Carpets*, Vienna, 1892; Vienna, Kaiserlich-Königlich Österreichisches Handelsmuseum, *Katalog der Ausstellung orientalischer Teppiche*, Vienna, 1891; Sarre Trenkwald, I, Pls. 1–5; S. Troll, *Altorientalische Teppiche*, Vienna, Angewandte Kunst Museum, 1951. Cf. with the carpet in the possession of Baron Maurice de Rothschild, Paris (Sarre-Trenkwald, II, Pls. 24–6, in colour).

100 Felt carpet (measurements unknown). East Asia, 8th C. or earlier. Japan, Nara, Shosoin Treasury. [25]
   Lit. Jiro Harada, *English Catalogue of Treasures in the Imperial Repository, Shosoin*, Tokyo, 1932; K. Erdmann, *Oriental Carpets*, fig. 167.

101 Woollen knotted carpet with flowering shrubs (427 × 200 cm.). India, 17th C. Carpets of the Maharaja of Jaipur are of this type. New York, Kevorkian Foundation (by kind permission of Mrs. Marjorie Kevorkian). Cf. Fig. 254. [26]
   Lit. M. S. Dimand, *The Kevorkian Foundation. Collection of Rare and Magnificent Oriental Carpets*, New York, 1966. Pl. XIII, in colour.

102 Silk knotted carpet (760 × 350 cm.). D, Persia, Kashan. Mid-16th C. From the possession of the Branicki family and formerly in Warsaw Castle. [27]
   Lit. A. U. Pope, *Survey*, Pl. 1195.

103 Woollen knotted carpet (length 350 cm. × width 410 cm.). F, North Persia, Tabriz, 16th C. Paris, Musée des Arts Décoratifs. [28]
   Lit. F. Sarre, *Altorientalische Teppiche*, Leipzig, 1908, Pl. VIII, p. 132; R. Koechlin and G. Migeon, *Islamische Kunstwerke*, Berlin, 1928, Pl. 83, in colour. The other half of this carpet is in the sacristy of Cracow Cathedral.

104 Silk knotted carpet brocaded (520 × 370 cm.). Persia (Isfahan), 17th C. The 'Coronation' carpet of the Danish Royal House. Copenhagen, Rosenborg Castle. [29]
   Lit. V. Slomann, 'The Coronation Carpet of the Kings of Denmark', *Bulletin of the American Institute for Persian Art and Archaeology*, New York, 1934, pp. 13 ff.

105 Woollen knotted carpet (802 × 412 cm.). D, North-west Persia, Tabriz, c. 1600. From the Castle in Dessau. New York, Metropolitan Museum. [30]
   Lit. A. U. Pope, *Survey*, Pl. 1137; K. Erdmann, *Oriental Carpets*, fig. 66.

106 Woollen knotted carpet (225 × 135 cm.). D, F, Central Anatolia, Konya, 13th C. Istanbul, Türk ve Islam Eserleri Museum Inv. Nr. 693. [31]
   Lit. See Nrs. 23–25; K. Erdmann, *Oriental Carpets*, fig. 5; Anon., *Eski Türk Halilarindan ve Kilimlerinden Örnekler*, Istanbul, 1961, Pl. I, in colour.

107 'Lotto' carpet in the altarpiece by Lorenzo Lotto, Venice, SS. Giovanni and Paolo. [32]

108 Anatolian carpet in *The Annunciation* by Carlo Crivelli, London, National Gallery. [33]

109 Anatolian carpet in a painting by Andrea Solario, *Portrait of the painter Domenico Morone*, Milan, Brera. [34]

110 Silk knotted carpet, brocaded (216 × 140 cm.). Persia (Kashan or Isfahan), 'Polish' carpet, 17th C. Venice, Treasury of St. Mark's. [36]
   Lit. A. U. Pope, *Survey*, Pl. 1245.

111 Silk knotted carpet, brocaded (215 × 136 cm.). Persia (Kashan or Isfahan), 17th C. Venice, Treasury of St. Mark's. The carpet was apparently presented to the Doge in 1622 by a Persian Embassy. [37]

112 Silk knotted carpet, brocaded (196 × 133 cm.). Persia (Kashan or Isfahan), 17th C. Venice, Treasury of St. Mark's. Provenance as Nr. 111. [38]

113 Woollen knotted carpet (127 × 63 cm.). F, Animal carpet with medallions, Persia, 16th C. Florence, Bargello. [39]

114 Woollen knotted carpet (253 × 177 cm.). Persia, end of 16th C. From the Palazzo Capponi in Florence. New York, Metropolitan Museum. [40]

115 Woollen knotted carpet (147 × 92 cm.). *F*, Prayer rug, West Anatolia, 18th C. From the Alaeddin Tomb in Konya. Istanbul, Türk ve Islam Eserleri Museum Inv. Nr. 287. The niche, hardly indicated, contains the symbols of the holy places in Mecca and Medina. [47]

116 Woollen knotted carpet in imitation of an animal skin (195 × 132 cm.). Anatolia, 18th C. Istanbul, Türk ve Islam Eserleri Museum Inv. Nr. 324. [48]
    Lit. K. Erdmann, *Oriental Carpets*, fig. 151; *Türkische Kunst*, exhibition catalogue, Darmstadt, 1965, Nr. 16. (Catalogue measurements incorrect.)

117 Woollen knotted carpet (194 × 150 cm.). West Anatolia, 18th C. Istanbul, Türk ve Islam Eserleri Museum Inv. Nr. 406. [49]
    Lit. Exhibition *Türkische Kunst*, exhibition catalogue, Darmstadt, 1965, Nr. 18.

118 Woollen knotted carpet (193 × 155 cm.). Anatolia, Ushak district, c. 1700. Istanbul, Türk ve Islam Eserleri Museum Inv. Nr. 698. [50]

119 Woollen knotted carpet (415 × 117 cm.). *D*, Central Anatolia, Konya? 18th C. Istanbul, Türk ve Islam Eserleri Museum Inv. Nr. 677. [51]
    Lit. Anon., *Eski Türk Halilarindan ve Kilimlerinden Örnekler*, Istanbul, 1961, Pl. IX.

120 Woollen knotted carpet (218 × 160 cm.). *D*, Asia Minor, Bergama district, 16th–17th C. From Sheikh Baba Yusuf mosque, Sivrihisar. Istanbul, Türk ve Islam Eserleri Museum Inv. Nr. 701. [41]
    Lit. K. Erdmann, *Oriental carpets*, p. 27.

121 Woollen knotted carpet (227 × 108 cm.). *F*, Asia Minor, 18th C. Istanbul, Türk ve Islam Eserleri Museum Inv. Nr. 291. [42]
    Lit. Anon., *Eski Türk Halilarindan ve Kilimlerinden Örnekler*, Istanbul, 1961, Pl. 32; *Türkische Kunst*, exhibition catalogue, Darmstadt, 1965, Nr. 57. (Catalogue measurements incorrect.)

122 Woollen knotted carpet, *F*, West Anatolia, Bergama district, 17th–18th C. Istanbul, Türk ve Islam Eserleri Museum. [43]

123 Woollen knotted carpet (140 × 135 cm.). *F*, West Anatolia, 17th–18th C. Istanbul, Türk ve Islam Eserleri Museum Inv. Nr. 280. [44]
    Lit. Exhibition *Türkische Kunst*, exhibition catalogue, Darmstadt, 1965, Nr. 58.

124 Woollen knotted carpet, West Anatolia, 18th C. Istanbul, Türk ve Islam Eserleri Museum. [45]

125 Woollen knotted carpet (200 × 150 cm.). Anatolia, Ushak district, c. 1700. Based on a Holbein carpet design. From the Sheikh Baba Yusuf mosque in Sivrihisar. Istanbul, Türk ve Islam Eserleri Museum. [46]
    Lit. K. Erdmann, *Oriental Carpets*, fig. 32; Oktay Aslanapa, *Turkish Arts*, Istanbul, 1960, Pl. IX, in colour.

126 Woollen knotted carpet with central medallion and fused corner pieces (165 × 115 cm.), Asia Minor, Ushak, 17th C. Istanbul, Türk ve Islam Eserleri Museum Inv. Nr. 11. [55]

127 Woollen knotted carpet. Multiple prayer rug (400 × 135 cm.). *D*, *F*, West Anatolia, Ushak 17th C. From the Sultan Selim mosque in Edirne. Istanbul, Türk ve Islam Eserleri Museum Inv. Nr. 776. [56]
    Lit. Anon., *Eski Türk Halilarindan ve Kilimlerinden Örnekler*, Istanbul, 1961, Pl. 5.

128 Woollen knotted carpet. Multiple prayer rug (121 × 102 cm.). *F*, *D*, West Anatolia, Ushak 17th C. From Sivrihisar. Istanbul, Türk ve Islam Eserleri Museum Inv. Nr. 555. [57]
    Lit. See Nr. 127 above, Pl. 8.

129 Woollen knotted carpet (488 × 215 cm.). West Anatolia, Ushak?, 18th C. Istanbul, Türk ve Islam Eserleri Museum Inv. Nr. 761. [58]
    Lit. Exhibition *Türkische Kunst*, exhibition catalogue, Darmstadt, 1965, Nr. 26.

130 Woollen knotted carpet. *D*, Caucasus, 18th C. Istanbul, Türk ve Islam Eserleri Museum. [59]

131 Woollen knotted carpet. Caucasian copy of a Persian Tree carpet with enthroned figures. 18th C. Istanbul, Türk ve Islam Eserleri Museum. [60]

132 Woollen knotted carpet (444 × 223 cm.). North Persia, c. 1700. From the Jerreh Pasha mosque in Istanbul. Formerly Istanbul Chinili Kiosk. [52]
    Lit. E. Kühnel, *Die Sammlung türkischer und islamischer Kunst in Tschinili Köschk*, Berlin, 1938, Pl. 36.

133 Woollen knotted carpet (910 × 255 cm.). *F*, India, 17th C. From the Sultan Yildirim Beyazid mosque in Bursa. Formerly Istanbul, Chinili Kiosk Inv. Nr. 3887. [53]
    Lit. E. Kühnel, cf. Nr. 132 above, Pl. 35.

134 Woollen knotted carpet, 'Vase' carpet (640 × 280 cm.). *D*, South Persia, 16th C. From the Mehmed Sokollu Pasha mosque in Istanbul. Formerly Istanbul, Chinili Kiosk Inv. Nr. 38. [54]
    Lit. E. Kühnel, cf. Nr. 132 above, Pl. 34. Carpets which reached Europe through the firms Weise and Mattieu and S. Haim may have come from the Chinili Kiosk.

135 Woollen knotted carpet (525 × 300 cm.). *D*. Caucasus—Northwest Persia, c. 1800. In the Istanbul art trade in 1930. [61]
    Lit. K. Erdmann, *Oriental Carpets*, fig. 112, pp. 48–9. Carpets of this kind were frequent in the Harems of the Palaces and in the mosques in Istanbul.

136 Woollen knotted carpet with central medallion and cartouche design. North-west Persia, c. 1600. In the London art trade. [62]
    Lit. K. Erdmann, *Europa und der Orientteppich*, Berlin Mainz, 1962, p. 100.

137 Silk knotted carpet (203 × 133 cm.). Persia, Isfahan, 17th C. Munich, Bavarian National Museum. [63]

138 Woollen knotted carpet, Ottoman (190 × 147 cm.). Cairo, 16th C. Frankfurt, Kunstgewerbe Museum. [64]
    Lit. K. Erdmann, *Orientalische Teppiche aus vier Jahrhunderten*, exhibition catalogue, Hamburg, 1950, Nr. 6.

139 Woollen knotted carpet, Star Ushak (305 × 185 cm.). Anatolia, first half 17th C. Cologne, Kunstgewerbe Museum. [65]
    Lit. K. Erdmann, *Oriental Carpets*, fig. 142.

140 Woollen knotted carpet (114 × 81 cm.). *F*, India, 17th C. Düsseldorf, City Art Collections. [66]
    Lit. See Nr. 138 above, Nr. 131. The other piece of this carpet is in the Victoria and Albert Museum, London. See A. F. Kendrick and C. E. C. Tattersall, *Handwoven Carpets, Oriental and European*, London, 1922, Pl. 32; F. R. Martin, *A History of Oriental Carpets before 1800*, Vienna, 1908, fig. 221.

141 Woollen knotted carpet, copy of a South Persian design (550 × 190 cm.). *D*, North Persia, 18th C. Essen, Folkwang Museum. *Lit.* See 138 above, catalogue Nr. 108. [67]

142 Silk tapestry carpet (248 × 161 cm.). Persia, Kashan, 17th C. Karlsruhe, Landes Museum. [68]
Lit. K. Erdmann, 'Persische Teppiche der Safawiden Zeit', *Pantheon*, Munich, 1932, pp. 227 ff.; idem, *Orientalische Teppiche aus vier Jahrhunderten*, exhibition catalogue, Hamburg, 1950, pp. 72–3.

143 Silk knotted carpet, 'Polish' carpet (measurements unknown), Persia, Isfahan, 17th C. From the church in Edemissen, Peine district. Hanover, Kestner Museum. [69]

144 Woollen knotted carpet with the arms of the Centurione and Doria (209 × 141 cm.). Anatolia, Ushak district, 17th C. Hamburg, Kunst und Gewerbe Museum. [70]
Lit. See Nr. 142 above, catalogue Nr. 20.

145 Woollen knotted carpet (280 × 175 cm.). Anatolia, Ushak, 17th C. Hamburg, Kunst und Gewerbe Museum. Only burned fragments remain from a similar, larger piece of the type in the Berlin Museums (See Bode-Kühnel, 3rd ed. fig. 74); K. Erdman, *Oriental Carpets*, fig. 40. [71]

146 Silk knotted carpet, 'Polish' carpet (205 × 140 cm.). Persia, Isfahan, 17th C. Hamburg, Kunst und Gewerbe Museum. [72]

147 Woollen knotted carpet (500 × 250 cm.). Anatolia, Ushak, 16th C. Hamburg, Kunst und Gewerbe Museum. Cf. the Count Stroganoff's Ushak (W. v. Bode, *Vorderasiatische Knüpfteppiche aus älterer Zeit*, Leipzig, *c.* 1904, p. 69, fig. 38). [73]

148 Woollen knotted carpet (237 × 153 cm.). North Persia, *c.* 1600. Kunst und Gewerbe Museum, Hamburg. [74]

149 Woollen knotted carpet (360 × 230 cm.). East Persia (?), beginning 17th C. Hamburg, Kunst und Gewerbe Museum. [75]
Lit. K. Erdmann, 'Ein persischer Teppich im Museum für Kunst und Gewerbe', *Jahrbuch der Hamburger Kunstsammlungen*, 1961, VI, pp. 149 ff.; A. U. Pope, *Survey*, Pl. 1215.

150 Woollen knotted carpet on silk foundation (188 × 114 cm.). India, 17th C. Hamburg, Kunst und Gewerbe Museum. [76]

151 Woollen knotted carpet, cut off at the figures above and below (604 × 365 cm.). *D*, *F*, North-west Persia, first half 16th C. Berlin Museums Inv. Nr. I 1. [77]
Lit. Bode-Kühnel, fig. 71 K. Erdmann, *Oriental Carpets*, fig. 50. This piece which was partially burned belongs to carpets woven in pairs. See chapter 'Carpet Pairs'. The companion piece is in the County Museum, Los Angeles; A. U. Pope, *Survey*, Pl. 1128.

152 Woollen knotted carpet (506 × 256 cm.). *D*, North Persia, second half 16th C. Berlin Museum Inv. Nr. KGM 73, 1195. A similar carpet is in the possession of Count Boucquoi in Vienna (Bode-Kühnel, 3rd ed., fig. 11). [78]

153 Woollen knotted carpet (490 × 265 cm.). *D*. Shortened by about 40 cm. North Persia, first half 16th C. Berlin Museums Inv. Nr. I 1313. [79]
Lit. K. Erdmann, *Oriental Carpets*, fig. 60; idem, 'Zwei Medaillonteppiche in der islamischen Abteilung', *Berliner Museen*, 1935, LVI, pp. 32 ff. K. Erdmann, 'Teppicherwerbungen der Islamischen Abteilung', *Berichte aus den preussischen*

Kunstsammlungen, Berlin, 1943, LXIV, p. 7, fig. 2, formerly Weissberger Collection, Madrid; K. Erdmann, *Orientalische Teppiche aus vier Jahrhunderten*, exhibition catalogue, Hamburg, Kunst und Gewerbe Museum, 1950, Cat. Nr. 99; O. Bernheimer, *Alte Teppiche des 16 bis 18 Jahrhunderts der Firma L. Bernheimer*, Munich, 1959, Nr. 87.
There are several related pieces. The Parish Watson carpet (A. U. Pope, *Survey*, Pl. 1120) is similar but, from the form of the shield-shaped pendant, is of later date. A green-ground carpet which I saw in 1937 at Haim's in Istanbul is related. Wulff's fragment, previously owned by Bardini, Florence (A. U. Pope, *Survey*, Pl. 119 in colour) belongs to this group which was formerly numerous. A similar fragment is in the Bardini Museum in Florence (M. and V. Viale, *Arazzi e Tapete Antichi*, Turin, 1952, Pl. 122). Another is in the collection of Dr. Ungar Endré in Budapest (Budapest Exhibition 1936, Cat. Nr. 1). The pieces in the Rath Museum in Budapest and in the Chinili Kiosk in Istanbul are unpublished.

154 Woollen knotted carpet (350 × 260 cm.). *F*, *D*, Central Persia (?) *c.* 1600. Berlin Museums Inv. Nr. KGM 88, 330 [80]
Lit. K. Erdmann, 'The Art of Carpet Making', *Ars Islamica*, Ann Arbor, 1941, VIII, pp. 169 ff.

155 Woollen knotted carpet (545 × 212 cm.). *D*, North Persia, beginning 17th C. Berlin Museums Inv. Nr. KGM 90, 10. [81]

156 Woollen knotted carpet (306 × 230 cm.). *F*, *D*, South Persia, 16th C. Berlin Museums Inv. Nr. I 5055. [82]
Lit. K. Erdmann, *Oriental Carpets*, Pl. IV, in colour. Sarre-Trenkwald, II, Pl. IX, in colour.

157 Woollen knotted carpet, 'Vase' carpet (540 × 235 cm.). *D*, South or Central (?) Persia, first half 16th C. Berlin Museums Inv. Nr. I 2656. [83]
Lit. A. U. Pope, *Survey*, Pl. 1229. A companion piece formerly in the collection of Lady Baillie (A. U. Pope, *Survey*, Pl. 1225, in colour. Another in the Cl. H. Mackay Collection, Sarre-Trenkwald, II, Pl. 7 and A. U. Pope, *Survey*, Pl. 1222). The Berlin piece was destroyed during the war, and the Mackay piece is in the Baltimore Museum.

158 Woollen knotted carpet, 'Portuguese' carpet (500 × 252 cm.). *D*, Persia, 17th C. Berlin Museums Inv. Nr. KGM 87, 974. [84]

159 Woollen knotted carpet (410 × 294 cm.). *F*, *D*, East Persia, 17th C. Berlin Museums Inv. Nr. KGM 99, 315. [85]

160 Woollen knotted carpet, 'Garden' carpet (630 × 300 cm.). *D*, *F*, North-west Persia, 18th C. Berlin Museums Inv. Nr. I 3089. [86]

161 Woollen knotted carpet, 'Dragon' carpet (678 × 230 cm.). *D*, Caucasus, early 16th C. Berlin Museums Inv. Nr. I 3. [87]
Lit. Sarre-Trenkwald, II, Pl. 3.

162 Woollen knotted carpet, 'Dragon' carpet (572 × 268 cm.). *D*, Caucasus, *c.* 1600. Berlin Museums Inv. Nr. KGM 81, 1018. [88]

163 Woollen carpet (228 × 228 cm.). *F*, Caucasus or North-west Persia, 17th C. Berlin Museums Inv. Nr. I 13. Cf. the Cartouche carpet in the McIlhenny Collection (K. Erdmann, *Oriental Carpets*, fig. 122). [89]

164 Woollen knotted carpet (313 × 187 cm.). Caucasus, end 18th C. Berlin Museums Inv. Nr. I 2840. [90]

165 Woollen knotted carpet, Ottoman carpet (290 × 217 cm.). Cairo, c. 1540–50. Berlin Museums Inv. Nr. I 10. [91]
Lit. K. Erdmann, 'Kairener Teppiche', *Ars Islamica*, Ann Arbor, 1938, V, pp. 179 ff. and 1940, VII, pp. 55 ff; idem, *Oriental Carpets*, fig. 129.

166 Woollen knotted carpet, Ottoman carpet (415 × 287 cm.). Cairo or Istanbul, c. 1600. Berlin Museums Inv. Nr. I 30. [92]
Lit. Sarre-Trenkwald, II, Pl. 53 (detail).

167 Woollen knotted carpet (430 × 268 cm.). *D*, Asia Minor, Ushak, 16th–17th C. Berlin Museums Inv. Nr. I 7. [93]

168 Woollen knotted carpet (436 × 229 cm.). *D*, Asia Minor, Ushak, 16th C. Berlin Museums Inv. Nr. I 19. K. Erdmann, *Orientteppiche*, fig. 42, in colour. [94]

169 Woollen knotted carpet (192 × 116 cm.). Kurdistan, 17th or 18th C. Berlin Museums Inv. Nr. I 946. [95]
Lit. K. Erdmann, *Orientteppiche*, fig. 26; F. Sarre, 'The Hittite Monument of Ivriz and a Carpet Design', *The Burlington Magazine*, London, 1908, XIV, pp. 113 ff.

170 Woollen knotted carpet (293 × 165 cm.). Spain, Alcaraz (?) end 15th C. Berlin Museums Inv. Nr. 90, 90. [96]
Lit. E. Kühnel, 'Maurische Teppiche aus Alcaraz', *Pantheon*, Munich, 1930, pp. 416 ff; K. Erdmann, *Oriental Carpets*, fig. 179.

171 Woollen knotted carpet, 'Animal' carpet (155 × 161 cm.). *D*, *F*, North Persia, 2nd half 16th C. Berlin Museums Inv. Nr. 73, 1198. Cf. the two carpets from the shrine of Ardebil, Bode-Kühnel, fig. 85. [97]

172 Woollen knotted carpet, Medallion carpet (167 × 167 cm.). *F*, North Persia, Tabriz (?), mid-16th C. Berlin Museums Inv. Nr. KGM 05, 120. [98]

173 Woollen knotted carpet Medallion carpet (402 × 180 cm.). *D*, North Persia, Tabriz, 16th C. Berlin Museums Inv. Nr. I 32. [99]
Lit. K. Erdmann, *Oriental Carpets*, fig. 59.

174 Silk knotted carpet, brocaded in gold and silver, 'Polish' carpet, (210 × 143 cm.). Central Persia, Isfahan, first half 17th C. Berlin Museums Inv. Nr. KGM 84, 495. [100]
Lit. K. Erdmann, *Orientteppiche*, Nr. 13.

175 Woollen knotted carpet, 'Isfahan' carpet (265 × 180 cm.). East Persia, Herat (?), c. 1600, Berlin Museums Inv. Nr. I 33. [101]
Lit. K. Erdmann, *Orientteppiche*, Nr. 12.

176 Woollen knotted carpet, 'Tree' carpet (197 × 130 cm.). North-west Persia, c. 1700. Berlin Museums Inv. Nr. I 25. [102]
Lit. K. Erdmann, *Orientteppiche*, Nr. 9.

177 Woollen knotted carpet, 'Holbein' carpet (242 × 137 cm.). Asia Minor, Ushak district, 16th C. Berlin Museums Inv. Nr. I 11. [103]
Lit. K. Erdmann, *Orientteppiche*, Nr. 30.

178 Woollen knotted carpet, 'Holbein' carpet (334 × 186 cm.). Asia Minor, Ushak district, 16th C. Berlin Museums Inv. Nr. I 21. [104]
Lit. K. Erdmann, *Orientteppiche*, Nr. 31. Carpets of this kind were included in pictures by Italian masters several decades before Holbein depicted them. Because this type appears in a painting by Lorenzo Lotto it is customary in America today to refer to these carpets as 'Lotto' carpets instead of 'Anatolian Arabesque' carpets. See Bode-Kühnel, *Vorderasiatische Knüpfteppiche*, 4th ed., figs. 17 and 19, for the naming of this group; *Heimtex*, 1957, IX, where W. Grote-Hasenbalg proposed calling this type 'Lattice carpets', a term which is insufficiently clear to be acceptable, though it defines certain peculiarities of the design; C. G. Ellis, Bode-Kühnel, 1958 (English edition), fig. 19 'Turkish Arabesque Carpet (Lotto Rug)'. The term 'Lotto' rug was first used by J. G. Lettenmaier *Das grosse Teppichbuch*, Munich, 1962; A. Riegl, *Orientalische Teppiche*, Vienna, 1891, p. 65; H. Jacoby, *Eine Sammlung Orientalischer Teppiche*, Berlin, 1923, p. 116; K. Erdmann, *Orientteppiche*, p. 13, Nr. 31; M. S. Dimand, *The Ballard Collection of Oriental Rugs in the City Art Museum of St. Louis*, St. Louis, 1935, Pl. 20; K. Erdmann, *Orientalische Teppiche aus vier Jahrhunderten*, exhibition catalogue, Hamburg, Kunst und Gewerbe Museum, Cat. Nr. 20; S. Troll, *Altorientalische Teppiche*, Österreichisches Museum für Angewandte Kunst, p. 14; M. Viale and V. Viale, *Arazzi e Tappeti Antichi*, Turin, 1952, p. 229 'ottagoni . . . con altrettante, figure intermedie a forma di croce'.

179 Woollen knotted carpet, Mamluk carpet (315 × 230 cm.). Cairo, beg. 16th C. Berlin Museums Inv. Nr. KGM 83, 571. [105]
Lit. K. Erdmann, 'Kairener Teppiche', *Ars Islamica*, Ann Arbor, 1938, V, pp. 179 ff. and 1940, VII, pp. 55 ff.

180 Woollen knotted carpet, 'Garden' carpet (310 × 178 cm.). North-west Persia, 18th C. Berlin Museums Inv. Nr. I 2239. [106]
Lit. K. Erdmann, *Orientteppiche*, Nr. 19; idem *Oriental Carpets*, fig. 125. In this carpet the fish in the central canal have become flowers and at the sides remnants of canal alternate with flower beds. Cf. Figs. 70–73.

181 Woollen knotted carpet, 'Synagogue' carpet (303 × 94 cm.). *D*, Spain 14th–15th C. Berlin Museums Inv. Nr. I 27. [107]
Lit. K. Erdmann, *Orientteppiche*, Nr. 45; F. Sarre, 'A Fourteenth Century Spanish "Synagogue" carpet', *The Burlington Magazine*, London, 1930, LVI, pp. 89–95.

182 Silk knotted carpet with gold and silver brocading, 'Polish' carpet (210 × 143 cm.). Persia, Isfahan, 17th C. Berlin Museums Inv. Nr. I 23. [108]
Lit. K. Erdmann, *Oriental Carpets*, fig. 82; idem, *Orientteppiche* Nr. 14; the pair to this carpet is illustrated by A. U. Pope, *Catalogue of a Loan Exhibition of early Oriental Rugs*, Chicago, 1926, Nr. 26.

183 Woollen knotted carpet (220 × 128 cm.). North Persia, c. 1600. Berlin Museums Inv. Nr. I 1934. [110]
Lit. K. Erdmann, *Orientteppiche*, Nr. 7. Cf. Figs. 155 and 173,

184 Woollen knotted carpet, 'Holbein' carpet (159 × 89 cm.). *F*, Asia Minor, Ushak, 15th C. Berlin Museums Inv. Nr. I. 6737. [111]
Lit. K. Erdmann, 'Neuerwerbungen der Islamischen Abteilung', *Berliner Museen*, 1940, LXI, pp. 47 ff. Fig. 2; B. Scheunemann 'Teppiche im sogenannten kleinen Holbeinmuster', *Forschungen und Berichte*, Berlin, 1958, II, p. 68. Cf. K. Erdmann, *Orientalische Teppiche aus vier Jahrhunderten*, exhibition catalogue, Kunst und Gewerbe Museum, Hamburg, 1950, Cat. Nr. 18; M. S. Dimand, *The Ballard Collection of Oriental Rugs in the City Art Museum of St. Louis*, St. Louis, 1935, Pl. XIV. For a Spanish copy of such a carpet see Fig. 271. Another frag-

ment is in the Palazzo Salvadore in Florence. In carpets of this type the octagons occur in two colours. Only in one piece in the Brukenthal Museum in Hermannstadt (Sibiu) three colours are found. (Illustrated by J. de Vegh-C. Layer in *Tapis Turcs*, Paris, n.d., Pl. 1.)

185 Woollen knotted carpet, 'Holbein' carpet (170 × 113 cm.). Asia Minor, Bergama district, 17th C. Berlin Museums Inv. Nr. I 29. [112]
   Lit. K. Erdmann, *Orientteppiche*, Nr. 28; idem, *Oriental Carpets*, fig. 37.

186 Woollen knotted carpet (294 × 165 cm.). Asia Minor, Ushak, 17th C. Berlin Museums Inv. Nr. I 9.   [113]
   Lit. K. Erdmann, *Orientteppiche*, Nr. 41.

187 Woollen knotted carpet, Prayer rug (172 × 127 cm.). Istanbul or Bursa, *c.* 1600. Berlin Museums Inv. Nr. KGM 89, 156.   [114]
   Lit. K. Erdmann 'Kairener Teppiche, Part II, Mamluken und Osmanen Teppiche', *Ars Islamica*, Ann Arbor, 1940, VII, pp. 55 ff.; idem, 'Weitere Beiträge zur Frage der Kairener Teppiche', *Berliner Museen*, new series, 1959, IX, pp. 12 ff.; E. Kühnel and L. Bellinger, *Catalogue of Cairene Rugs and Others Technically Related*, Textile Museum, Washington, 1957.

188 Woollen knotted carpet, Mamluk carpet (196 × 130 cm.). *F*, Cairo, beginning 16th C. Berlin Museums Inv. Nr. KGM 91, 26. [115]
   Lit. K. Erdmann, *Orientteppiche*, Nr. 35.

189 Woollen knotted carpet (396 × 398 cm.). *F*, Caucasus, 16th–17th C. Berlin Museums Inv. Nr. I 12.   [116]
   Lit. K. Erdmann, *Orientteppiche*, Nr. 24; Sarre-Trenkwald, II, Pl. 5.

190 Woollen knotted carpet, Prayer rug, Turkish Court Manufacture (183 × 122 cm.). Istanbul or Bursa, dated 1610–11. Berlin Museums Inv. Nr. I 15, 64.   [119]
   Lit. Bode-Kühnel, p. 78, fig. 51; K. Erdmann, *Oriental Carpets*, fig. 139; idem, 'Weitere Beiträge zur Frage der Kairener Teppiche' *Berliner Museen*, new series, 1959, IX, pp. 12 ff.

191 Woollen knotted carpet, 'Holbein' carpet (226 × 230 cm.). *D*, *F*, Asia Minor, Ushak district, 16th C. Berlin Museums Inv. Nr. KGM 86, 1172.   [121]

192 Woollen knotted carpet, Medallion Ushak (350 × 190 cm.). *D*, Asia Minor, *c.* 1700. Berlin Museums Inv. Nr. I 4928.   [123] Cf. chapter 'Carpets with European Blazons'.

193 Woollen knotted carpet, 'Garden' carpet (270 × 170 cm.). North-west Persia, 18th C. Berlin Museums Inv. Nr. KGM 82. 706. Cf. chapter 'Garden Carpets'.   [125]

194 Woollen knotted carpet (427 × 195 cm.). *D*, Spain, 15th C. Berlin Museums Inv. Nr. KGM 86, 602.   [126]

195 Woollen knotted carpet (447 × 226 cm.). Persia, Tabriz or Qazvin, *c.* 1600. Berlin Museums Inv. Nr. I 7/56. (From the A. Cassirer Collection.)   [127]
   Lit. Bode-Kühnel, fig. 74. The A. Cassirer Collection is at present in the Art Institute, Detroit.

196 Woollen knotted carpet, Medallion carpet (224 × 198 cm.). *F*, North Persia, Tabriz, 16th C. Berlin Museums Inv. Nr. I 32/60. [128]
   Lit. See literature under fig. 154: *Berliner Museen*, 1963, XII, pp. 40 ff.

197 Woollen knotted carpet, 'Dragon' carpet (290 × 160 cm.). Caucasus, end 18th C. Berlin Museums Inv. Nr. I 8/59.   [129]
   Lit. K. Erdmann, *Oriental Carpets*, fig. 99; Cf. Figs. 161, 162, pl. VII above; idem, 'Later Caucasian Dragon Carpets', *Apollo*, London, 1935, XXII, pp. 21–25.

198 Woollen knotted carpet, 'Holbein' carpet (118 × 114 cm.). *F*, West Anatolia, 16th C. Berlin Museums Inv. Nr. I 33/60.   [130]
   Lit. See chapter on 'Holbein' carpets, pp. 52 ff. O. Bernheimer, *Alte Teppiche des 16 bis 18 Jahrhunderts der Firma L. Bernheimer*, Munich, 1959, fig. 2; K. Erdmann, 'Teppicherwerbungen der Islamichen Abteilung', *Berliner Museen*, 1962, XII, part 2, fig. 3. Cf. K. Erdmann, *Oriental Carpets*, fig. 45.

199 Woollen knotted carpet (185 × 118 cm.). West Anatolia, Ushak, 17th C. Berlin Museums Inv. Nr. I 9/60.   [131]
   Lit. K. Erdmann, 'Teppicherwerbungen der Islamichen Abteilung', *Berliner Museen*, 1962, XII, part 2, fig. 3; U. Schürmann, *Bilderbuch für Teppichsammler*, Munich, 1960, Pl. 5.

200 Woollen knotted carpet (130 × 107 cm.). Border *F*, *D*, South Persia, beginning 17th C. Formerly Sarre Collection, Berlin Musems Inv. Nr. I 67/62.   [136]

201 Woollen knotted carpet (253 × 213 cm.). *D*, India, 17th C. Berlin Museums Inv. Nr. I 41/63.   [138]

202 Woollen knotted carpet (250 × 232 cm.). *F*, Anatolia, Ushak, 16th C. Berlin Museums Inv. Nr. I 72/62.   [139]

203 Woollen knotted carpet (390 × 170 cm.). Morocco, 19th C. Berlin Museums Inv. Nr. I 76/62. See P. Ricard, *Corpus des Tapis Marocains*, Paris, 1923–27.   [141]

204 Woollen knotted carpet with silver and perhaps gold brocading (see below), *D*, 'Animal' carpet, Persia. Tabriz, 2nd half 16th C. Baron E. de Rothschild Collection.   [220]
   Two of the four Animal carpets from this collection were exhibited in Paris in 1893 and on that occasion were discussed by G. Marye in the *Gazette des Beaux Arts*, Paris, 1894, p. 70. The same pieces were again exhibited in Paris in 1903 at the 'Exposition du Pavillon de Marsan', cat. Nr. 667/668. This exhibition was discussed by G. Migeon in the *Gazette des Beaux Arts*, 1903, XIX, p. 366 and *Les Arts Livr.* 1903, XVI, p. 30 and by F. Sarre in the *Repertorium für Kunstwissenschaft*, Stuttgart, 1903, XXVI, p. 532. Unfortunately neither illustrations nor exact descriptions are included, which makes identification difficult. All four carpets are of the same type and it is to be asumed that they are knotted in wool on a silk foundation, as is customary in this type. Should the pile be of silk, as suggested in the publications above, it would be unusual. Probably some details such as the script and some flowers were brocaded in silver. This type is extant in a number of examples and can be divided into two groups. Closely related is a carpet in the von Pannwitz Collection in Schloss Hartekamp (Holland) and a fragment in the Carrand Collection in the Bargello in Florence. On the other hand the Rothschild carpets are also related to a number of pieces which can be grouped round the Salting carpet in the Victoria and Albert Museum. If the four Rothschild carpets belong to the first group, they must have been made during the second half of the sixteenth century in North-west Persia, probably Tabriz. If they belong to the second group, they are Turkish copies of carpets of the first group, and were made about 1800. (From the author's notes of 1938.)

205 Woollen knotted carpet with brocading (on silk foundation) (250 × 170 cm.). Persia, Tabriz, 16th C. Paris, Musée des Arts Décoratifs. [221]

Lit. M. Koechlin-R. Migeon, *Cent Planches d'Art Musulman*, Paris, n.d., Pl. LXXXVI; A. U. Pope, *Survey*, *Pl.* 1146; Free translation of the verses by Wahrmund in A. Riegl, *Orientalische Teppiche*, Vienna, 1892, Pl. LXXI; Cf. verses from well-known poets in an Animal carpet fragment in the Bardini Museum in Florence and in the Salting carpet in the Victoria and Albert Museum; the verse (trans. M. Hassan) in a brocaded silk carpet in the Arab Museum Cairo (F. Sarre, *Altorientalische Teppiche*, Vienna, 1908, Pl. II); the verse (trans. H. Demel) in a Persian Animal carpet in the Angewandte Kunst Museum, Vienna (Sarre-Trenkwald, I, Pl. 6); the verse (trans. Wahrmund) in the carpet in the Gobelins Museum, Paris (A. Riegl, *Orientalische Teppiche*, Vienna, 1892, Pl. LXXIV). The following verse occurs in the Tree carpet in the Poldi Pezzoli Museum in Milan (Sarre-Trenkwald, II, Pl. 29): 'Happy is the carpet which, during the longed-for banquet, lies like a shadow under the King's feet' and 'A carpet is like a tulip hedge, which cannot be harmed by the autumn wind'. Cf. also the verse in the carpet in Leningrad (A. Riegl, *Orientalische Teppiche*, Vienna, 1892, Pl. XI) and the words in the carpet of the Rothschild Collection in Paris (idem, Pl. XCVII).

206 Woollen knotted carpet with brocading (225 × 158 cm.). Persia, 2nd half 16th C. Formerly von Pannwitz Collection, Schloss Hartekamp, Holland. [222]

Lit. K. Erdmann, *Oriental Carpets*, fig. 53; Sarre-Trenkwald, II, Pl. 35.

207 Woollen knotted carpet, 'Hunting' carpet (570 × 365 cm.). *D*, Persia, Tabriz, signed Ghiyath eddin Jami, dated 949 H. (A.D. 1542/3), Milan, Poldi Pezzoli Museum. [224]

Lit. K. Erdmann, *Oriental Carpets*, fig. 52; Sarre-Trenkwald, II, Pl. 22, 23 detail in colour; A. U. Pope, *Survey*, Pl. 118.

208 Detail of the above. [225]

209 Detail of Vienna 'Hunting' carpet. [226]

210 Chronogram in the upper border of the Prayer carpet, Fig. 190. [227]

211 Woollen knotted carpet, Kurdish copy of a Caucasian 'Dragon' carpet (435 × 180 cm.). *D*, signed Hasan Beg, dated Muharram 1101 H. (Oct. A.D. 1689), Washington, Textile Museum. [228]

Lit. K. Erdmann, *Oriental Carpets*, fig. 101.

212 Woollen knotted carpet. Persia, signed Ustad Yusuf Kermani 1191 H. (A.D. 1776/7) *D*, Belgrade, private possession. [229]

Lit. K. Erdmann, 'The Art of Carpet Making', *Ars Islamica*, Ann Arbor, 1941 VIII, p. 130, fig. 1; cf. the dated carpet of the Princess Lichnowsky (H. Jacoby, *Eine Sammlung orientalischer Teppiche*, Berlin, 1923, fig. 17), and the carpet signed by Riza the Kermani (J. de Vegh and C. Layer, *Tapis Turcs provenant des églises et collections de Transylvanie*, Paris, n.d., c. 1925).

213 Woollen knotted carpet, Arabesque carpet (437 × 142 cm.). *D*, Persia, dated 1794, New York, McMullan Collection. [230]

214 Woollen knotted carpet, Prayer rug (155 × 133 cm.). Anatolia, Ushak district, dated 1721. [231]

215 Woollen knotted carpet (198 × 115 cm.). Anatolia, Ladik, dated 1794. New York, Metropolitan Museum. [232]

216 Woollen knotted carpet. Anatolia, Ghiordes with embroidered inscription M. Hissen 1736. In the Evangelical Church, Rosenau, Transylvania. [233]

Lit. E. Schmutzler, *Altorientalische Teppiche in Siebenbürgen*, Leipzig, 1933, Pl. 33.

217 Woollen knotted carpet, Caucasus, Kazak, dated 1331 H. (A.D. 1913), Hamburg, private possession. [234]

218 Woollen knotted carpet (130 × 75 cm.). Caucasus, Daghestan, dated 1293 H. (A.D. 1876/7). South Germany, private possession. [235]

Lit. K. Erdmann, *Orientalische Teppiche aus vier Jahrhunderten*, exhibition catalogue, Hamburg, Kunst und Gewerbe Museum, 1950, Nr. 118.

219 Woollen knotted carpet, Prayer rug (156 × 117 cm.). Caucasus, Daghestan, dated 1284 H. (A.D. 1867/8). North Germany, private possession. [236]

Lit. K. Erdmann, *Oriental Carpets*, fig. 110; catalogue, Hamburg (cf. 218 above) Nr. 117.

220 Woollen knotted carpet. North-west Persia, Tabriz, 16th C. Brooklyn Museum, cf. Fig. 82; a further fragment of this carpet is in the Musée des Tissus in Lyons, Inv. Nr. 674. [327]

Lit. J. K. Mumford, *The Yerkes Collection of Oriental Carpets*, New York, 1910, Pl. VII, in colour. E. Kühnel (*Berliner Museen*, new series, VIII, 1957, p. 11) suggests that, besides Tabriz which was occupied several times by the Turks in the 16th century the new capital Qazvin also had a court manufactory of carpets.

221 Woollen knotted carpet (256 × 256 cm.). *D*, *F*, India, 16th C. Glasgow Art Gallery, Burrell Collection. [238]

Lit. K. Erdmann, *Oriental Carpets*, fig. 170; May H. Beattie, 'The Burrell Collection of Oriental Rugs', *Oriental Art*, London, 1961, new series, VII, pp. 3 ff.

222 Woollen knotted carpet, border fragment. India 16th–17th C. Glasgow Art Gallery, Burrell Collection. [239]

Lit. May H. Beattie, 'The Burrell Collection of Oriental Rugs', *Oriental Art*, London, 1961, new series, VII, Nr. 4, p. 3; K. Erdmann, 'Der Indische Knüpfteppich', *Indologen-Tagung 1959*, p. 104. A second frgament is in Stockholm in the National Museum. 'The design of these border fragments is said to be based on the legendary Wak Wak or Talking Tree. According to the Emperor Akbar's biographer the weaving of fine carpets began in India during his reign (1556–1605) so that such pieces could hardly have been woven much before the end of the 16th or the beginning of the 17th century'. Catalogue *The Rug in Islamic Art*, Leeds, Temple Newsam House Museum, 1964, Nr. 35.

223 Silk knotted carpet (360 × 135 cm.). India, 17th C. Put together from two pieces, the smaller of which was bought in Madrid in 1871 and the larger in Paris in 1888. [240]

Lit. Goupil Auction, 1888, Pl. 4; W. von Bode und E. Kühnel, *Vorderasiatische Knüpfteppiche aus alter Zeit*, fig. 48; idem, 1921, fig. 53 (the mistake of locating this carpet in the Musée des Arts Décoratifs in Paris arose from an error in the account of the Goupil auction, in the *Revue des Arts Décoratifs*, Paris, 1888/9, p. 216).

224 Woollen knotted carpet (estimated to be 2100 × 900 cm.). *F*, India, 17th C. Said to come from the Chihil Sutun in Isfahan. Formerly Haim Collection in Istanbul. [241]

225 Silk tapestry carpet (whole piece *c.* 450 × 240 cm.). *F*, Persia, Kashan, *c.* 1600. Formerly Dresden Kunstgewerbe Museum. [242]

Lit. 'Persische Wirkteppiche der Safawidenzeit', *Pantheon*, Munich, 1932, V, pp. 227 ff. The middle section of this carpet is in Cologne, Kunstgewerbe Museum (K. Erdmann, *Europa und der Orientteppich*, Berlin/Mainz, 1962, fig. 49).

226 Woollen knotted carpet, Ottoman carpet (200 × 213 cm.). *F*, Cairo, 16th–17th C. London, Victoria and Albert Museum. [243]
  Lit. K. Erdmann, *Oriental Carpets*, fig. 134; A. F. Kendrick and C. E. C. Tattersall, *Handwoven Carpets, Oriental and European*, II, Pl. 39.

227 Woollen knotted carpet, Ottoman carpet. Cairo 16–17th C. Paris, Musée des Arts Décoratifs. [244]
  Lit. A. Riegl, *Altorientalische Teppiche*, Vienna, 1892–5, Pl. 68.

228 Woollen knotted carpet, Ottoman carpet (248 × 436 cm.). *F*, Cairo, 16th–17th C. Vienna, Angewandte Kunst Museum. [245]
  Lit. C. G. Ellis, 'Gifts from Kashan to Cairo', *Textile Museum Journal*, Washington, Nov. 1962, p. 33.

229 Woollen knotted carpet (333 × 178 cm.). *D*, Persia, Tabriz, 16th C. From the shrine of Ardebil. Formerly Sarre Collection. New York, Metropolitan Museum. [246]
  Lit. Sarre-Trenkwald, II, Pl. 38; Bode-Kühnel, fig. 85; F. Sarre, *Altorientalische Teppiche*, Leipzig, 1908, Pl. VII, in colour. The pair is also in the Metropolitan Museum (formerly Rockefeller Collection).

230 Woollen knotted carpet, Ottoman carpet (190 × 132 cm.). Cairo, 17th C. Berlin Museums Inv. Nr. I 6355. [249]
  Lit. K. Erdmann, *Oriental Carpets*, fig. 135; the design only occurs occasionally, mostly in larger carpets (carpet in the Museum of Cairo University and fragment in the Victoria and Albert Museum).

231 Woollen knotted carpet with duplicated medallion design, 'The Chelsea carpet' (540 × 316 cm.). *D*, North-west Persia, Tabriz, mid-16th C. London, Victoria and Albert Museum. [250]
  Lit. K. Erdmann, *Oriental Carpets*, Pl. III; Sarre-Trenkwald, II, Pls. 15, 16, detail in colour. The name arose from the fact that the Museum acquired the carpet from a dealer in the Chelsea district of London.

232 Woollen knotted carpet (300 × 292 cm.). *F*, *D*, Persia, second half 16th C. Florence, Bardini Museum. Based on the design of the 'Chelsea carpet', see above. [251]
  Lit. K. Erdmann, 'Il Tappeto con figure d'animali nel Museo Bardini a Firenze', *Dedalo*, Milan, XI, March 1931, pp. 647 ff. For further examples of design relationships cf. the white-ground carpet of Count Boucquoi in Vienna (Bode-Kühnel, 3rd. ed. fig. 11), and Fig. 152 for a later variation of the design; the silk Kashan carpet in the Gulbenkian Collection (K. Erdmann, *Oriental Carpets*, fig. 69), also the fragmentary replica knotted in wool in the Musée des Arts Décoratifs in Paris, formerly O. Homberg Collection (*Les Arts*, Paris, 1904, 36, p. 47); the Animal carpet of Count Schwarzenberg, Vienna (Bode-Kühnel, 3rd ed. fig. 13) with the carpet in the Hermitage, Leningrad (Catalogue of the Islamic Collections, 1952, Pl. 18, in Russian); the carpet in the Mortimer Schiff Collection (K. Erdmann, 'Ein wiedergefundener Teppich', *Ars Islamica*, Ann Arbor, 1934, I, pp. 121 ff.) with the carpet in the Gobelins Museum, Paris (A. Riegl, *Orientalische Teppiche*, Vienna, 1892, Pl. 74); the pair of Shah Abbas carpets, 'Polish' carpets, of Mrs. Rainey Rogers (A. U. Pope, *Survey*, Pl. 1261) and the pair of which one is in the Deering Collection and the other in Hardwick Hall. (A. U. Pope, *Survey*, Pl. 1246).

233 Silk knotted carpet (124 × 109 cm.). Persia, Kashan, 16th C. Paris, Louvre. [252]

234 Woollen knotted carpet (505 × 240 cm.). *D*, North Persia, 16th C. Milan, Poldi Pezzoli Museum. [253]
  Lit. Sarre-Trenkwald, II, Pl. 29, 30, detail in colour; A. U. Pope, *Survey*, Pl. 1154.

235 Woollen knotted carpet, Wagireh (pattern sample) for a carpet in the Ferahan design (142 × 102 cm.). Sultanabad or Hamadan district, *c.* 1900. Hamburg, Kunst und Gewerbe Museum. [254]

236 Woollen knotted carpet, Wagireh, probably for an Anatolian carpet (95 × 54 cm.). Turkey, *c.* 1870. Sweden, private possession. [255]

237 Woollen knotted carpet, Wagireh for a Bijar. Persia, 19th C. [256]
  Lit. G. Griffin Lewis, *Practical Book of Oriental Rugs*, Philadelphia/London, 1911, p. 318.

238 Woollen knotted carpet, Wagireh for a Heriz. Persia, end 19th C. [257]
  Lit. W. Grote-Hasenbalg, *Der Orientteppich, seine Geschichte und seine Kultur*, Berlin, 1922, p. 118, fig. 70.

239 Woollen knotted carpet, Wagireh for a Bijar, Persia, 19th or 20th C. [258]
  Lit. A. U. Dilley, *Oriental Rugs and Carpets, a Comprehensive Study*, New York/London, 1931, p. 102, Pl. XXIII.

240 Woollen knotted carpet, Wagireh with a Herati design. Persia, 19th C. [259]
  Lit. Henry Hildebrand, *Der persische Teppiche und seine Heimat*, Zurich, 1951, pp. 28 ff.; cf. A. E. Hangeldian, *Tappeti d'Oriente*, Milan, 1959, p. 22.

241 Woollen knotted carpet, 20th C. Wagireh after a Persian carpet of the 17th C. (see 242) Petag Ltd., Frankfurt. [260]

242 Silk knotted carpet, Persia. One of this set of rugs from the Mausoleum of Shah Abbas II in Qum is dated 1670/71. (See A. U. Pope, *Survey*, Pl. 1259a.) [261]

243 Woollen knotted carpet (84 × 70 cm.). Wagireh for an Anatolian carpet, Turkey, end 19th C. Berlin Museums Inv. Nr. I 9, 59. [262]

244 Woollen knotted carpet. Wagireh for a North Persian carpet. 18th C. *c.* 1930 in the Rhineland trade. [263]

245 Woollen knotted carpet (135 × 85 cm.). Wagireh for a Caucasian carpet, Berlin Museums Inv. Nr. I 24/61. [264]

246 Woollen knotted carpet. Wagireh for a Medallion Ushak (?). *c.* 1946 in the Stockholm trade. [265]

247 Woollen knotted carpet (142 × 97 cm.). Wagireh (?) for a Seichur carpet, Kuba, beg. 19th C. (?). Cologne, Dr. U. Schürmann. [266]

248 Woollen knotted carpet (176 × 162 cm.). Wagireh for a Persian Arabesque carpet, probably *c.* 1800. Florence Sundt Collection. [267]

249 Detail of Fig. 213. [268]

250 Woollen knotted carpet (311 × 130 cm.). *F*, Multiple-niche prayer rug. Anatolia, Bergama district, 16th C. Istanbul, Türk ve Islam Eserleri Museum Inv. Nr. 744. [269]

Lit. Türkische Kunst, exhibition catalogue, Darmstadt, 1965, Nr. 6; O. Aslanapa, *Turkish Arts*, Istanbul, 1960, Pl. 13, in colour.

251 Woollen knotted carpet (242 × 272 cm.). Ottoman carpet, Cairo, 16th C. Formerly L. Bernheimer Ltd., Munich; In the Cologne art trade in 1960. [270]

Lit. K. Erdmann, *Oriental Carpets*, fig. 131; A survey of the literature in K. Erdmann, 'Neuere Untersuchungen zur Frage der Kairener Teppiche', *Ars Orientalis*, Ann Arbor, 1961, IV, pp. 65 ff.; Cf. the correspondence between Albrecht Dürer and Willibald Pirkheimer about the square shape of the carpet (K. Erdmann, *Europa und der Orientteppich*, Berlin/Mainz, 1962, p. 49).

252 Woollen knotted carpet (diameter *c*. 300 cm.). Mamluk carpet, Cairo, 16th C. This carpet is published here for the first time by courtesy of Sg. Piero Barbiero of Genoa; cf. the round Ottoman carpet in the Corcoran Gallery of Art, Washington (K. Erdmann, *Europa und der Orienttepich*, Berlin/Mainz, 1962, fig. 27). [271]

253 Woollen knotted carpet in form of a cross with European arms. Ottoman carpet, Cairo 16th C. San Gimignano, Communale Museum; Cf. a fragment of a cross-shaped carpet in the stores of the Berlin Museums (K. Erdmann, 'Weitere Beiträge zur Frage der Kairener Teppiche', *Berliner Museen*, new series, 1959, IX, pp. 12 ff). [272]

254 Woollen knotted carpet of unusual shape. India 17th C. Many such shaped carpets are in the possession of the Maharaja of Jaipur. Cf. the design in Fig. 101. [273]

255 Woollen knotted carpet. Cross-shaped 'Vase' carpet, South Persia, 16th C. From the mosque in Qum. [274]

256 Silk knotted carpet (188 × 127 cm.). Persia. Signed by Ni'matullah from Joshegan, dated 1082 H. (A.D. 1671) from the mausoleum of Shah Abbas II at the mosque in Qum. [275]

Lit. A. U. Pope, *Survey*, Pl. 1258A. See Bode-Kühnel, fig. 103.

257 Silk knotted carpet, 12 sided. *D*, Persia, 17th C. From the mausoleum of Shah Abbas II in the mosque in Qum. [276]

258 Woollen knotted carpet, octagonal. Persia, end 17th C. Formerly Satterwhite Collection. [277]

259 Woollen knotted carpet, 'Triclinium' carpet. Persia, 19th C. In the American art trade in 1914. [278]

260 Silk knotted carpet, Shah abbas carpet, 'Polish' carpet, with unidentified European arms (482 × 217 cm.). *D*, Persia, 17th C. Formerly in the possession of the Czartoryski family. New York, Metropolitan Museum. [279]

Lit. Mańkowski, *Polskie Tkaniny i Hafty XVI–XVIII*, Wieku, Wroclaw, 1954.

261 Silk tapestry carpet with the Polish arms of King Sigismund III (Vasa) (238 × 132 cm.). *D*, Persia, Kashan, datable 1601/2. Munich, Residenz Museum Inv. Nr. Wc3. [280]

Lit. T. Mańkowski, 'Note on the Cost of Kashan Carpets at the Beginning of the Seventeenth Century', *Bulletin of the American Institute for Persian Art and Archaeology*, New York, 1936, VI, pp. 152 ff.

262 Woollen knotted carpet with the arms of the English family Montagu (275 × 183 cm.). One of a set, two of which are dated 1584 and 1585 respectively, in European figures in the end kilim. European, perhaps Flemish copy of an Anatolian carpet. Duke of Buccleuch and Queensberry. [281]

Lit. C. E. C. Tattersall, *A History of English Carpets*, London, 1934; May H. Beattie, 'Britain and the Oriental Carpet', *Leeds Arts Calendar*, 1964, Nr. 55, pp. 4 ff.

263 Woollen knotted carpet, 'Bird' carpet, with the arms of the Archbishop of Lwow (Lemberg) (284 × 188 cm.). Anatolia, Ushak, beginning 17th C. Stockholm, Lundgren Collection. [282]

Lit. C. J. Lamm, 'Ein türkischer Wappenteppich in schwedischem Besitz', *Kunst des Orients*, Wiebaden, 1955, II, pp. 59 ff.; K. Erdmann, *Europa und der Orientteppich*, Berlin/Mainz, 1962, fig. 41.

264 Woollen knotted carpet with the impaled arms of the Kretkowsky and Güldenstern families (235 × 161 cm.). Polish copy of an Ottoman carpet, 17th C. [283]

Lit. T. Mańkowski, 'Influence of Islamic Art in Poland', *Ars Islamica*, Ann Arbor, 1935, II, p. 105, fig. 9.

265 Woollen knotted carpet with the arms of the Girdlers' Company of London. *D*, India, Lahore, 1632. [284]

266 Woollen knotted carpet with the arms of the English family Fremlin. *D*, India, 17th C. [285]

Lit. V. Robinson, *Eastern Carpets*, I, London, 1882.

267 Woollen knotted carpet, octagonal (430 × 345 cm.). *D*, South Persia, 17th–18th C. Formerly Bernheimer Collection, Munich. [286]

Lit. O. Bernheimer, *Alte Teppiche des 16 bis 18 Jahrhunderts*, Catalogue, Munich, 1959, Nr. 62.

268 Woollen knotted carpet, Spain, Alcaraz, 15th C. Philadelphia Museum of Art, Inv. Nr. 55.65.21. See A. van de Put 'Some Fifteenth Century Spanish Carpets', *The Burlington Magazine*, London, 1911, XIX, pp. 344 ff. [287]

269 Woollen knotted carpet with octagons (413 × 233 cm.). Spain, Alcaraz, 15th C. Cleveland, the Cleveland Museum of Art, Inv. Nr. 52.511. Cf. E. Kühnel, 'Maurische Teppiche aus Alcaraz', *Pantheon*, Munich, 1930, pp. 416 ff.; R. B. Serjeant, 'Material for a History of Islamic Textiles up to the Mongol Conquest', *Ars Islamica*, Ann Arbor, 1951, XV/XVI, pp. 29 ff. [289]

270 Woollen knotted carpet with wreaths (300 × 160 cm.). Spain, Alcaraz or Cuenca, 16th C. Berlin, Staatliche Museums. [290]

Lit. K. Erdmann, *Oriental Carpets*, p. 178.

271 Woollen knotted carpet with geometric design in off-set rows (463 × 106 cm.). Spain, Alcaraz, 15th C. Boston, Museum of Fine Arts. [291]

Lit. K. Erdmann, *Oriental Carpets*, fig. 175. Cf. with an Anatolian prototype, Fig. 13.

272 Woollen knotted carpet after an Anatolian model, in the manner of Fig. 52 (325 × 177 cm.). Spain, Alcaraz (?) 16th C. Formerly North American art trade. [292]

Lit. K. Erdmann, *Oriental Carpets*, fig. 177.

273 Spanish carpet of the Lotto type in a miniature of a manuscript of the Theseide, 3rd quarter 15th C. Vienna, Hofbibliothek. [293]

Lit. K. Erdmann, 'Eine unbeachtete Gruppe Spanischer Knüpfteppiche des 15 bis 17 Jahrhunderts', *Belvedere*, Vienna, 1932, XI, pp. 74 ff.

274 Woollen knotted carpet in a textile design. Spanish Alcaraz (?) 16th C. London, Victoria and Albert Museum. [294]

275 Fragment in the cut weft-loop technique (46 × 26 cm.). From Old Cairo (Fostat), 9th–11th C. Berlin Museums Inv. Nr. I 6688. See C. J. Lamm, 'The Marby Rug and some Fragments of Carpets found in Egypt', *Svenska Orientalsällskapets*, Årsbok, 1937, pp. 51 ff. [295]

276 Woollen knotted carpet. Copy of an Anatolian prayer rug (285 × 185 cm.). Spain, Cuenca. *c.* 1700. Madrid, Arqueologico Nacional Museum. [296]

277 Woollen knotted carpet, copy of a Medallion Ushak. Spain, Cuenca, *c.* 1700. Count de Welczeck Collection. [297]
Lit. J. Ferrandis Torres, *Exposición de Alfombras Antiguas Españolas*, Madrid, 1933, Pl. XLI.

278 Woollen knotted carpet (332 × 245 cm.). Spain, Madrid, Santa Barbara, end 18th C. Livinio Stuyck Collection. [298]

279 Woollen knotted carpet (220 × 117 cm.). Spain, Alpujarra, 18th C. Cologne, Kunstgewerbe Museum. [299]
Lit. K. Erdmann, *Orientalische Teppiche aus vier Jahrhunderten*, exhibition catalogue, Kunst und Gewerbe Museum, Hamburg, 1950, Nr. 140, fig. 49.

280 Woollen knotted carpet after an Anatolian model. Poland, 18th C. Cracow Museum. Cf. A. Riegl 'Zur Frage der Polenteppiche', *Mitteilungen des K. K. Österreichischen Museums für Kunst und Industrie*, Vienna, 1894, pp. 225 ff.; T. Mańkowski 'Influence of Islamic Art in Poland', *Ars Islamica*, Ann Arbor, 1935, II, pp. 93 ff., fig. 13. [300]

281 Woollen knotted carpet with a European design (257 × 156 cm.). Poland, end 17th C. Formerly Berlin, Sarre Collection. [301]

282 Finnish Rya. 19th C. Helsingfors, National Museum. [302]
Lit. U. T. Sirelius, *The Ryijy Rugs of Finland*, Helsingfors, 1926. In this richly illustrated book the earliest carpet is dated 1695 and the latest 1836.
A. F. Kendrick and C. E. C. Tattersall, *Handwoven Carpets, Oriental and European*, I, p. 72, II, Pl. 83.

283 Woollen knotted carpet, Masurian carpet (246 × 165 cm.). East Prussia, dated 1792. Private possession Perkunen, Lyck district, East Prussia. [303]
Lit. K. Hahm, *Ostpreussische Bauernteppiche*, Jena, 1937, Pl. XXXI. The examples mentioned by Hahm cover the period 1706 to 1827.

284 Woollen carpet, double weave (410 × 170 cm.). *D*, East Prussia, Masurian carpet, dated 1818. Berlin Museums Inv. Nr. 17Q1. [304]
Lit. K. Hahm (see Fig. 283), Pl. 41.

285 Woollen knotted carpet, Italy, probably 19th C. Rome, private possession. [305]
A. Sautier, *Italian Peasant Rugs*, Milan, 1923, Pl. III.

286 Woollen knotted carpet (300 × 110 cm.). Italy (?) 18th C. Munich, L. Bernheimer Ltd. [306]
Lit. A. Sautier, *Italian Peasant Rugs*, Milan, 1923, fig. 305; O. Bernheimer, *Alte Teppiche des 16 bis 18 Jahrhunderts* Catalogue, Munich, 1959. Nr. 122. The Rumanian carpets are only related to this group in certain instances. (A. Tzigara-Samurcas, *Tapis Roumains*, Paris, n.d. (*c.* 1930) Pl. 27/8.)

Illustrations Check List

Giving Fig. numbers in German edition with corresponding illustration numbers in English edition
Figs. 1–22 have the same numbering in both editions

German	English	German	English	German	English	German	English	German	English
23 =	99	80 =	154	137 =	Col. Pl. XV	194 =	74	251 =	232
24 =	Col. Pl. III	81 =	155	138 =	201	195 =	75	252 =	233
25 =	100	82 =	156	139 =	202	196 =	76	253 =	234
26 =	101	83 =	157	140 =	Col. Pl. XVI	197 =	77	254 =	235
27 =	102	84 =	158	141 =	203	198 =	78	255 =	236
28 =	103	85 =	159	142 =	23	199 =	79	256 =	237
29 =	104	86 =	160	143 =	24	200 =	80	257 =	238
30 =	105	87 =	161	144 =	25	201 =	81	258 =	239
31 =	106	88 =	162	145 =	26	202 =	82	259 =	240
32 =	107	89 =	163	146 =	27	203 =	83	260 =	241
33 =	108	90 =	164	147 =	28	204 =	Col. Pl. II	261 =	242
34 =	109	91 =	165	148 =	29	205 =	84	262 =	243
35 =	Col. Pl. IV	92 =	166	149 =	30	206 =	85	263 =	244
36 =	110	93 =	167	150 =	31	207 =	86	264 =	245
37 =	111	94 =	168	151 =	32	208 =	87	265 =	246
38 =	112	95 =	169	152 =	33	209 =	88	266 =	247
39 =	113	96 =	170	153 =	34	210 =	89	267 =	248
40 =	114	97 =	171	154 =	35	211 =	90	268 =	249
41 =	120	98 =	172	155 =	36	212 =	91	269 =	250
42 =	121	99 =	173	156 =	37	213 =	92	270 =	251
43 =	122	100 =	174	157 =	38	214 =	93	271 =	252
44 =	123	101 =	175	158 =	39	215 =	94	272 =	253
45 =	124	102 =	176	159 =	40	216 =	95	273 =	254
46 =	125	103 =	177	160 =	41	217 =	96	274 =	255
47 =	115	104 =	178	161 =	42	218 =	97	275 =	256
48 =	116	105 =	179	162 =	43	219 =	98	276 =	257
49 =	117	106 =	180	163 =	44	220 =	204	277 =	258
50 =	118	107 =	181	164 =	45	221 =	205	278 =	259
51 =	119	108 =	182	165 =	46	222 =	206	279 =	260
52 =	132	109 =	Col. Pl. V	166 =	47	223 =	Col. Pl. XVII	280 =	261
53 =	133	110 =	183	167 =	48	224 =	207	281 =	262
54 =	134	111 =	184	168 =	49	225 =	208	282 =	263
55 =	126	112 =	185	169 =	50	226 =	209	283 =	264
56 =	127	113 =	186	170 =	51	227 =	210	284 =	265
57 =	128	114 =	187	171 =	52	228 =	211	285 =	266
58 =	129	115 =	188	172 =	53	229 =	212	286 =	267
59 =	130	116 =	189	173 =	54	230 =	213	287 =	268
60 =	131	117 =	Col. Pl. VI	174 =	55	231 =	214	288 =	Col. Pl. XX
61 =	135	118 =	Col. Pl. VII	175 =	56	232 =	215	289 =	269
62 =	136	119 =	190	176 =	57	233 =	216	290 =	270
63 =	137	120 =	Col. Pl. VIII	177 =	58	234 =	217	291 =	271
64 =	138	121 =	191	178 =	59	235 =	218	292 =	272
65 =	139	122 =	Col. Pl. IX	179 =	60	236 =	219	293 =	273
66 =	140	123 =	192	180 =	61	237 =	220	294 =	274
67 =	141	124 =	Col. Pl. X	181 =	62	238 =	221	295 =	275
68 =	142	125 =	193	182 =	63	239 =	222	296 =	276
69 =	143	126 =	194	183 =	64	240 =	223	297 =	277
70 =	144	127 =	195	184 =	65	241 =	224	298 =	278
71 =	145	128 =	196	185 =	66	242 =	225	299 =	279
72 =	146	129 =	197	186 =	67	243 =	226	300 =	280
73 =	147	130 =	198	187 =	68	244 =	227	301 =	281
74 =	148	131 =	199	188 =	69	245 =	228	302 =	282
75 =	149	132 =	Col. Pl. XI	189 =	70	246 =	229	303 =	283
76 =	150	133 =	Col. Pl. XII	190 =	71	247 =	Col. Pl. XVIII	304 =	284
77 =	151	134 =	Col. Pl. XIII	191 =	72	248 =	Col. Pl. XIX	305 =	285
78 =	152	135 =	Col. Pl. XIV	192 =	73	249 =	230	306 =	286
79 =	153	136 =	200	193 =	Col. Pl. I	250 =	231		

Index of Carpets

Abbasid 212–13
Alpujarra 215, 281
Anatolian 89, 95, 117, 148, 151, 154, 158
Aniline dyed 27, 190
Animal, Anatolian 17 ff., 24, 48 ff., 52, 142
Animal, Persian 24, 29, 37, 61, 64, 72, 78, 80, 92, 100, 138, 152, 177, 182
Arabesque 118, 121, 129, 148, 172, 195, 196
Ardebil 28, 29 ff., 33, 34, 36, 37, 91, 138, 163, 182, 197

Bergama 22, 49, 55, 56, 57, 89, 95, 98, 109, 145, 148, 172, 174
Beyshehir 119
Bijar 191
Bird 23, 37, 83, 85, 111, 117, 118, 147, 156, 170, 208
Branicki 91

Cairene 95, 149, 154, 198, 208
Cartouche 29, 89, 177, 182
Caucasian 28, 75, 85, 89, 103, 104, 109, 117, 118, 119, 125, 132, 133, 147, 170, 177, 194
Central Anatolian 41 ff.
Central Asian, Turfan 211
Chanakkale 22, 109
Chess-board 117, 148
Chinese 118, 199
Chintamani 81 ff., 111, 112, 117, 156
Copies 23, 27, 84–85, 116, 159, 169, 170, 205 ff., 208, 217

Daghestan 109, 174
Damascus *see* Mamluk
Dragon 34, 36, 83 ff., 89, 100, 103, 104, 109, 118, 119, 125, 132, 138, 147, 148, 153–4, 170
Dragon and Phoenix 17, 18, 49, 95, 143, 218

European 27, 205 ff., 215 ff.
Ezine 22

Felt 66, 91
Figure 71 ff.
Finnish Rya 217
Floral 103, 113, 118
Forgeries 81 ff.
Fostat *see* Old Cairo

Garden 37, 66 ff., 89, 108, 131, 142, 150
Gendje 109
Gerus 195
Ghiordes 49, 110, 156, 170, 172

Hamadan 190, 192
Herat 130, 140, 182, 189, 192
Hereke 80
Heriz 191, 194
Holbein 21, 22, 25, 52 ff., 57 ff., 100, 109, 116, 141, 145, 148, 149, 151, 154, 169, 210, 218
Hunting 28, 34, 61, 72 ff., 100, 117, 152, 168, 179

Indian 23, 29, 70, 75, 91, 108, 117, 121, 170, 177, 178, 199, 208
Indo-Isfahan 117, 118, 158
Isfahan 37, 89, 90, 116, 117, 118, 139, 140, 157, 158
Italian peasant 217

Joshegan 70, 10

Karabagh 174, 194
Kashan 30, 61 ff., 68, 74, 89, 92, 100, 115, 117, 128, 143, 168, 170, 179, 183, 184, 185, 189, 198, 206
Kazak 109, 148, 173, 174
Kerman 70, 157, 174
Kirshehir 110
Konya 34, 41 ff., 48 ff., 52, 95, 104, 109, 143, 218
Kuba 109, 172
Kufic script border 24, 44, 52, 55, 60, 119, 151, 210, 218
Kula 49, 111, 119
Kurdish 136, 170

Ladik 111, 155, 172, 174
Lotto 22, 57 ff., 100, 109, 116, 117, 118, 119, 148, 184, 208, 211

Mamluk (Damascus) 22, 23, 36, 37, 52, 79, 89, 97, 100, 116, 117, 119, 120, 134, 142, 143, 147, 148, 151, 154, 198, 199
Marby 18, 49, 217
Morocco, North Africa 97, 159
Masurian 216, 217
Medallion, Persian 26, 29, 37, 64, 73, 78, 92, 103, 108, 120–1, 127, 128, 138, 139, 143, 144, 152, 153, 168, 177, 182, 188
Medallion, Ushak 59, 103, 111, 113, 118, 120, 136, 150, 158, 184, 194, 207, 214
Miniatures, carpets in Oriental 24 ff., 71
Mujur 111

Nigde 103
Nomad 111, 119, 142
North Persian 69, 70, 126, 127, 128, 133, 138, 139, 144, 152, 177

Old Cairo (Fostat) 18, 36, 43, 44, 45, 51, 52, 59, 95, 109, 143, 211
Ottoman 23, 89, 98, 100, 109, 117, 118, 125, 134, 135, 146, 147, 148, 151, 170, 181, 184, 187, 198, 217

Paintings, carpets in 17 ff., 95–96
Polish 205, 208
'Polish' *see* Shah Abbas
Portuguese 37, 75, 90, 108, 130
Prayer 28, 78 ff., 100, 102, 111, 114, 117, 118, 143, 146, 149, 155 ff., 169, 170, 172, 173, 214
Prayer, multiple niche 102, 156, 157

Qazvin 30, 68, 177, 230

Samarkand 119, 197
Scroll 26, 128, 158, 196
Shah Abbas 36, 37, 89, 92, 99 ff., 106, 116, 117, 120, 130, 139, 144, 148, 157, 169–70, 178, 184, 206

235

Index of Museums and Collections